ROUTLEDGE LIBRARY EDITIONS: WORK & SOCIETY

Volume 8

RURAL EMPLOYMENT

RURAL EMPLOYMENT

Trends, Options, Choices

IAN HODGE
AND
MARTIN WHITBY

Routledge
Taylor & Francis Group
LONDON AND NEW YORK

First published in 1981 by Methuen & Co. Ltd

This edition first published in 2024
by Routledge
4 Park Square, Milton Park, Abingdon, Oxon OX14 4RN

and by Routledge
605 Third Avenue, New York, NY 10158

Routledge is an imprint of the Taylor & Francis Group, an informa business

British Library Cataloguing in Publication Data
A catalogue record for this book is available from the British Library

ISBN: 978-1-032-80236-7 (Set)
ISBN: 978-1-032-81308-0 (Volume 8) (hbk)
ISBN: 978-1-032-81328-8 (Volume 8) (pbk)
ISBN: 978-1-003-49926-8 (Volume 8) (ebk)

DOI: 10.4324/9781003499268

Publisher's Note
The publisher has gone to great lengths to ensure the quality of this reprint but points out that some imperfections in the original copies may be apparent.

Disclaimer
The publisher has made every effort to trace copyright holders and would welcome correspondence from those they have been unable to trace.

RURAL EMPLOYMENT

Trends, Options, Choices

IAN HODGE AND
MARTIN WHITBY

METHUEN
LONDON AND NEW YORK

First published in 1981 by
Methuen & Co. Ltd
11 New Fetter Lane, London EC4P 4EE

Published in the USA by
Methuen & Co.
in association with Methuen, Inc.
733 Third Avenue, New York, NY 10017

Photoset in Great Britain by
Rowland Phototypsetting Limited, Bury St Edmunds, Suffolk
and printed at the University Press, Cambridge

British Library Cataloguing in Publication Data

Hodge, Ian
Rural employment.
1. Labor supply
I. Title II. Whitby, Martin
331.1'173'4 HD5707

ISBN 0-416-73080-9

CONTENTS

TABLES

FIGURES

ACKNOWLEDGEMENTS

A number of people have contributed materially to the production of this volume in several ways. We owe a substantial debt to Ken Thomson who read and commented on the complete text in draft. Useful comments on particular chapters were received from Ken Willis and Lionel Hubbard (Chapter 2), Arnold Grayson (Chapter 5) and Mark Shucksmith (Chapter 6). Our thanks are also due to Ian Whitby for the diagrams in the text. Despite this liberal help all errors and omissions remain our own responsibility.

Ian Hodge
Martin Whitby

PART I

Rural development: problems and policies

1
INTRODUCTION

The main thesis of this book is that rural labour markets are at the core of the problem of rural depopulation in developed countries: the success of policies seeking to moderate the process of population decline will be closely related to the policy-maker's ability to influence labour markets constructively. The renewal of rural population is not simply a matter of the balance of births over deaths: migration in search of work has been a major cause of rural decline and its reversal, to bring about economically viable communities, must be related to the availability of employment in rural areas. The emergence of *socially* viable communities is a higher level objective which we take as given. As economists we can offer little on this except to say that economic viability will usually be a *necessary*, but not a *sufficient* condition for social survival.

The book brings together a number of separate applied disciplines to focus on the problems of choosing appropriate policies for rural areas. Demographic processes can describe the sequence of events which led rural areas to their present state. They are further used here to examine the impact of policies on rural areas. At times we have found ourselves making professional contact with geographers, in our interest in the spatial distribution of activities. Because of our policy orientation we have drawn from, and occasionally criticized, the pronouncements of planners and politicians, whether in local or central governments in the UK or state and federal governments in the USA and Australia. Despite such an eclectic array of branches our main disciplinary roots are those of the applied economist seeking to assist societies to make the best choice of policies from the competing alternatives available.

Our sub-title, 'Trends, Options, Choices', describes the types of phenomena we deal with, but may give a misleading impression of the sequence of the book. At various stages we shall indeed be discussing trends, options and choices, but not necessarily in that order. Part I of the book deals with all three. It starts, in the remainder of this chapter with some conceptual material which underpins later arguments. Then, in Chapter 2, we present a case study designed to portray the general processes of rural demographic change, followed by an attempt to assess the most recent trends concentrating on the so-called 'population turnaround' which has been noted in several countries. In Part II we review the employment trends in five broad industrial groups, and, in the process, form some views about the options available for increasing rural employment. Finally, in Part III, we turn to problems of choice. In Chapter 9 we outline the economic processes at work in determining the relationship between induced changes in employment and the rest of the regional economy. Chapter 10 consists of a brief résumé of the application of economic appraisal techniques to employment generating projects. Then follow two case studies which use the techniques in Chapters 11 and 12. In Chapter 13 regional policy approaches to employment generation are reviewed and Chapter 14 contains a discussion of some problems of implementation. Finally we present a concluding summary statement.

In the rest of this chapter we set the scene for the remainder of the book, by presenting some conceptual material which underlies much of its argument. In particular we attempt to clarify the term 'rural', to delineate the process of rural decline and to outline a simple theory of labour markets.

What is rural?

There are two main approaches to defining rural areas currently in use, both of which have disadvantages. First, rural areas may be defined on the basis of a more or less static governmental administrative rule. For example, in the UK, particularly up to 1974 and 1975,[1] rural areas are those with local governments designated as rural. They thus reflect an administrative classification at some earlier date and because some rural areas are taking on urban

1 The dates of local government re-organization respectively in England and Wales, and Scotland.

characteristics at varying rates, the usefulness of such a classification is limited. If we could point to a particular date when the classification did apply across the board, this would be useful as a baseline for describing trends, but no such single date can be identified.

The second approach to defining rural, which has been applied in the USA, is to base the definition on a measure of the size of human settlements. In the USA settlements of 2500 are taken as the upper size limit of rural populations. The total population classified as rural in these terms has stayed roughly constant at 54 million over the period 1950–75 (Ford, 1978). During the same period the 'farm population' (those living and working on farms) fell from 23 million to 9 million. Defining rural in terms of settlement size will allow rural statistics to reflect sensitively any internal changes, but will also complicate the measurement of overall trends as areas move into and out of the urban category. However, modern data handling systems would allow the presentation of statistics on a number of different bases, which would reduce this problem to one of interpretation of the results.

The proportion of a country's population designated as rural tends to decline in the initial stages of development, but to reach a plateau as the economy matures. One point in this process is the stage at which the country becomes 'urban-dominant' – when the share of the rural population falls below 50 per cent of the total. Great Britain reached this stage of development in 1851. The order in which some other countries passed this threshold, according to their census date nearest to it, was:

Argentina	1914
United States	1920
Australia	1921
New Zealand	1921
Denmark	1930
Canada	1931
France	1931
Chile	1940
Cuba	1943
Norway	1946
Netherlands	1947
Greece	1950
Spain	1950
Sweden	1950

Taiwan	1950
Uruguay	1950
Israel (first census)	1951
Finland	1960
Japan	1960
Mexico	1960
Switzerland	1960
USSR	1960
Venezuela	1960

Source: Davis (1969)

The same author projected the entry of Austria, Brazil, Columbia, Czechoslovakia, Ireland, Italy, Poland and South Africa into the urban-dominant group by 1970. All of these dates are based on the individual countries' own definitions of urban and rural: they do not therefore necessarily refer to precisely consistent situations in all cases. It is worth noting that many developed countries have only recently become urban-dominant. For the most part the evidence presented here is taken from the UK, USA, Canada, Australia and New Zealand: countries which all became urban-dominant fifty or more years ago. The conditions in those five countries will generally be replicated throughout the developed world, however, and parts of many countries which have not yet passed through from rural-, to urban-dominance, will exhibit similar characteristics and problems to those described here.

It is also possible to define 'rural' in terms of more continuous variables such as average population density, occupational structure or the dominant form of land use. Such measures would offer a way round the obvious limitations of the simple urban/rural dichotomy. The idea of a continuum of measurable characteristics changing continuously along a scale from urban to rural has been developed, particularly by geographers and sociologists. This approach allowed Cloke (1977) to calculate an 'index of rurality' for districts in England and Wales in 1961 and 1971. The index is more fully described in Chapter 13 below: here we should note that it provides a numerical measure of rurality at the district level, which may be used in further examination of the characteristics of counties in England and Wales. For example, the correlation between these and the county median of district rurality can be calculated, and the relevant correlation coefficients for three years are shown in Table 1.1.

Table 1.1 Correlations between rurality and county income and unemployment rate: England and Wales, 1976–8

Year	*Rurality/ Unemployment*	*Rurality/ Income*
1976	− 0.6959	0.6252
1977	− 0.6934	0.7308
1978	− 0.7038	0.5133

Sources: Index of rurality – Cloke (1977). Unemployment – *Employment & Productivity Gazette.* Income – Inland Revenue, *Survey of Personal Incomes*

These coefficients are large enough to indicate some relationship, possibly causal. The county median index of rurality ranges from the highly rural −12 to the most urban county +15. Note, however, that the two ends of this continuum are labelled urban and rural from prior information; the index itself is calculated mechanically. Because of this chosen direction of the scale the negative correlation between rurality and unemployment indicates that the more rural the county the higher the unemployment. By contrast the positive coefficient between rurality and incomes indicates that incomes fall as counties become more rural. Because the majority of incomes come from employment these correlations suggest that the structure of rural employment is dominated by low-wage industries. Further, the fact that employment in several of these industries is declining suggests that most of the unemployment in rural areas is structural in origin; that is, it arises because of changes in the structure of the economy.

A practical alternative, which falls between the administratively simple urban-rural dichotomy and the continuously changing index, as devised by Cloke, has recently been put forward by Gilg (1980). He advocates the use of a three-way classification of rural areas as urban dominated, intermediate and extreme rural. Such a classification would be particularly useful in that the problems to be dealt with in the three types of area are quite different. For the most part it is the problems of the extreme rural areas that are under discussion here, at least as far as the UK is concerned, as these are the main depopulating areas.

The concept of development

Development has received much attention during the last two decades from those concerned with less developed countries, but its relevance in the developed world has only been recognized comparatively recently. From the development literature we could define development to mean:

- an increase in aggregate income, or output
- an increase in *per capita* income, or output
- an improvement (however defined) in the distribution of wealth or income
- an increase in the range of choices open to the individual
- an improvement in the quality of life

There is clearly a degree of potential overlap between these concepts: for example an increase in incomes would probably bring with it a wider range of individual choice, and perhaps a general improvement in the quality of life. However, these concepts also differ widely in the ease with which they can be defined and measured. As a starting point we could take it that the above possibilities are listed in declining order of measurability and hence of usefulness for analytical purposes.

It is also evident that some of the above measures are aggregates, which are influenced by population growth, whereas others are *per capita* measures which are standardized for the rate of change of population. Which type of measure is used will depend upon the use to which it is put. If populations of different sizes are compared it will be appropriate to use a standardized *per capita* measure. If the same region is being considered under a range of hypothetically different situations, each with the same population size, then aggregate measures will be acceptable.

Another aspect of development is the normative overtones it commonly carries with it. The current usage of the word virtually always implies that development is a 'good thing' which is worth striving towards. However, we should note that development is not achieved without costs. Some of these costs are easily measured and can be incorporated in the concept used. Other costs are not so easily assessed and may simply have to be listed separately.

Rural development and rural change

Rural development differs from development studied at the national level, in that rural areas are sub-regions of the nation state. This introduces complications into the problems of measuring development because activities aimed at promoting development in one region may generate other, desirable or undesirable, effects outside that region. A simple case would be where taxpayers in all regions are paying for policies introduced in rural areas. In examining rural developments, particularly those promoted by public policies, the point of view taken by the researcher may be critical. In taking a truly 'national' point of view he would count all policy expenditures inside and outside the region, giving them equal weight. At the other extreme, a rural xenophobe might ignore all effects outside rural areas and recognize only those within it. Indeed, such a position might be partially defended on the grounds that regional policies are intended to transfer income from one region to another. An intermediate position would be to recognize all expenditures, whether within or outside the region, to be important and to record them separately. The policy-maker could then add his own weights to the estimated values before making a decision.

More complicated concepts must be introduced where particular expenditures in one region 'leak' away to others, because they are spent on imports into the region, whilst part of the expenditure is multiplied up by being spent on goods and services produced within the region. The concept used here is that of the 'regional multiplier', which is broadly an estimate of the extent to which income generated in a region further enhances other incomes in that region because it is spent on indigenously produced goods and services. We return to consider multipliers and leakages in more detail in Chapter 9.

An example of the multiplier at work can be seen from an application of Myrdal's 'principle of circular and cumulative causation'. In Figure 1.1 the sequence begins with a decline in agricultural employment which has two separate effects. On the one hand, this decline promotes emigration, which leads to a reduced rate of natural increase because of a disturbance to the age/sex structure of the population, and hence to a further drop in population. On the other, the initial fall in population also brings a

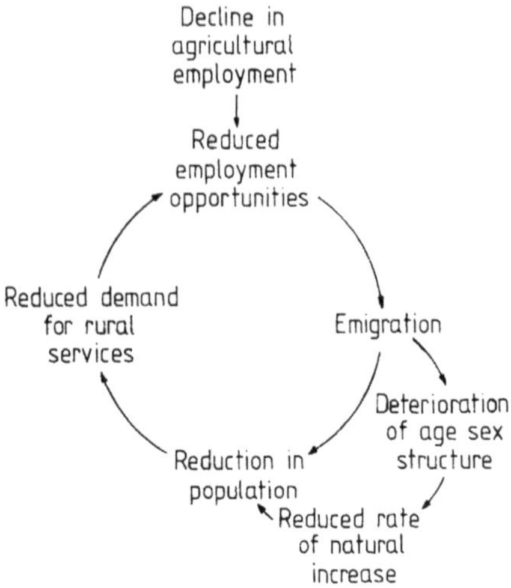

Figure 1.1 The principle of circular and cumulative causation

reduced demand for services (the multiplier effect) and hence further reduced employment opportunities. Through the interaction of these two sets of factors the process of population decline is able to continue until whole areas are uninhabited or very sparsely populated.

This model also brings out two interrelated themes of this book, the demographic nature of rural development and the working of rural labour markets. The demography of rural depopulation is discussed at some length in the next chapter and rural labour markets are examined in Part II, by broad industrial groups. But since labour markets are an integral part of the development process, and are touched on at various stages in the book, we present a brief outline of their workings here.

Labour markets

In the labour market for a particular industry employers seek to hire the services of workers with a particular set of skills. The amount employers are prepared to offer as wages will be determined by the cost of other inputs which might be substituted for labour, the technical ease with which that substitution can be made and the demand for the product. Any change in these basic conditions will mean that an employer could profitably vary his use of labour. A decrease in the price of capital goods or the introduction of a new machine which can increase the output of a man will lead him to employ fewer workers: a rise in the price of his output, whether due to a poor harvest or a sudden increase in consumers' incomes, will encourage him to employ more workers for the following season. Such factors combine to determine the employer's and the industry's demand for labour: that is, the varying number of workers they will willingly employ at each different price. Generally, the higher the wage level, the fewer workers we would expect employers to hire.

On the other side of the labour market, workers offer their services for hire. Whether or not they will accept a particular wage will be determined by their relative enthusiasm for the alternatives available to them. Workers will have to be offered some incentive to work under noisy, dangerous or dirty conditions or for long or uncertain hours. This will be more true if more highly paid, or pleasanter, work is readily available to them. Workers' preferences for particular types of work will be influenced by their education and training, and by their previous work experience. At a more basic level age, sex and health may constrain entry into particular types of work. This complex of factors combines to determine the wage which workers are prepared to accept for working in a particular industry, and the numbers of workers offering themselves for work at a range of wage levels. Generally it would be expected that the higher the wage, the more workers would be coming forward for employment.

The situation we have just described is summarized diagrammatically in the market diagram, Figure 1.2. The employers' demand curve, DD, indicates his declining willingness to hire workers as wages rise. The workers' supply schedule, SS, states that more employees will come forward for employment the higher the wage offered. Only one wage and quantity employed, W_E and Q_E satisfy these conflicting sets of aspirations simultaneously. Where the two curves intersect, an equilibrium occurs, at which the number of workers demanded by employers precisely matches the number willing to supply work at the going wage rate.

It is important to note that each of the two curves shows only the relationship between wages and number of workers, whether

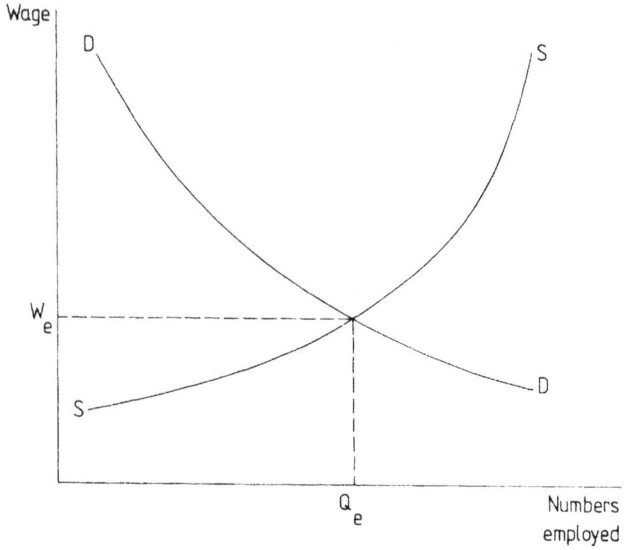

Figure 1.2 Labour demand, supply and wages and employment

demanded or supplied. The position of these curves depends upon the range of factors discussed above, which, in reality, are unlikely to remain constant for long periods. The stability of the equilibrium solution thus depends upon the stability of the underlying determinants of the two curves. If these two curves are constantly shifting position, the equilibrium levels of employment and wage will also change constantly. Actual wages and employment will probably adjust to these moves rather more slowly so that they will diverge from equilibrium. Such divergences may become substantial where markets fail to adjust over a long period. Such failures may arise, for example, where workers are reluctant to move between jobs in different locations in response to favourable wage differentials. This reluctance might be a reflection of, say, the perceived costs of travel associated with the move.

Apart from such causes of disequilibrium, there will also be wage differences between locations and industries because of different strengths of demand expressed by employers or different levels of enthusiasm for various work situations expressed by employees. Such differences may reflect the particular sets of skills required by employers, as in the differential between lorry drivers and postmen, or the unpleasantness of the job, as in the difference between dustmen and farm workers. Once established, such sets of differentials may be slow to change, as we shall see in the case of farm employment. This persistence is partly because wages in developed countries are the outcome of collective bargaining between employers and trade unions. In the bargaining process much use is made of the concept of comparability as an argument, with the result that differentials tend to persist strongly.

Another manifestation of disequilibrium is the presence of unemployment in the economy. Steeply rising unemployment during the 1970s has led to controversy as to its sources and origins in both the USA and the UK. This debate has been ably summarized by Davies (1979). Current forecasts for the UK (see, for example, Timbrell, 1980) suggest very substantial increases in unemployment may be expected throughout the 1980s. On central assumptions, Timbrell predicts an unemployment rate of 12.5 per cent in 1991, which is more than double the 1979 actual rate of 6 per cent. Moreover there will be substantial differences between regions in the increases projected, with the more rural regions of Wales, the South West and East Anglia expected to have particularly high rates of unemployment. If workers moved instantaneously, in response to wage differentials there would be no reason, in terms of the individual labour markets as described above, why unemployment should arise. Generally unemployment will arise wherever the supply of labour exceeds demand for it at the prevailing wage rate. This may be because friction in the market slows adjustment, because of structural changes, in, for example, the changing pattern of demand for goods, or possibly because of deficiencies in the demand for labour due to a falling level of economic activity.

Rural labour markets do not necessarily exhibit high rates of unemployment as measured in the statistics. In the UK the most common measure of unemployment is derived from statistics relating to the collection of state unemployment benefit. In the USA, by contrast, a survey technique is used to assess numbers unemployed who are judged to be actively seeking employment. Thus measures of unemployment between the two countries would not be comparable. Generally the US method produces larger estimates of unemployment than the UK method because in the latter case people who are seeking employment are not necessarily drawing unemployment benefit. An indicative measure of numbers who might become employees may be obtained from the *activity rate* which is the number of people in or seeking employment as a percentage of the total number in the employable age range. Typical UK activity rates for men tend to be of the order of 80 to 90 per cent whereas for women they are only half that value. During the 1960s and 1970s female activity rates have tended to move upwards whilst male activity rates have fallen somewhat. These trends are repeated in rural areas, though the rural activity rate for men is currently above the urban rate and the reverse is the case for women.

The coefficients quoted earlier showed a strong tendency towards higher unemployment as counties became more rural. Nevertheless, rural labour markets in Britain do exhibit relatively low unemployment rates compared with the more depressed urban areas. This is consistent with the generally high activity rates for men, who dominate total employment, and low activity rates for women, who also exhibit low rates of unemployment. They thus give an appearance of being relatively 'tight' labour markets in which high levels of wages might be expected. The fact that rural incomes are low must be explained by other factors, of which two are particularly important. First, the tightness of rural labour markets, as indicated by unemployment rates, is to some extent illusory when migration is occurring. Emigration might be seen as a process whereby rural areas can transfer their unemployed to other areas. Even if the migrants remain unemployed at their destination, they may still prefer this to being unemployed in rural areas, not least because it may be a necessary stage in finding a new job. A more accurate measure of the pressure of demand for labour in depopulating areas may be obtained from the sum of unemployment and emigration. Second, the level of incomes is low, partly because the structure of employment in rural areas is dominated by low income industries in which manual and semi-skilled occupations are more important than in the sophisticated large firms found in urban industrial concentrations. These two factors would go a long way towards explaining the low level of rural incomes.

Rural change: good or bad?

The above summary of the process of rural change describes a sequence of adaptation to changing economic pressures. Three distinct views of the desirability of this process are possible. First, it could be argued that this is a normal process of modernization; that the minor share of the population left in rural areas should be allowed to follow its own interests wherever these may lead. From this point of view the resulting depopulation would be acceptable and might even be welcomed. Second, it could be argued that areas undergoing such a transformation need help to adjust; that at least the people left behind must be assisted in moving to demographically viable areas and perhaps others discouraged from moving into the most severely depopulating areas. Third, the consensus might be that rural areas should be occupied and that action must be taken to retain people there or to encourage immigration to replace those who have left: clearly, such a policy approach would be the most costly in terms of public expenditure but it might nevertheless be defensible if the expected benefits from maintaining population levels exceed the perceived costs of doing so.

In practice governments in developed countries have varied their approaches among the three types listed. Generally, rural depopulation has been accepted in many areas with little effort expended to ameliorate its effects or arrest it. Occasionally, ameliorative policies have been pursued which attempt to offset the worst effects of depopulation. Also, occasionally, more thorough attempts have been made to halt the process of decline. Which of the three types of strategy is pursued most vigorously is ultimately a matter for political choice. Such choices, however, have wide repercussions throughout the economy, an understanding of which would improve the appropriateness of the decisions involved.

Creation of new or increased employment opportunities in rural areas is by no means a simple task for the policy-maker. Whilst the search for appropriate policies proceeds, many influences are at work which tend to exacerbate the problems. However, the potential benefits remain, both in terms of providing employment *per se* and of maintaining and developing rural societies. The options are available but require the commitment of both finance and initiative. The best ways of tackling these problems can only be discovered through an understanding of the processes of rural change and development, the economic activities involved and the evaluation and planning of the alternatives.

2
DEMOGRAPHIC CHANGE

In this chapter we seek to paint a broad picture of the processes of demographic change in rural areas and the way in which they interact. As demographic changes are very much the concern of this study we begin with a description of demographic development in one hypothetical rural area. We then turn to examine actual recent demographic changes, particularly the recent phenomenon of return migration to rural areas.

Demographic processes

In order to illustrate the demographic processes at work in rural areas we have assembled a simple model of a rural population which will indicate the tendencies which are found. This approach seems more useful than attempting to persuade the various data sets relating to rural populations in different countries to yield the general story we wish to tell. The interested reader will be able to find such works easily enough for his own country. Meanwhile we present a general picture of Poverdale, an imaginary rural region which nevertheless exhibits all of the general features of rural depopulation.

The age and sex distributions of the population of Poverdale in 1930 and 1980 are presented in Table 2.1 where it will be seen that within the total population of just over 2000 in 1930, women were slightly more numerous than men and that they tended to live longer, as indicated by the greater proportion of women in the older age ranges. However, from 1930 an improvement in life expectancies occurred and this, combined with age-selective out-migration and a drop in birth rate, has had the effect of changing the age/sex distribution of the population quite dramatically by 1980. This is best seen in Figure 2.1 which presents the data of

Table 2.1 Age and sex distribution of the population of Poverdale, 1930 and 1980

Age range	*0–4*	*5–14*	*15–24*	*25–34*	*35–44*	*45–54*	*55–64*	*65–74*	*75 and over*	*Total*
1930										
Number of males	100	200	200	180	150	90	50	25	5	1000
Number of females	90	180	180	180	170	130	80	40	10	1060
Total	190	380	380	360	320	220	130	65	15	2060
1980										
Number of males	42	97	106	110	113	116	110	80	53	827
Number of females	40	91	92	82	83	93	99	91	91	762
Total	82	188	198	192	196	209	209	171	144	1589

Table 2.1 in the form of a 'population pyramid'. The shape of the pyramid in 1930 is typical of slowly growing populations dominated by moderate expectations of life. Despite the improvement in life expectations from 1930 onwards, selective out-migration of

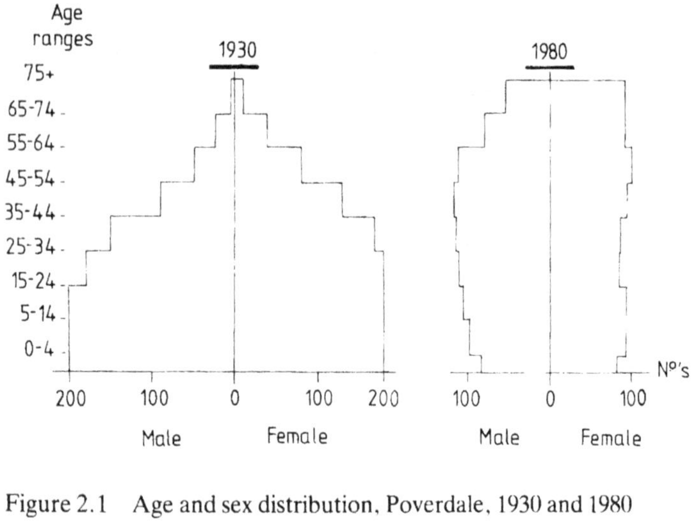

Figure 2.1 Age and sex distribution, Poverdale, 1930 and 1980

the younger elements has reduced the total population by some 500 over the half-century.

The annual age-specific mortality, fertility and migration rates for this period are recorded in Table 2.2. The mortality and fertility rates experienced in Poverdale are similar to those in rural Britain for this period. For example, they show a somewhat poorer life expectation in most age ranges, compared with the regional mortality rates for East Anglia and South West England in 1978 (OPCS, 1980a, 1980b). Birth rates for females aged 15–50 average 5.6 per cent which is a little below the 5.95 per cent in East Anglia and 5.65 per cent in the South-West in 1978. It is notable that rural birth rates are very much higher than urban in the USA (see, for example, Beale, 1978). Differences between the sexes in the age-specific mortality rates reflect differences in work experience and the risks associated with child-bearing. The migration rates are by no means high for particular parts of rural Britain: many areas have experienced much higher rates, sometimes resulting in the virtual disappearance of whole communities within a decade or two. Sex differences here indicate the propensity of women to migrate younger than men. The greater aggregate rate for women (a weighted 0.48 per cent for women compared with a weighted 0.71 per cent for men) explains the greater net decline in their numbers, despite their lower mortality rates in every age range.

The effect of these rates of change on the age distribution of the population of Poverdale can be seen in the 1980 pyramid of Figure 2.1. It is also possible to calculate what the 1980 population would

Table 2.2 Annual age-specific mortality, fertility and emigration rates: Poverdale, 1930–80

	Percentage rates								
Age range	*0–4*	*5–14*	*15–24*	*25–34*	*35–44*	*45–54*	*55–64*	*65–74*	*75 and over*
Mortality									
Male	0.05	0.03	0.08	0.1	0.3	0.8	2.5	6.0	15.0
Female	0.03	0.15	0.03	0.06	0.15	0.5	1.2	3.0	12.0
Fertility			8.0	10.0	2.0				
Emigration									
Male			1.0	1.0	1.0				
Female			2.5	2.5					

have been under different demographic regimes. Of particular interest are the effects of a higher and a zero migration rate which are shown in Figure 2.2. Here we repeat the 'actual' pyramid for 1980 and adopt two migration assumptions – one involving no migration at all and the other, out-migration at double the 'actual' rate (see Table 2.2). This brings out the impact of migration on the age distribution. Comparing the actual pyramid with the 'no migration' pyramid shows that the main effect is on the younger age ranges. Comparing the actual and the high migration situations shows that high migration would have produced an even more top-heavy pyramid more dominated by old people.

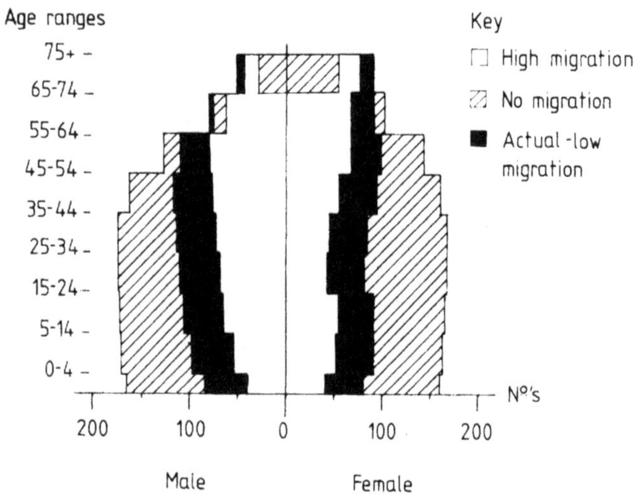

Figure 2.2 Effect of migration states on age and sex distribution, Poverdale, 1980

The qualitative effect of these different demographic regimes can also be summarized in dependency ratios which are calculated as the proportions of the total population in the under 15 and the 65-and-over age ranges taken together. For the different age distributions portrayed in Figures 2.1 and 2.2 the dependency ratios are:

1930		0.316
1980	– no migration	0.321
	– actual migration	0.368
	– high migration	0.391

Thus, even without migration, the improved life expectations from 1930 onwards would produce an increase in dependency ratio. Further increases follow directly from the onset of selective migration.

The total effect of the different migration regimes on the population of Poverdale may be summed up in terms of the net changes in population from 1930 to 1980, as in Table 2.3.

Table 2.3 Net change in population under three migration states: Poverdale, 1930–80

	Male	*Female*	*Total*
No migration	+178	+139	+317
Actual migration	−174	−298	−472
High migration	−447	−585	−1032

These estimates indicate that, had there been no out-migration, the population of Poverdale would be nearly 800 larger in 1980 than otherwise. By contrast, a higher (doubled) rate of migration would have produced a further net reduction of 560, compared with the actual population. It would be possible to assess what migration rates could have been sustained without any net decline in population from these numbers. This would involve experimenting with rates between the zero and the actual rates of migration until the desired terminal population was reached.

We return to Poverdale in Chapter 12 when various possible futures for the community are considered. At this point it is worth underlining the simplifications which are embodied in the analysis so far. First, all birth, death and migration rates have been assumed constant over the half century under consideration. In practice birth rates sometimes change quite suddenly, often in ways which cannot easily be explained. They would be most unlikely to remain constant over so long a period, but, in the interests of simplicity, and since birth rates for small rural areas do not change in any particular known way over time, the assumption is useful for this analysis. Death rates, by contrast, tend to decline gradually over time, under the influence of improved medical practices, public health and nutrition. Introduction of changing mortality rates into this analysis would have made the results more realistic, but would also have complicated the process of separating out the components of demographic change. The assumed constancy of migration is perhaps the most unreal of the assumptions, because migration may be undertaken for a variety of reasons and in response to rapidly changing economic and other opportunities. Further, age specific migration in one period is likely to promote a migration response in the next period. For example, an increased exodus of young women in one period might lead to the migration of somewhat older young men, in search of wives. Neither sequences such as this, nor the shorter term fluctuations in migration rates can be depicted by the rigid structure of rates chosen here. They should therefore be seen as averages, round which substantial fluctuations would be expected.

A second simplifying assumption has also been made in the context of migration, namely that there has been no migration into Poverdale over the half century. This assumption could be more realistically phrased, without altering the numbers resulting, by saying that all migration rates are net of immigration. Clearly there will be some migration into a community such as Poverdale and the possible effects of a substantial increased population are discussed in Chapter 12. Meanwhile the more general phenomenon of return migration, which has been observed in many developed countries, is discussed in relation to actual experience below.

Recent demographic patterns

The foregoing discussion of demographic processes in rural areas relates mainly to the experience of developed countries before 1971. That year saw the last population census in several countries, including the UK, and changes since then are only now becoming clear. For the UK, the post-1971 migration situation has been usefully surveyed by Champion (1981) on the basis of official mid-year estimates of population. At the county level Champion points to 'strong evidence of tendencies towards counter-urbanisation' in the 1970s. This has been particularly evident in some of the remote areas of Scotland which have gained population as a result of oil developments. In peripheral areas of the UK this population flow was not continuous but was characterized by a surge at the beginning of the 1970s and some slowing up of the flow in the middle of the decade.

A similar turnaround has occurred in the pattern of migration in a number of other countries where rural areas have in fact experienced significant rates of immigration. This change has been well documented in the USA (see for instance, Beale, 1977; McCarthy and Morrison, 1977) although it is also occurring in a significant number of other countries (Vining and Kontuly, 1978). Beale comments that 'growth is occurring in hundreds of counties that conventional analysis in the 1960s would have consigned to continued demographic stagnation and decline'. Between 1970 and 1975, the highest population growth and immigration rates have been in the lowest population density classes, illustrating the penetration of these trends into the most remote and hitherto least settled areas. This same pattern appears to be continuing in the most recent period for which data are available (Dillman, 1979). A large number of factors have been suggested as contributing to this change. Dillman (1979) has listed those indicated in a number of studies, including:

1 spillover of population into non-metropolitan counties adjoining metropolitan ones;
2 decentralization of manufacturing in pursuit of lower land and wage costs;
3 early retirement coupled with higher retirement incomes;
4 increased pursuit of leisure activities;
5 levelling off of the loss of farm population;
6 an increase in alternative lifestyle agriculturalists;
7 narrowing traditional gaps in urban and rural lifestyles;
8 energy and mineral exploitation;
9 increased fear of crime and concern with urban disamenities.

Some of the movement towards rural areas is the direct result of economic pressures, such as the expansion of energy exploitation boosting the populations in some settlements in Northern Queensland, Australia or the movement of firms in response to relative prices. Other causes relate to a preference for rural living and there is evidence that this has recently become increasingly widespread, either due to increasing 'anti-urbanism' or due to a greater preference for rural lifestyles and leisure activities. These aspects of rural living have tended also to become more available both due to increased incomes, especially amongst the retired, and to the reduced inconveniences associated with living in a rural location (e.g. more widely available electricity supplies and colour TV reception, and better road access to urban centres). Migrants to rural areas also appear to be motivated to a greater extent by non-employment factors (Williams and Sofranko, 1979). One final point which has been suggested (Hoch, 1979) is that high marginal income tax rates, accentuated by a progressive tax structure under conditions of inflation, could encourage the substitution of an improved quality of life for money income.

The longer term implications of this recent change are unknown. They are unlikely to have the same consequences for all areas. Dillman (1979) also quotes a national survey undertaken in the USA in 1974 which found that whereas 40 per cent of the population lived in cities of more than 50,000 only 21 per cent preferred to live there. However, the percentage of people who would opt for living more than 30 miles away from a city of 50,000 or greater is only slightly more than now lives there: 21 per cent actual versus 26 preferred. We should beware, therefore, of assuming that this 'population turnaround' will automatically solve the problems of the remoter rural areas.

More precise documentation of the migratory flows of the 1970s must await the next population census. The 1981 census will allow a fuller analysis of these events than has been possible so far, but the results of such work are unlikely to be available before the mid-1980s. Meanwhile it is clear that past and present rural depopulation will continue to cause concern in particular areas and policies aimed at offsetting if not reversing its worst effects will continue to be introduced.

3
PRIORITIES AND OBJECTIVES OF POLICY

Possible policies

From the discussion in the previous chapters it can be seen that rural depopulation might be deemed undesirable and indeed it is well known that the governments of many developed countries do find it so. What, then, can be suggested in the way of policies to ameliorate the situation? Part III of this book is devoted to discussion and evaluation of such policies but at this stage we review the possibilities in general terms.

First, it is obvious that there is the option of doing nothing about rural depopulation and of letting it proceed unchecked. In fact this is the option which is implicitly chosen in most situations. This is to say that while governments accept that there will be depopulation in most of their rural areas, it is only in some that concerted efforts have been made to stem the rate of depopulation. In comparatively few have they actually managed to halt it. Nevertheless, we include this option as a base line against which other potential policies may be evaluated.

The next possibility is to accept that rural depopulation will occur and attempt to mitigate the consequences of it by subsidizing the services which would otherwise not be provided in a population which is seriously depleted. In principle it is also possible that this can arrest or check further depletion. This route is one which has been followed in the UK and other countries. It is a policy direction which has often been easiest to adopt because it involves only minor adjustments to existing policies, which may be attractive as a means of appeasing rural pressure groups. For example, the educational response to rural depopulation in the UK has been to allow *per capita* educational costs to rise slowly over time. Nevertheless, at some stage it has to be decided whether or not a school shall be continued and, generally, this level has been set at less than ten pupils. Urban schools operate with average pupil to teacher ratios in excess of thirty which means that the extra costs of rural education become very substantial before a closure is brought about. Even when schools are closed it is still a great deal more expensive to educate rural children when they must be transported to the nearest school, which may be thirty miles away. We shall have more to say about rural services at a later stage. For the present we should note that it is one of the ways in which governments may seek to check rural depopulation and they are doing it, in effect, by subsidizing the income of rural people.

Why not subsidize the incomes of rural people more directly? In fact this is what is done in many respects in a number of countries through agricultural policies which have for years augmented farmers' incomes by raising the level of prices they receive for their produce or by lowering the price they have to pay for their inputs. Such policies are well known and well documented; it is interesting that they have proved comparatively ineffective in checking rural depopulation and the reasons for this will be analysed more fully in Chapter 4. Meanwhile we should note that agriculture provides a good example of an industry which may be subsidized if we are trying to increase rural incomes, simply because agriculture is an industry which is very closely tied to rural areas. Forestry is another such industry, but apart from these two there are very few which could be subsidized across the board as a means of increasing rural incomes. It has often been suggested, and is well worth considering, whether rural depopulation might more efficiently be checked simply by paying a direct income support to rural people. This has most commonly been put forward as an alternative to agricultural support although it would bring substantial administrative problems. Nevertheless, it may well prove that the direct subsidy to rural incomes might be a more effective way of retaining people in rural areas than paying them to produce agricultural commodities when surpluses of these commodities exist or subsidizing them to undertake other rural activities.

Finally there is the policy alternative to which this book is directed, that of taking direct action to promote employment. This could take a number of forms, such as those already mentioned in agriculture and forestry. Other possibilities arise in industrial employment and service provision. Each of these activities is considered at length in Part II. Our concentration on rural employment, as opposed to other aspects, derives from the belief that the provision of employment and earning potential to rural inhabitants represents the most satisfactory approach to establishing acceptable conditions in the countryside in the longer term. The availability of jobs is the major factor influencing people of working age to live in remoter areas and thereby in achieving self-sustaining rural communities.

Before we discuss the potential of various economic activities individually to provide employment, we examine the objectives and role of government in influencing rural employment and some general policies which seek to broaden the range of jobs in the countryside.

The role of government

Government intervenes in a mixed economy, principally for two classes of reason: firstly to improve the efficiency of the market system, that is to raise the value of the output of the economy, and secondly to influence the distribution of welfare within the community. The potential gains in efficiency from the encouragement of economic activity in rural areas derive largely from the utilization of resources which would otherwise remain idle. In a perfectly operating market system, opportunities for using such resources profitably would not exist. However, because of inflexibility and immobility, the market does not always work effectively, especially in the case of labour. While the proportions of the work force registered as unemployed in rural areas may be below those in some urban areas, other potential sources of labour may also be included. These are, firstly, those who in the absence of locally available employment would leave the area in a possibly unsuccessful search for work elsewhere, and, secondly, women whose spouses work in rural areas and who would be willing to work if employment was available. This latter group tends not to register as unemployed, and is therefore not evident in the unemployment statistics. Finally, people who have previously left the area may be willing to return if employment opportunities are available.

The movement of population from rural areas may mean that

there is under-utilized infrastructure remaining which could be put to use if the local population was increased or maintained, so avoiding the need for new facilities to be provided elsewhere. Weighed against this is the generally higher cost of providing services in rural areas.

Finally, it is possible that land or other natural resources may be under-utilized. This could be the case where lack of knowledge of the opportunities, where high initial capital costs or where the long wait before benefits are achieved, prevent the development of otherwise profitable enterprises by private investors. These can provide a rationale for public investment programmes or incentives such as are given for the construction of large-scale water resource development projects. Opportunities also exist for the development of areas for recreation, particularly where this involves people undertaking new, unfamiliar enterprises, such as on farms.

Some economic activities achieve benefits beyond those which are measured by the market value of their output. In these circumstances a free market will tend to lead to a lower level of production of these products than is socially desirable. This is the externality problem (see Whitby and Willis (1978) for a further explanation). An example is in the production of timber which may be valued as a strategic reserve in case of blockade as well as providing a suitable area for recreation. Where such external benefits occur government may intervene to encourage the expansion of their production. Similarly, the valuation of a characteristic countryside may encourage the promotion of particular agricultural technologies. Benefits from rural development could also be experienced beyond rural areas. The encouragement of economic activity in the countryside might be seen as a way of reducing the pressures which are exerted in the larger towns and cities where the concentration of population generates increased congestion costs. These are the familiar costs associated with such factors as traffic congestion, pollution and excessive pressure on public services. Clearly this is only one side of the argument as other factors, such as the lower cost of providing services, are also relevant. We must also be careful in generalizing too much in this respect as clearly some inner-city areas are experiencing just the opposite of these problems. Policies are pursued in a number of countries to encourage the re-establishment of economic activities in the inner-cities of the larger urban areas which have also lost population and employment.

The second main area of government action arises from a desire to alter the distribution of welfare which results from the market allocation of resources. The pattern of economic change in rural areas tends to result in circumstances which are often not considered acceptable. These concern the generally low level of incomes for many rural workers, the limited range of economic and social opportunities and the poor quality and high costs of services. We would include, within this distributional category, efforts to maintain alternatives to the increasingly predominant urban lifestyle. This is sometimes regarded as the primary objective of policies in the remoter rural areas (Grieve, 1972) and may be viewed as a shift of welfare towards those with an inclination towards rural life. This second area is probably the more common justification for policies specifically aimed at developing the economies of some regions relative to others.

Objectives of policy

The consideration of the potential role of government in rural areas suggests the objectives which government policies have. These may be of varying significance under different circumstances but may generally be listed as:

1. the utilization of resources which would otherwise remain idle but which may be profitably utilized in the economy, especially labour and land;
2. the increase in the range of employment opportunities which are open to the local labour force;
3. the maintenance or development of an acceptable local service base and social environment for rural residents;
4. an improved standard of living and quality of life in assisted areas;
5. reduction of pressures on urban areas.

The formal objectives of government involvement are not often specifically detailed before policies are initiated. Often policy statements include such objectives as 'maintaining population' or 'improving the environment' in certain areas. For instance, the objectives given to UK Development Commission assistance provided in the Eastern Borders (see Chapter 11) were 'to stimulate new growth and other activity in the area so as to provide a better environment and to arrest depopulation' (Scottish Office, 1966). However, the rate of depopulation and the quality of the environment are only of significance to the extent that they influence individuals' welfare and, presumably therefore, are not themselves the ultimate policy objectives. Furthermore, the relative priorities of different objectives are invariably not indicated and those objectives which are given are specified without identifying why the populations or economies of these areas should deserve special attention above and beyond those in other areas. We face the problems of this lack of clear objectives when we come to the evaluation of policies.

Policy instruments for local development

The policies aimed at rural development are as diverse as the economic activities which may be used as the vehicle for development. They are also implemented by a range of agencies which may either be responsible for particular activities, such as the UK Forestry Commission, or they may be concerned with a particular area, such as local authorities or development agencies. It is not possible, therefore, to discuss all these policies and the objectives at which they were aimed. Policies relating to specific activities are considered in Chapters 4 to 8.

A government has at its disposal a wide range of instruments which may be employed with the objective of encouraging local economic developments. These may be characterized by the degree to which the policy is related to the specific economic activity which is being promoted. They range from the improvement of an area as a location for all forms of economic activity to the undertaking of a specific economic activity by government itself. Some possible instruments are shown in Table 3.1.

The first group of instruments are concerned with making specific areas more attractive locations for the development of economic activity. This may be achieved either through the improvement of the quality of the public services in that area or the ease of access to it by reducing the costs of obtaining local services, or by giving publicity to the area, so that its potential benefits, typically the availability of space, attractive environments and

Table 3.1 Instruments for the promotion of economic initiatives

To specific areas	*To specific activities*	*Direct intervention*
Providing infrastructure Subsidizing local services Data collection and analysis Area promotion	Provision advance factories Input subsidies Grants for establishment and development of specific enterprises Feasibility studies Advice and training courses Protecting rural products Creating favourable tax position Research activities	Undertaking primary production Relocation of public sector employment Public investment Public works

labour force, may be weighed against the perhaps better known costs.

A greater number of options is available for the provision of assistance to specific activities, ranging from the overall protection of particular products throughout the economy to the provision of premises for a particular company. Many of these options, as well as the third group, the direct undertaking of an economic enterprise by government itself, are considered later in the context of the individual activities.

Rural employment policies in the United Kingdom

A wide range of the objectives of government in the UK have had and continue to have direct impact upon the level of employment in the economic activities which are located in rural areas. Efforts to increase farm productivity, to influence wages paid to farm employees or to achieve certain levels of national self-sufficiency in food production – all have direct implications for employment in agriculture. Less directly, other policies, such as those influencing urban labour markets, may have indirect effects on rural employment. Some policies, though, have had as a specific objective, usually in association with others, the support or development of employment in economic activities in rural areas. Most commonly, these have been in the context of the maintenance of traditional rural activities or the introduction of new ones, in order to maintain or encourage 'viable' rural communities. This type of objective has been given to policies associated with a wide range of activities, including agriculture, industrial development, forestry and tourism. Policies concerned with employment in particular activities are discussed in Part II.

While regional policies have provided assistance to particular areas suffering from high rates of unemployment, legislation aimed at promoting rural development in general derives from the Development and Road Improvement Funds Act, 1909. This Act established a fund from which advances could be made for a number of purposes. These included aiding and developing agriculture and rural industries, the promotion of forestry, reclamation and drainage of land and the general improvement of rural transport. An early review of the workings of the Development Commission, which had been established to make allocations from the fund (Development Commission, 1920), recognized the need for non-farm employment opportunities to be provided not only for women and children but also for men whose time is only taken up for parts of the year by work in the fields. The scheme was novel to the extent that it sought to embody in a statute the conception of the economic development of the UK although this was restricted in the main to agricultural and fishery resources. Over the period of operation of the fund, its scope has been considerably altered, although it is still broadly true that any scheme which is calculated to benefit the rural economy may be eligible for assistance, provided that no other statutory provision for helping it exists (Development Commission, 1976). The main types of activity currently regarded as suitable for assistance include the provision of business management and technical advice and limited credit for small manufacturing and servicing industries in the rural parts of England, the provision of factory premises, the support of pioneering and experimental schemes, the work of voluntary or self-governing bodies which help to enrich social or intellectual life for country people and surveys of rural conditions or research projects bearing on the rural economy. Since 1975 and 1976, the Development Commission's activities in Scotland and Wales have been given up to the Scottish and Welsh Development Agencies respectively. A more recent review of the Commission's work has been provided by the Development Commission (1976). Throughout this period, however, limited funds have been available to the Commission and its efforts have largely gone unnoticed, except perhaps through the work of the Council for Small Industries in Rural Areas.

Rural employment policies in the United States

The USA has also suffered problems which have resulted from the decline in the level of employment in certain rural areas and policies have been suggested for easing these. Cochrane (1965) describes the Rural Development Program which was announced in the USA in 1955. The programme contained a number of recommended lines of action to aid low-income and part-time farm families. These included the increase of industrialization of low-income areas through appropriate actions by state and local leaders, surveys of local labour-supply conditions and making fuller use of the abundant forest products in some areas. However, it was later argued (Bishop, 1960) that the poor organization and meagre support given to the programme suggested that the nation was unconcerned over the welfare of its under-employed citizens. Between 1961 and 1965, the Area Redevelopment Act provided (1) loans to support job-creating commercial and industrial enterprises, (2) grants and loans for public facilities, (3) technical assistance to bridge the knowledge gap, and (4) retraining programmes to fit workers to new jobs (Tweeten and Brinkman, 1976). Programmes which were organized under this act were also criticized for being spread too thinly across the country and so never reaching the critical mass of resources needed in any one area to overcome the forces responsible for economic decline. This act was replaced in 1965 by the Public Works and Economic Development Act, which created the Economic Development Administration (EDA). This provided for the creation of multi-county 'economic development districts' and each of these had to have one or more 'growth centres'. The majority of funds went for grants to finance public works and development facilities. Assistance was also given to private firms. Tweeten and Brinkman provide an assessment of the success of the EDA. They indicate that while the EDA was cost-effective in providing employment, it did not have a great impact on the overall level of non-metropolitan under-employment. However, the EDA economic development districts have increased in number from 6 to 214, which include over 70 per cent of counties in continental USA. At the same time the level of funding has decreased significantly (Hansen, 1980). The result has been a wide scattering of funds in relatively small amounts. Hansen concurs with Tweeten and Brinkman's view of the present position that 'at this point it is apparent that micropolitan areas have no federal development policy at all, only a confused set of piecemeal programs'.

Rural employment policies in Australia

An alternative objective of rural development lies in the encouragement of the development of previously sparsely or even unsettled areas, and is illustrated in policies pursued in rural Australia. While relatively little effort has been made to encourage the retention of population or the creation of employment in the country towns which have seen considerable population decline, policies have sought to encourage settlement in the remoter parts of the country, especially in the north.

Two major types of policy have been involved. Firstly there are the closer settlement policies which have provided openings for new settlers, especially for returned servicemen, by the breaking up of large estates and the prevention of the undue aggregation of holdings. The considerable potential for government influence in land policy derives from the fact that only about 10 per cent of Australia's land area is held freehold, the bulk of the remainder being leased from the government. Thus restrictions on leases can be used to achieve public objectives in land utilization. Under some forms of land title, landownership cannot be transferred where this would result in the occupier holding more than the 'home maintenance area' or 'living area', which is designated as the area which would be sufficient for the maintenance in average seasons and circumstances of an average family (Lewis, 1971). It was hoped that such policies would lead to greater support for local service industries and make possible improved amenities in country towns. Apart from the problems of defining the home maintenance area, it left occupiers of such units in serious difficulty during the inevitable fluctuations of fortune in Australian agriculture. Further problems arose from the limit to farm size while technological change was increasing the optimal farm size, and from rising income aspirations. Paradoxically too, these schemes have been in operation at the same time as structural adjustment policies were developed elsewhere to promote farm amalgamation and the exit of farmers from agriculture. Some legislation still provides for limits on the extent of aggregation permitted.

The second type of policy concerns the development of new lands. The process of clearing and improving areas for both dryland and irrigation farming is one which has continued since European settlement. As we have already mentioned, governments may invest in large-scale development projects where, for a variety of reasons, private investment is not forthcoming. In Australia, both federal and state governments have provided public funds for the clearance of native vegetation and the establishment of pastures and cropping over vast areas of land. Funds have also been devoted to many water resource development schemes. Details of major agricultural developments since World War II are given by Hoffman (1967).

Disagreement over the wisdom of large-scale land clearance and irrigation in the remote parts of Australia has promoted considerable debate (see for example, Forster, 1961; Hutton, 1967; Campbell, 1962; Davidson, 1965). To many, however, the value of such projects was unquestioned, for instance MacDonald has commented 'The average Australian has little doubt that north Australia needs to be and can be developed' (Foreword in Kelly, 1966). Davidson (1965) has listed six general motives for northern development:

1 concern that unoccupied Australian land could be occupied by neighbouring countries in southern and eastern Asia;
2 the need for a large population to defend the area;
3 a belief that valuable resources, in the form of land, water and minerals, are being wasted;
4 the contribution which the area could make to supplying food to the undernourished areas of the world;
5 the potential for the production of tropical crops which could save Australian imports;
6 the need for development to raise the standard of living of the aboriginal.

He goes on to show that the non-economic objectives are not met through large-scale development and that the economic arguments only support minor improvements in the pastoral industry. He ascribes the reason for the undertaking of large-scale development in the area to lie in the failure of those responsible for research and development to realize that 'development is an economic process'.

The largest, and most controversial northern development scheme has been the Ord River Project in Western Australia. Davidson was not optimistic about its potential: 'It is possible that no settlement in Australia's history has been commenced with so little chance of success.' The debate which took place at the initiation of the project has been reviewed by Lloyd (1965). The original scheme was to be undertaken in a number of stages. The first of these was completed in 1967 and included the development of about 12,000 hectares for irrigation farms. Stage two involved the construction of the Ord River Dam to form a major storage reservoir which provides for the development of a further 40,000 hectares for irrigation in Western Australia and construction of a channel to the Northern Territory border with sufficient capacity to serve another 20,000 hectares. This second stage was completed in 1971, although until 1975, with the exception of beef cattle fattening, commercial agricultural production consisted almost exclusively of cotton. For a number of reasons, especially the rising cost and ineffectiveness of insect control, this has now virtually ceased. The total area of crops irrigated reached a peak in 1967/8 of about 5500 hectares. In 1974/5 it was estimated to be 2000 hectares (Department of Natural Resources, 1976). Events would appear to have justified Davidson's pessimism.

More recently, the issues have been less topical, and more formal economic analyses of potential development projects, including the consideration of multiple objectives, have been undertaken (Wesney and Woolcock, 1978). The knowledge of the full cost to the community of water or land development projects need not be the sole criterion by which decisions are made. It does, however, clearly indicate the costs of achieving any 'non-economic' benefits which may be ascribed to a project.

Costs of rural employment policies

We have dealt with policy issues so far from a rather one-sided viewpoint; largely as if governments simply identified their objectives, implemented their policies and the desired results came to pass. We will now briefly dispel this idealism, leaving the detailed evaluation of policies to Chapter 10, where there is further consideration of many of these issues.

The implementation of policies to achieve the objectives discussed earlier does involve a range of costs as well as benefits. For instance, investment in one type of production or in one area generally means that it must be foregone elsewhere in the economy. Similarly a likely reason for the absence of manufacturing developments in remoter rural areas is that the cost of transporting the raw materials and finished products exceed such costs in alternative locations, thus rendering the production process less profitable. If companies are 'bribed' to locate in these less favoured locations, then the costs of production will be higher and this cost must be borne. Finally, charges for public services tend to be levied on an average cost basis, i.e. each consumer is charged the same rate, regardless of the cost of supply. Thus, while an increase in the population in rural areas does raise the cost of providing public services such as electricity and post, it does not increase government income and so these extra costs must be borne by all consumers or, through the exchequer, by the taxpayer.

In order to achieve the objectives indicated above, it is not necessary to stimulate economic development in every settlement. Within an area there will be a range of settlements of different sizes, each, dependent upon its size, providing a range of services which are available to those living around the centre and who have access to it. Settlement patterns are discussed at some length by Whitby and Willis (1978). Thus in order to maintain a basic level of service provision in a region, it is necessary to ensure that the residents have access to at least one centre offering the range of services which is regarded as basic. Clearly, what this range is and what represents 'accessible' must be determined by the policy-makers in the light of the numbers involved and costs of supplying services. Furthermore, as mentioned at the opening of this chapter, in many areas governments choose to do nothing about rural depopulation. Efforts to maintain levels of population and service provision in all settlements, thereby enforcing a rigid size structure which happened to be in existence at some rather arbitrary point in time, would be likely to face extremely high costs and very little chance of success. Various approaches to guiding initiatives to specific centres have, therefore, been adopted in an attempt to overcome these difficulties. In this context, we may briefly mention two issues: economies of scale in service provision and growth centres. The first of these concerns the relationship between the *per capita* cost of providing services and the size of settlement. It is commonly held that as settlement size increases, service costs decrease and various studies have examined this (Gilder, 1979). The second concerns the belief that development can be more successful if concentrated on specific centres or nodes, as a result of agglomeration economies. Growth centres may attract new technology and innovative managers leading to self-sustaining growth. (The study of growth centres has been reviewed by Moseley, 1974.) These two issues complement each other in suggesting that settlement policies should direct development and new growth towards chosen locations and such policies have been widely followed. Woodruffe (1976) has reviewed a number of such policies which have been implemented in Britain.

Constraints to rural development policies

Our final concern in this chapter is with constraints. Even if policies to stimulate rural employment are seen to be valuable and worthwhile, their full implementation might be limited by the constraints in the policy system. Economic activities require a variety of resources, the lack of which could provide strict limits to potential rural employment levels; the outstanding example is that of manpower. Without forcing people to migrate to the countryside, it will not usually be possible to achieve rapid increases in population levels. Of course, other factors are important too: land for agriculture and forestry, raw materials for processing, or markets for final products. The extent of what is achievable from a given set of resources is termed the feasibility constraint. For instance, while it may be grossly expensive to have farms worked entirely by human labour, it is technically feasible. There are other constraints such as the extent of finance or other resources. The schemes which we are considering involve the commitment of public funds, which have a variety of alternative uses. We cannot therefore presume the costs of all possible projects, even though they may be shown to provide certain benefits, will necessarily be accepted by government. It has to be shown that they are in some way more worthwhile than the alternative uses of those funds. The optimal allocation of funds within the public sector will be achieved where the value to society of the last £1 of expenditure is the same in all areas. The problem also has ramifications beyond the public sector, for, from a national point of view, it needs to be established that the funds could not be put to better use in the private sector. Concern that in general public sectors have become too large and that they have an excessive, debilitating effect on the entire economy is currently widespread. Consequently, pleas for any expansion of public expenditure are viewed with considerable circumspection. This attitude further supports the need for more formal analysis of proposed projects so as to identify more accurately their costs and benefits.

Lastly, we include the institutional constraints which limit the degree and extent of economic initiatives which can be taken. These are really just another form of feasibility constraint. They arise from restrictions over their areas of involvement of particular agencies or from ineffectiveness within the organization, leading to a failure to exploit opportunities or to co-ordinate the initiatives which are undertaken. We examine the institutional aspects of rural employment initiatives in chapter 14. Meanwhile, in Part II, we largely concentrate on the potential of various activities to provide jobs. Nevertheless, the constraints to expanding employment which must be faced are very real, and should be borne in mind.

PART II

Rural employment: actual and potential

In the next five chapters we describe in some detail the development of employment in a number of rural industries. The initial intent of these chapters was to indicate the relative importance of industries as employers, to give some impression of the trend of employment in industries, to explain these levels and trends in economic or sociological terms and finally to indicate which factors are likely to be important in determining the future level of employment in each industry. In an ideal world, where any information needed was available, such chapters would start with statistics on the level of employment and the rate of earnings in each industry. They would then proceed through an examination of the demand for the industry's products through the technology available for production to the factors determining the supply of labour and then, having described the labour market for that industry, we should be in a position to give a prognosis of its future performance as an employer. However, this format has only been possible with the first two chapters, which relate to the traditional rural land-using industries, agriculture and forestry. Because of their nature these industries are well supplied with data and have been thoroughly documented with economic and sociological studies.

The next industry treated is recreation and tourism (Chapter 6) which is entirely different from the first two in being a 'service' industry which does not produce physical products. We have thus departed from the normal sequence of examination from primary industries, in this case agriculture, forestry and extractive industries, through secondary industries which manufacture and process the output of primary industries to tertiary industries which supply services rather than physical products. The reasons for departing from this tradition are that tourism and recreation are integrated with agriculture and forestry. In rural areas the demand for recreation is closely related to the form of land use: also recreation and tourism has become, to a degree, a joint product with that of the agricultural and forestry industries. It is thus much more difficult to assemble data on the level of rural employment in recreation and tourism as can be seen from the chapter.

Next, in Chapter 7, dealing with industrial processes, we have again departed from the primary/secondary classification in combining primary extractive industries together with manufacturing industries in rural areas. This is appropriate because of basic similarity of these industries as employers in rural areas. Because many different industries are involved and the rural 'share' of their employment is usually small, it is difficult to assess the quantitative importance of industrial employment.

Finally, in Chapter 8 we deal with a complex set of economic activities under the heading 'service industries'. Such industries have become increasingly important as employers in recent years and their activities also feature in much of the discussion about rural settlement patterns. They are thus accorded a chapter to themselves.

4
AGRICULTURE

This chapter begins with a summary of the declining agricultural employment situation, focusing particularly on the developed countries and the characteristic of their agricultural labour forces. The adjustment of the farm labour force to changing circumstances brought about by economic growth is then reviewed in terms of the demand for and supply of labour in agriculture, leading to some tentative conclusions as to the future of farm employment. Finally, employment in industries associated with agriculture is considered.

The decline in agricultural employment is a well-known process in most developed countries of the world: indeed it is an integral part of the development process as described in Chapter 1. As economies diversify labour tends to transfer from primary industries, of which the main one is usually agriculture, to other sectors. The general impression can be confirmed from the recent cross-sectional data in Table 4.1. The world proportion of employment in agriculture can be seen to have fallen substantially over the twelve years to which the table relates. Then, comparing the developed and the developing countries, it is apparent that not only is the share of the labour force in agriculture in developed countries smaller but it is also declining more rapidly. In the next three lines of Table 4.1 it can be seen that the share of the economically active population in agriculture is very small in North America but remains substantial in Europe, although that proportion has declined rapidly too. In Oceania, which includes some developing countries as well as the more advanced economies of Australia and New Zealand, the share of employment in agriculture has fallen somewhat more slowly.

Turning to individual developed countries, it can be seen that few of them had more than a quarter of their labour force in agriculture as recently as 1965. Thus only Ireland, Spain and Italy,

Table 4.1 Agriculture's changing share of the labour force

	Per cent of economically active population in agriculture	
	1965	*1977*
World	54.2	46.2
Developed countries	23.4	13.6
Developing countries	69.4	60.7
North America	5.6	2.7
W. Europe	24.6	11.4
Oceania	10.3	6.8
Canada	10.7	5.6
USA	5.1	2.4
Belgium-Luxembourg	6.6	3.4
Denmark	14.4	7.7
France	17.9	9.5
GDR	15.3	10.2
Ireland	31.4	22.0
Italy	24.8	12.5
Netherlands	9.4	5.8
Norway	15.7	8.5
Spain	34.0	18.9
Sweden	11.0	5.6
Switzerland	9.4	5.6
UK	3.4	2.2
Australia	9.6	6.2
New Zealand	13.2	9.7

Source: FAO Production Yearbook, vols. 31 and 32

of the countries shown, had such a share of labour on farms. By 1977 the situation had changed, and those three countries had a good deal less than a quarter of their labour force in agriculture. At the other extreme come the UK and the USA with very small shares of their labour forces in agriculture. But what is particularly notable is that, in virtually all of the developed countries, the share of employment in agriculture fell by between a third and one-half over the period 1965–77. In the more strongly agricultural countries, such as Ireland and New Zealand, it could be argued that the share of agricultural employment has fallen more slowly. In the case of New Zealand the proportion of employment is now below 10 per cent and may be expected to fall further.

The data in Table 4.1 have been taken as a broad indication of the trend in agriculture's share of the labour force. However, there are a number of other important differences between countries which should also be noted because they are directly relevant to the pace of change in agriculture's employment share. Thus it is important to understand the significance in different countries of employment and self-employment, of family workers, of the age structure of the farm work force, of changes in farm business size and related institutional factors, and of the relationship between full-time and part-time farming. These aspects of agricultural employment will be dealt with in turn before we review agricultural employment in terms of demand and supply, so that views may be formed of agriculture's future role as an employer.

In Table 4.2 statistics relating to the importance of farmers, family workers and hired workers in the agricultural labour force are presented. A number of points emerge from this table. First the substantial importance of farmers, that is proprietors and tenants of farms, emerges very clearly. In most of the countries for which data are available the number of workers classified as farmers amounts to more than half of the total. It should be noted, in this connection, that there is some general uncertainty as to the precise meaning of the word 'farmer'. In many cases this is a comparatively high status occupation to which many would aspire; consequently some of those claiming to be farmers under one definition might not in fact be full-time commercial farmers in the normal sense of the word. The data must therefore be interpreted with some caution.

An important difference between countries arises in the share of the work force accounted for by family workers. These are often very important in agriculture, as members of the farm family tend to work on the farm, often for low remuneration, in the expectation of eventually taking it over when the present proprietor retires or dies. This proportion of the work force also tends to be large because of the comparatively high fertility of farm families. Consequently farmers may employ several members of the family for a substantial part of their careers. An interesting difference between the UK and most of the rest of the countries depicted in Table 4.2 is in the importance of hired workers. In the UK more than 35 per cent of the workers accounted for by agriculture come into this category. Generally the explanation of the greater importance of hired workers in the UK is in the relatively large size

Table 4.2 Farm labour use by type of worker: various countries

		Farmers (000)	*Family workers (000)*	*Hired workers (000)*	*Total (000)*	*Hired workers as per cent of total*
USA	1971	3275.1[a]		1161.2[c]	4436.3	26.9
	1978	2680.9[a]		1255.7[c]	3936.6	31.9
Canada	1971	273.0	110.0	99.0	481.0	20.6
	1977	239.0	84.0	145.0	468.0	31.0
Australia	1971	224.0	14.0[d]	127.0	366.0	34.7
	1976	252.0	34.0[d]	100.0	385.0	26.0
New Zealand	1970	65.6	16.2	27.0[c]	108.8	24.8
	1976	75.7	20.3	37.6[c]	133.6	28.1
UK	1973	288.0[b]	94.0	238.0[c]	630.0	37.8
	1979	304.0[b]	63.0	199.0[c]	558.0	35.7

Sources: USA: *Agricultural Statistics*, United States Department of Agriculture, 1978.
Canada: *Selected Agricultural Statistics of Canada,* Agriculture Canada, 1978.
Australia: Australian Bureau of Statistics.
New Zealand: *New Zealand Official Yearbook*, 1973 and 1979.
UK: *Annual Review of Agriculture*, 1978 and 1980.

Notes: a. Including farmers (from the same source there were 2.9 million farms in the USA, in 1971 and 2.7 million in 1977).
b. Including part-time farmers.
c. Excludes casual workers.
d. Formally classified as 'helpers' who receive no payment in cash or in kind.

of farm business, which in turn is often attributed to historical factors such as the enclosure movements in the seventeenth to nineteenth centuries. These movements drastically reformed the landholding structure in the UK, dispossessing large numbers of small peasant farmers and generating a large group of 'landless labourers' who then worked on a contract wage for larger farmers. This section of the agricultural work force behaves much like other manual workers, pursuing higher wages and better employment opportunities as they arise. Thus the main changes in the UK agricultural labour force which have been observed since World War II have centred on the rapid decline of the hired (non-family) section of the agricultural labour force, as the demand for labour has declined.

The data in Table 4.2 show the continuation of this trend in the UK, although at a slower rate than was observed during the 1960s. The situation has, however, been quite different in the USA,

Canada and New Zealand, where the hired work force has actually increased over the period shown. New Zealand differs from the others in that all categories of employment increased there. This would be partly attributable to the fact that she is still establishing new farms but also to the general recession in New Zealand where serious general unemployment has appeared for the first time during the 1970s. However, there is uncertainty as to the trends shown for New Zealand because of statistical reclassification, particularly of working wives, and a steep increase in the number of small, mainly part-time, farms. After allowing for these factors the trends in total labour use in New Zealand are probably downwards. The North American farm labour force shows an increase in the number of hired workers, whilst farmers and family workers have declined. This shift in emphasis towards hired workers is probably a response to the favourable development of farm incomes during the 'commodity crisis' of 1972/3 which enabled farmers to employ more hired workers and allow family members to take more leisure, retire, or move to other occupations. Examination of the more recent annual statistics shows that, with the passing of the commodity boom years, the longer-run trend of a declining hired work force has reasserted itself in North America. The steep decline in the proportion of hired workers in Australia is explained in terms of an increasing proportion of persons classified as 'helpers' who are associated with the business but receive no wages, salary or payments in kind. Although the statistics do not make this explicit it is probable that most helpers will be family members.

The above changes in farm employment yield a somewhat static view of the labour force because they are the net result of contrary flows into and out of agriculture. Recruitment to farm work typically occurs at young ages and the industry usually takes on many more young workers than are needed to maintain the mature farm work force in later years. Consequently there must be a subsequent displacement of young workers which takes place either by transferring them to self-employed status, as farmers, or by their movement to other industries. Often this transfer is associated with rural to urban migration, and because the outflow from agriculture tends to be dominated by young workers, the labour force left behind is often thought to be an ageing one. For example, in Figure 4.1 data relating to the age distribution of farm workers in England are presented. The area in each block of the histogram is proportional to the total number in each age range so that the vertical axis measures the number of workers in each year of the age range. The smooth curve is a crude estimate of a continuous distribution of ages which would fit these numbers.

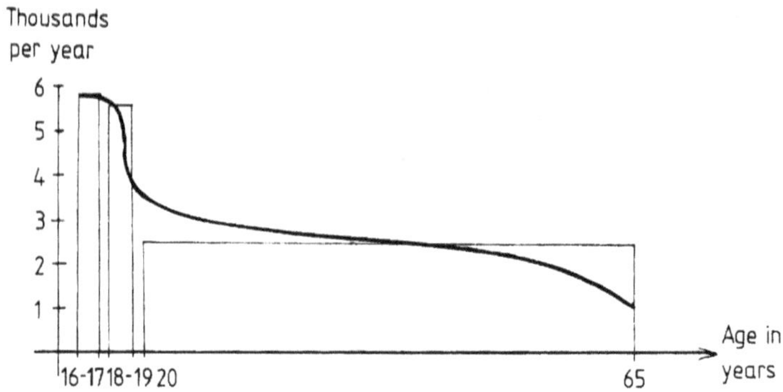

Figure 4.1 Age distribution of farm workers in England, 1979

It has not been drawn to represent an ageing population of farm workers because there is no clear-cut evidence that this is happening. It can, however be seen that there are *on average* many more young workers in the labour force than are needed to replace the mature workers. The fact that the number of adult workers is also declining means that even fewer replacements will be needed in future. From this diagram it appears that recruitment is running at roughly twice the rate needed to maintain the existing hired labour force. However, this does not mean that 2000–3000 young workers will actually have to leave farming each year. A substantial proportion of these workers may become farmers. In practice it is not possible to tie the static census data in Figure 4.1 to gross migratory flows because we do not know what is the real rate of movement into and out of the hired work force. Some fragmentary evidence is available. For example, according to the UK Ministry of Agriculture (MAFF, 1980) 9000 whole-time male and female hired workers had left school within the year preceding the census. Since the majority of these will have been male (they outnumber young women in the census in the ratio of 6.6:1) it is likely that the over-recruitment of workers is even higher than suggested by the census data. Recruitment to the ranks of self-employed farmers takes place at later ages and the numbers required for this rôle during the decade ending in 1971 were estimated by Whitby (1977) at 4358 per annum. However, this estimate relates to England and Wales in an earlier period and the data were taken from a different source. It was almost certainly an underestimate and for these reasons, cannot be closely compared with the numbers above.

Data for the age distribution of hired farm workers in the USA, from Rowe (1979), are reproduced as Figure 4.2. This figure allows comparison of age distributions between the different ethnic groups contributing to the work force. As with Figure 4.1 the percentages have been divided by the age ranges to which they relate so that the average percentage within each year of the range is portrayed by the vertical height of the columns. The workers represented here are those with 150 and more days work in 1977, that is effectively full-time workers. The contrast in age structure between the three ethnic groups is striking here. The Whites have an age distribution similar to that in Figure 4.1, with an excess of recruitment in the earlier years apparently being offset by movement out of this category of work in the 20s and 30s. There is evidently either late recruitment of Hispanics or there has been a recent decline in recruitment. After age 44 their numbers rise and then fall across the age groups reflecting either past swings in the recruitment/retirement balance amongst young workers or a cultural pattern (such as the return of women to full-time work after raising a family). The age distribution of Blacks and Others is yet more uneven than that of Hispanics. This may be connected with the sharp decline in the number of Blacks and Others during the decade preceding this survey, noted by Rowe. It is notable that the only evidence of an ageing farm work force here is amongst the Hispanics, who have a particularly large proportion of workers in the 45–54 year age range.

In contrast with the UK, the agricultural labour force in the more recently settled countries of North America and Australasia have tended to operate with a family farm structure since the earliest settlement. With the exception of certain farming systems where a more 'plantation' type of economic structure has pervaded (for example the southern United States, where the labour force was initially provided by slaves) and some of the larger farming enterprises in other countries, the family farm has been the norm.

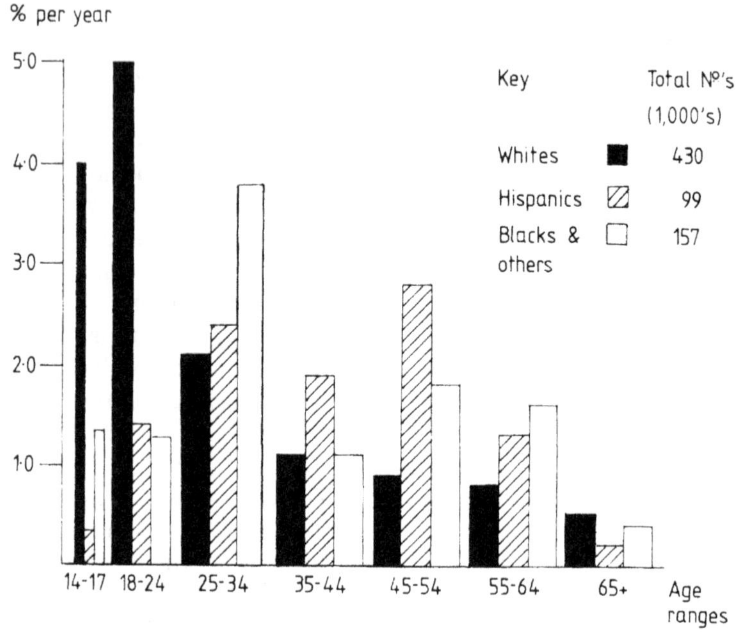

Figure 4.2 Age distribution of hired farm workers in US agriculture by ethnic groups

Family workers would be expected to exhibit a closer attachment to the farm than hired workers, although this may not appear in migration statistics because of the way the attachment is expressed. Belonging to the family business may mean returning to it when off-farm conditions are adverse, rather than staying permanently on the farm.

Because of the seasonal demand for labour and the importance of self-employment in agriculture the commitment of labour to the industry is variable. Mobile gangs of seasonal workers are a familiar feature of developed agriculture: so too are part-time farms. The latter may be variously defined as farms where the proprietor has a non-farm source of income or where the farm resources at his disposal would be insufficient to employ one full-time man. Part-time farming has received a great deal of attention from agricultural economists and rural sociologists, particularly in Europe (see Gasson, 1977, for a review). Here, the main interest is in the flexibility it brings to the labour market. Thus attempts to generate employment through public works in rural areas may simply serve to enhance the incomes of part-time farmers without changing the status of the unemployed at all. Part-time farming may represent a transitional phase in the migration process in which farmers and their families become oriented towards urban society. It may reflect the post-migration situation with one or two family members retaining an interest in the farm, but perhaps no longer resident there, after the rest of the family have left.

Part-time farming is familiar in most developed countries. For example, in Australia, Reithmuller and Spillman (1978) have published a study of off-farm employment in the grazing industry. They found that those with off-farm employment had significantly less capital, smaller numbers of livestock equivalents, more debts, and obtained a lower return to their capital and management. They were able to separate part-time graziers into three groups from the motivational point of view, depending on whether they were concerned to reduce debts, to generate capital for development or to augment household income. The remoteness of graziers from urban centres would generally discourage the urban fringe form of part-time farming, in which residence on the farm is a major reason for owning the business, as is common in Europe and North America.

Quite recently an historic mode of part-time farming has reappeared in the form of rural self-sufficiency. The number of people moving into rural areas seeking a balanced lifestyle through the adoption of intermediate technology to feed, clothe and house themselves is not known. The present wave of such migrations appears to have begun, in the UK at least, in the 1960s, but its underlying ideology is much older, deriving from authors such as Kropotkin and Thoreau. Perhaps such notions are less strange in countries such as the USA where the family farm has been a goal related to national development, almost for centuries. In a review of 'rural revivalism' Larson (1978) divides the 'refugee participants' in the US movement into two categories 'homesteaders' consisting of nuclear families and 'group communes'. The latter were thought to number some 25,000 with 250,000–300,000 members in rural USA in 1973.

Nevertheless, it is unlikely that the number of people involved in this movement is yet sufficient to substantially alter the balance of rural land use or employment in agriculture in the UK. Similar arguments relating to intermediate technology have also received widespread attention since Schumacher's (1973) influential work. These notions have received little support amongst agricultural economists in developed countries. A succinct review of the prospects for intermediate technology in US agriculture has been published by Barkley (1978).

Theories of labour adjustment

The process of labour transfer from agriculture to the rest of the economy has been studied by a number of authors. Thus Bellerby's (1956) work on the incomes in agriculture in a number of countries relative to those outside it during the period up to World War II remains a classic. Other more econometric work has been carried out for the USA (Schuh, 1962; Galloway, 1968; Hathaway and Perkins, 1968) and Britain (Cowling *et al.*, 1970; Tyler, 1973; Dawson, 1980). Sociologists have also taken considerable interest in the process of labour transfer from agriculture and have attempted to provide a detailed explanation of the process at a more individualistic level. A recent volume edited by Ford (1978) provides a useful survey of the USA whilst a number of studies (Nalson, 1968; Gasson, 1973; Newby, 1977) present information relating to the UK. Some authors have applied more strictly demographic techniques to available data in order to analyse the process of recruitment to and retirement from farming (Kanel, 1961; Whitby, 1977).

The economic theory developed to explain the process of labour transfer focuses on two groups of factors: those affecting the demand for labour in agriculture and those affecting the supply of it. These two groups of factors will simultaneously determine the number of workers in the industry and their rate of earnings. On the demand side the wages that farmers are prepared to offer their workers are conditioned by the technical feasibility of substituting other inputs (mainly capital) for labour, the price of those inputs relative to the cost of labour and the expected price of agricultural output. The supply side of the farm labour market is dominated by variables such as the employment prospects elsewhere in the economy, working conditions on farms and workers' expectations as to their future relative earning potential in agriculture.

Labour demand

The technical substitution of capital for labour is as old as agriculture itself. For example the displacement of draft animals by tractors made it possible for one man to undertake the workload of two or three men and a large number of animals. Further, by releasing the land formerly occupied by draft animals it was possible to greatly increase the output of human food from the agricultural area.

The substitution process was further encouraged by the fact that the new capital inputs offered to farmers often allowed work to be undertaken which previously had not been possible. Thus cultivations were not simply now done by tractor power, they were actually done better because they could be more precisely timed and could be more quickly done, and in some cases led to fewer problems of soil compaction than occurs with draft animals. Other forms of technical development have been just as dramatic: for example, the introduction of ever-higher yielding varieties of the major crop plants have added substantially to yields. The capacity of the new varieties to respond to fertilizer has promoted higher productivity per unit area and has enabled further increases in output per man. Perhaps the slowest to benefit from these technical changes has been the pastoral livestock sector, where the necessity for detailed observation of stock behaviour has tied up more labour, although even here the introduction of machinery has had a dramatic impact. For example, milking machines, operated in carefully designed modern buildings, now allow one man to milk more than a hundred cows where with hand-milking he would have been unlikely to milk more than ten.

In the most extensive types of agricultural production the shepherd/cowboy/musterer/pastoralist has now had his productivity increased by the introduction of machinery which extends his personal mobility – four-wheel drive vehicles, snowmobiles, bulldozers, jet-boats, helicopters and light areoplanes – so that one person can now cover a vastly increased area of land.

The possibilities for labour substitution in the more intensive livestock industries have expanded dramatically since World War II. The most striking change of all has perhaps been in the poultry industry, where scientific breeding systems, effective disease control and the evolution of sophisticated housing systems have led to the emergence of an industry in which one person can manage many thousands of birds. Similar techniques have now been extended to pig-meat production and this leaves ruminant livestock as the last of the traditional animal production sectors. Following the introduction of the milking machine and scientific breeding systems based on artificial insemination, the dairy sector may now make progress in more sophisticated feeding systems involving the automatic monitoring of each cow's yield and relating its feed intake to its performance. Such systems are already spreading through developed agriculture. The inescapable requirements for individual handling persist most stubbornly in the sheep sector, where shearing continues to impose a peak demand for labour in the annual production cycle. In Australasia this peak has largely been met by the emergence of efficient contract gangs whereas in Europe shearing continues to be dealt with on the individual farm, possibly with help from neighbours. This fact alone probably limits the size of sheep enterprises in Europe. It seems that sheep probably lend themselves least to reductions in labour use and here changes are most likely to come through the introduction of improved veterinary techniques and housing and, to a lesser extent, through automatic handling devices.

Because of these technical changes in the quality of inputs, general movements of the price of agricultural inputs are difficult to record. Thus the quality of the purchased farm inputs has improved at varying rates over time, and the result is that it is generally difficult to say what has happened to their prices. Exceptions to this are the price of tractors and fertilizers in the UK which have been the subject of careful economic analysis (Rayner, 1968; Lingard and Rayner, 1975). These studies have tried to establish a 'constant quality index' for the price of tractors and fertilizer. Comparing such an index with the movement of the official price index for these inputs then allows measurement of the improvement in their quality. In these two cases the conclusion that the quality of tractors and fertilizer in the UK improved at nearly 4 per cent per annum is reached. Thus the remaining change in price, which was in fact downwards, could be attributed to other market forces such as shifts in supply. The importance of this is that it emphasizes the attractiveness of substituting other inputs for labour in the past.

Will such new technical possibilities continue to appear indefinitely? The importance of this question has been raised in the recent context of the so-called energy crisis, as a result of which some commentators have suggested that the imminent depletion of oil reserves will bring about a more or less complete industrial reorganization in the developed world. This important question cannot be fully dealt with here but it must not be ignored. Oil is a major component of the inputs in developed agricultural systems, although as Renborg (1979) has forcefully pointed out this does not allow us to draw strong policy prescriptions from 'energy accounting studies'. Most developed agricultural systems are indeed high energy systems (although pastoral New Zealand is an important exception to this as shown by Brown and Pearson, 1977). The oil crisis of the 1970s has drawn attention to this dependence on fossil fuels and has led to gloomy predictions as to the future of agriculture. In this connection it is important to separate dependence on oil from the general importance of fossil fuels. Thus the disappearance of oil might suggest that an alternative to the internal combustion engine would have to be found if agricultural systems as we now know them were to survive. But in practice its effects would be far more widespread than this. It would mean that other energy sources would have to be adapted to the manufacture of inputs including fertilizers, machinery and buildings and, at present rates of consumption, the energy required for these inputs is considerably larger than that consumed as liquid fuel. For British agriculture the sensitivity of different farm enterprises to increasing energy prices has been examined by Parsons *et al.* (1978).

We should note that high oil prices have also had some impact on the output of farm products. The initial increase in prices has been felt mainly in the renewed interest in energy crops. Energy can be obtained from many conventional crop plants, including sugar beet and cane, cassava, potatoes and trees. Since the onset of high oil prices there has been research on growing some of these plants for energy production, often on cheaper land than they usually occupy. There has also been work on the possibilities of new crops particularly suited to substitution for oil. A plant which has found particular favour in low rainfall conditions is jojoba (Walters *et al.*, 1979) and another is guayule (Vietmeyer, 1980). These crops produce, respectively, oil (of particular importance as a substitute for sperm whale oil) and natural rubber. Such novel crops, although not producing mineral oil or petroleum substitutes, may nevertheless reduce the pressure of demand for oil which is a potential substitute for them.

Having examined the technical possibilities of substitution for labour and the trend of input prices, we may now turn to the final variable on the demand side of the agricultural labour market, the expected price of farm output. Prediction of this variable raises similar issues to the problem of predicting energy futures. On the one hand the neo-Malthusians see a world in which food supplies fail to keep up with demand and, as a result, some drastic structural changes in agriculture, usually involving a dramatic increase in agricultural employment are predicted. The neo-Malthusian view was given a boost by the energy crisis which directed attention to the problems of depletable resources of all kinds, including, for example, phosphate and potash fertilizers as well as energy. The prevailing view here seems to be that there are sufficient reserves of these plant nutrients to maintain developed agriculture over a substantial period and hence we do not predict dramatic changes in the rate of growth of output in agriculture. In the developing world there are undoubtedly situations where Malthusian conditions can be found; the question for developed agricultural systems is whether the demand for their output will grow sufficiently to change the gradual long-term downward drift of output prices.

During much of the 1970s and throughout the whole of the 1960s the problem for developed agricultural systems has been the antithesis of Malthusian shortage, namely that of disposing of surpluses. Apart from the brief commodity crisis of 1972/3, when short harvests in Russia coincided with a number of other events, resulting in a doubling of world commodity prices in real terms (see Harris, 1974, for a full account of these factors), the general long-run trend of real commodity prices has been downwards. Thus increasing production in the developed countries has commonly led to the appearance of embarrassing surpluses. In North America these surpluses were generally accumulated in the form of grain; in Europe dairy products and beef have been the main surplus commodities, though others such as sugar and grain have also been important.

The coexistence of surpluses in the developed world and problems of starvation and malnutrition in the developing world is a problem which has now vexed the political system for some decades. This coexistence has led to the argument that 'whilst the world is starving it would be immoral for any country to attempt to curb its agricultural production' being enthusiastically supported by those with a vested interest in the continued expansion of developed agriculture. Nevertheless it has come to be recognized, mainly as a result of examination of the American experience in using its grain surpluses for aid purposes, that it is not easy to solve these twin problems together. Without involving ourselves in the detail of these arguments we would therefore suggest that, from the point of view of policies to be pursued in developed countries, it is inappropriate to assume that problems of world underdevelopment will encourage governments to promote the expansion of agricultural production. Rather, governments will be concerned to promote the continued transfer of resources out of their relatively efficient agricultural systems and into some other form of employment.

This discussion underlines the central dilemma of agricultural price policies. If they are effective in raising farm-gate prices above their long-run equilibrium level, then they will attract resources into agriculture. These resources, however, will not necessarily consist of labour: high farm-gate prices may well encourage capital investment. The extra resources in agriculture will then lead to extra production and a tendency to depress output prices. Such a sequence of responses has led to considerable interest in so-called structural policies which, essentially, seek to encourage the transfer of resources out of agriculture. Structural policies in the UK have met with very little success in the fifteen years over which they have been implemented. Nevertheless this type of policy which is aimed at adjustment continues to attract attention and some funds.

Policy instruments quite different from the more common end price/structural adjustment form are also used on a more limited scale, but may make more contribution to employment generation. These are the explicitly regional policies of the type pursued within the EEC under its less favoured areas directive. These policies operate in the most depressed agricultural regions, mostly in mountainous or remote areas. They tend to work by injecting money into infrastructural investment, thus generating work in itself, and, further, they usually relate to specific farming activities. The main subsidies paid under this directive in the UK are the livestock compensatory amounts, which are paid to hill farmers. Such subsidies are applied in areas where the technical substitution possibilities are limited and the range of feasible outputs narrow. Tracy (1976) points out that the official aim of these policies, 'to ensure the continued conservation of the countryside in mountain areas and in certain other less-favoured areas' and to avoid 'large scale depopulation of farming and other rural areas', is significantly different from those of the EEC's structural directives.

Thus, in the long term, there will be no incentive for governments to attempt to increase the real price of agricultural output, and since the developing world is unable generally to compete in world markets for agricultural commodities, their need for food is unlikely to be translated into effective demand and hence into increases in price on world markets. Accordingly we would expect that the long-term tendency for the price of farm output to decline will continue, albeit with occasional interruptions due to short-term events and the introduction of mistaken policies which ignore these longer-term tendencies.

Labour supply

The number of workers willing to offer themselves for farm employment at any given level of wages (the supply of labour), will be conditioned by the relative attractiveness of other jobs. The strength of these attractions may be reflected in the level of relative wages, in the likelihood of obtaining non-farm employment and in working conditions on farms.

On average non-farm wages are higher than those paid to farm workers. However, in the UK, at least, young farm workers have fared as well as their non-farm counterparts in that they have been able to earn comparable wages. Nevertheless older workers have been less favoured and the average relationship between farm workers' and manual industrial workers' wages has been about 70 per cent in the post World War II period. It is, however, notable that on average the relative earnings of farm workers have improved somewhat in the last five years of the 1970s and this is thought to be attributable partly to the unprecedentedly high level of farm output prices coinciding with UK entry into the Common

Market and the commodity crisis of 1972/3. It may also be that industrial wages have grown less rapidly than farm workers' wages under the influence of incomes policies during the 1970s.

Farm work has traditionally been the subject of romantic myths and folklore. Yet the fact is that farm work has been and still is boring, exhausting and often dangerous. Farm workers tend to work much longer hours on average than other manual workers. They must be prepared to respond to the seasonal pressures of work on farms which often demand a high level of extra effort when soil, weather or crop conditions are right or when crises occur in particular enterprises. Where there are family workers kinship ties may serve to provide the sense of commitment which is needed to produce the response needed. Where the work is done by hired workers with no family connection, wages and other incentives must be available at a sufficient level to retain the work force. In Britain and many other developed countries, housing may be provided for farm workers at a nominal rent. On farms producing commodities requiring little or no processing there is also the possibility of providing perquisites, or payment in kind. In England and Wales in 1978 (MAFF, 1979) half of all regular whole-time hired men (i.e. including family workers) received a house with their job as part payment. However the imputed value of the rental, together with all other perquisites, averaged only 2.4 per cent of total earnings. To some extent this percentage is low because the house rental is very low – employers recognize this and argue that a market rent for the house, or the cost of providing it is a good deal higher than the rent charged. In the USA 25 to 30 per cent of hired workers (excluding family workers) receive either housing or room and board as part-payment (USDA, 1979).

It has been argued that good labour relations are a potent reason for the attachment of farm workers to agriculture, despite the low wages many of them obtain and their adverse working conditions. This view has it that the small number of workers on farms makes for close contact between employer and employee. In working together to surmount the challenges of adverse weather or markets, worker and employer develop a common sense of purpose which enables them to avoid the conflicts which are more familiar in industrial situations. The form of this somewhat paternalistic idyll has been analysed by Newby (1977) for East Anglia, a traditional arable region where the dominant type of farm enterprise has led to the development of a particular type of worker/employer relationship. In other parts of the UK smaller farms and the greater importance of livestock enterprises has supported the persistence of a more family-based business structure. Such a structure will make for more complex relations because it introduces longer term questions concerning ownership and control of the business. The existence of bonds between worker and employer does serve to hold workers in agriculture once they have become committed to the industry. However, as is evident from the age distribution data above, there is a large number of predominantly young workers who are only loosely attached to the hired farm work force. Those who do not move out to farm in their own right will have left agriculture because they are not satisfied with the maximum rate of earnings which most of them will reach in their twenties, or because they find non-farm work more attractive.

The future of farm employment

The continuing decline of the farm work force has led some commentators to ask 'When will it end?' To this the answer must be when either

the real price of farm output rises,
or the real cost of capital inputs rises,
or the general level of unemployment rises,
or the relative level of farm wages rises,
or the taste of potential farm workers for the lifestyle associated with farm work changes,
or some combination of these events.

During the post-war period these variables have been at such a level as to allow a continuing stream of young workers to leave agriculture and for the total volume of employment to decline continuously.

At the time of writing, the recent period of high commodity prices, a deepening industrial recession and, to a lesser extent, the rural revivalism referred to above, have all combined to produce some slowing down in the rate of decline of the hired work force. However, the widely predicted decline in real commodity prices may, if it materializes, lead to a renewal of the transfer of labour from agriculture, perhaps even at rates as high as those experienced in the 1960s.

Industries associated with agriculture

The modernization of agriculture has been accompanied by an increase in the economic interdependence between it and other industries. Farm inputs are now purchased from the chemical and engineering industries and a range of transport, communication and professional services are also required. On the output side the share of sales requiring further processing beyond the farm-gate has increased with the spread of manufactured food products and convenience foods. The new industries on which agriculture now depends are not necessarily tied to rural areas, indeed in many cases their dependence on economies of scale (agricultural machinery) or imported inputs (fertilizers) often makes it unlikely that they will locate in rural areas. Only for some industries, such as food processing, the balance of advantage may still favour rural locations when transport costs, availability of raw materials and of labour are taken into account. However, the degree of interdependence between agriculture and the rest of the economy varies from country to country. Of the developed countries considered in this chapter Britain and New Zealand probably represent extremes in terms of interdependence, and are therefore worth examining in some detail.

In Table 4.3 the value of sales and purchases by the two agricultures are compared. British agriculture sells a much bigger total volume than New Zealand, although the ratio of sales volume in the two countries is not very different from the ratio of their total labour forces as recorded in Table 4.2. However, the major difference between the two countries is in the ratio of purchases to sales. Clearly New Zealand farmers make much less use of purchased inputs than their British competitors. This is largely accounted for by differences in the farming systems of the two countries. New Zealand agriculture is dominated by ruminant livestock production for export. The New Zealand climate is one in which grass and clovers grow well and the grassland obtains its nitrogen (unlike most other intensive agricultures) from legumes rather than from the chemical industry in the form of fertilizer. New Zealand does not have a very large arable sector and nor does

Table 4.3 Value of purchases from other industries and sales by agriculture: United Kingdom, 1973, and New Zealand, 1972

	UK, 1973 *£m*	*NZ, 1972* *$m (NZ)*
Purchases from other industries	1,820.3	384.8
Sales to all buyers	3,387.1	1,143.8
Ratio of purchase to sales	1:1.86	1:2.97

Source: UK: COI (1978). NZ: Department of Statistics (1979)

Note: In 1972 NZ $1 was officially valued at £0.467.

it have major intensive livestock sectors based on feeding concentrated feed to pigs and poultry. These differences are brought out more precisely in Table 4.4, which compares the percentage distribution of sales and purchases in the two countries.

In this table we see that New Zealand agriculture buys almost nothing from the food processing sector, but sells more to it than the UK. The low inputs of feed are accounted for by its lack of intensive livestock enterprises and the sales by the fact that much of the output must be processed prior to export. Oil and chemicals are more important in New Zealand, despite its small use of nitrogen fertilizer. New Zealand agriculture also spends less on buildings and construction than UK agriculture. New Zealand farmers do apply phosphate at high rates and transport, using oil, is a major item of cost. It is notable that New Zealand agriculture is slightly more dependent on direct imports than UK agriculture. On the sales side, UK agriculture sells least to the food processing sector and more into direct consumption (final domestic demand). New Zealand agriculture also sells more than UK direct to export and sells a very small share to final domestic demand.

What can we infer from this table about the employment impact of expanding agriculture in either of the two countries? First we may note that the UK is likely to have a much larger impact on non-farm employment because it buys more, per £ of sales, from other industries. In either country the biggest volume of sales is with the food processing sector and this is the industry which would increase its activity most in response to agricultural expansion. The extent of the response in terms of rural employment is dependent on two other factors which are not present in the table, namely the production technology in the industries affected and

Table 4.4 Percentage distribution of agricultural purchases and sales by industrial sector of origin or destination: United Kingdom, 1973, and New Zealand, 1972

	Purchases from industry by agriculture in		*Sales to industries by agriculture in*	
	UK	*NZ*	*UK*	*NZ*
Forestry, hunting, fishing	0	0	0	0
Mining, quarrying	0.2	0.3	0	0
Food, drink, tobacco	47.4	2.8	50.1	65.7
Oil, chemicals	14.8	24.5	0	0
Metals, engineering	3.1	7.1	0	0
Textiles, leather, clothing	0.7	1.9	1.1	1.2
Bricks, timber, construction	6.5	3.5	0	0.2
Paper, printing	0.8	1.5	0	0
Gas, water, electricity	2.1	3.0	0	0
Transport, communications	4.7	12.7	0.2	0
Distributive trades	2.7	12.4	0	0.8
Miscellaneous services	6.4	17.6	1.2	0.4
Imports/exports	10.6	12.7	4.8	16.8
Final domestic demand	—	—	42.6	14.9
Total purchases or sales	100.0	100.0	100.0	100.0

Sources: UK: COI (1978). NZ: Department of Statistics (1979)

Notes: 1. The row headings have been aggregated from the original sources to correspond as far as possible.
2. Percentages have been rounded to total 100.0.

their location. The location data on manufacturing and service industries are not comprehensive enough to allow isolation of the specifically *rural* effect of agricultural expansion on employment. The evolution of agriculture towards more complex interactions with the rest of the economy will go some way towards offsetting the decline in farm employment. However, it is unlikely that the new jobs in associated industries will be as many as those lost in agriculture and the new industrial jobs will not necessarily be located in rural areas. We return to consider the determinants of industrial location in Chapter 7.

5
FORESTRY

Forestry is similar to agriculture in the basic technical process underlying it, which combines carbon dioxide and water with solar energy in the production of plant material. Land using natural growth processes are at the technical core of forestry, as they are in agriculture, but there are a number of reasons why forestry merits separate treatment.

Modern commercial forestry has developed from a gathering technique applied to natural forest. Indeed the majority of the world forest cover today is still natural forest. A proportion of this is in the process of commercial exploitation but it would be quite unrealistic to compare the world's forest system, based on exploitation of past natural growth processes, with agriculture in developed countries which has now reached a very high level of sophistication and control. At most three-quarters of the world's forest area is capable of being exploited for commercial wood production. Of this a major share will be upgraded natural forest which has been subject to commercial exploitation with replanting or natural regeneration. Earl (1975) estimated that only 13 per cent of the annual increment of timber in the world was utilized in 1970, and that the percentage might rise to 19 by 1985. This would suggest that there is still massive scope for increasing the amount of timber extracted from forests, even before changes in existing management are introduced, and that analysis relating to the future of forestry should bear this in mind. However, the supply of particular types of timber, especially hardwoods, may be threatened unless effective conservation measures are implemented. The UK Forestry Commission (1977) suggests that the rate of removal of timber could be doubled in the USA, trebled in Canada and increased by a factor of nearly two in Europe and Oceania over the next fifty years. These rates of growth are somewhat modest, in relation to expected rates of growth of income and manufacturing production, but reflect a biological process which is governed by the life cycle of the tree itself. In the UK, forest rotations of fifty to sixty years are normal for conifers whilst broad-leaved trees require a hundred or more years. Other countries are more favoured in the rates of growth they can achieve; the faster growing species used in New Zealand reach maturity in thirty years. Indeed some tree species in the tropics have been reported as reaching maturity in eight years. Shortening the rotation with faster-growing strains and species is one important way in which timber production can be increased.

Another important difference with agriculture is the very basic interdependence between forestry production and other aspects of land management. In several countries a major reason for retaining natural forests, or replanting cleared areas, is the protection of watersheds from soil erosion, the reduction of flood damage and improvement of water yield. In New Zealand several million hectares of natural forest are retained for this reason. Soil conservation is also an important factor in forest management in the Alpine regions of Europe. On the other hand forests may actually reduce the quantity of water yielded by a catchment.

In the UK, the argument has been put forward that planting certain upland watersheds with trees reduces water run-off and hence the yield of river systems and reservoirs, constituting a measurable cost of afforestation (Centre for Agricultural Strategy (CAS), 1980). This interdependence between water gathering and afforestation may thus provide an important constraint upon the spread of forest planting as well as on the exploitation of existing forests.

The spatial scale of individual forest activities is often much larger than is typical in agriculture. Developed countries commonly have a state forest enterprise of some kind which manages their forest resources. In the UK, the Forestry Commission is the country's biggest single landowner and owns and manages nearly half of the country's 2 million hectares of forest. It is also responsible for administering 'Dedication Schemes', covering a further 0.6 million hectares of woodlands, under which private owners manage them according to an agreed plan. Part of the reason for the large size of operations in forestry is that there are economies of scale to be obtained. The scope for reaping scale economies has increased in recent decades as machines for carrying out various timber operations, particularly relating to planting and harvesting, have been developed. In addition to economies of scale in production, there are also economies in marketing. Thus 'downstream' industries, such as paper and board manufacture and timber processing, tend to operate with large plant which requires a substantial, steady flow of raw material. In such a situation the primary producer who can offer such a flow has a marketing advantage over his smaller competitor. However, the further spread of thermo-mechanical pulp mills, which are more economical at smaller sizes than chemical mills, is expected by the end of this century (Forestry Commission, 1977). This might encourage the rural location of the new smaller mills, nearer to their raw material sources.

The importance of scale economies in forestry may explain why mixed farming and forestry enterprises have been slow to establish despite their many advocates. Hard evidence on the economic advantages of integration has been slow to appear and such studies as are available (see for example Maxwell *et al.*, 1979) reach somewhat tentative conclusions. It is probably also true that the long time period of production favours a larger scale of business organization because of the financial needs of commercial forestry. Thus if the production process requires thirty or more years to complete a cycle, the larger organization maintaining a mixed-age stand of trees producing a steady stream of timber can achieve a more even cash flow.

The aggregate demand for forest products is also quite different from that for farm output. In developed countries the demand for agricultural products is income inelastic: indeed, for a number of agricultural products the elasticity of demand, at the farm-gate, is negative. This low elasticity implies that, as incomes grow, consumers will choose to spend a declining share of their income on the product in question. By contrast the income elasticity of demand for forest products is relativey high. Thus the UK Forestry Commission recently projected world demand, through to 2025, using income elasticities of demand for industrial wood products of the order of 0.7 for the first half of the period and 0.5 for the second. Such elasticities would imply that 2 per cent annual compound growth in incomes would be associated with a 45 per cent growth in expenditure on wood products in the first period and 32 per cent for the second.

Employment in forestry

The demand for labour in forestry will be determined by similar variables to those noted in the agricultural context. These will, however, be modified in their operation by the factors discussed above. Under the heading of demand we should note first the strength of demand for forest products, then the variation in employment over the forest rotation and its relation to the age structure of plantations, followed by the rate of technical progress in forestry production. These forces are summarized by reference to some recent forecasts for the UK. The supply side of the forestry labour market is then briefly reviewed and some estimates of employment in processing industries 'downstream' from the forest. Finally some forecasts of forest employment in Australia are noted, for comparison with those relating to the UK.

One of the more difficult variables to forecast, in the economic evaluation of forestry projects, is the level of timber price. The attractiveness of forest investments will be more sensitive to the price level assumed in countries where a low discount rate (see Chapter 10) is combined with a relatively short time horizon. Even in the UK where the time horizon is typically fifty or sixty years, different assumptions as to price levels would be important at low discount rates. During the past decade price expectations appear to have changed somewhat in that substantial increases in timber prices are now being forecast. Thus the Treasury's (1972) study concluded that no increase in timber prices should be incorporated in its calculations. The more recent Forestry Commission Study (1977) nevertheless incorporated alternative price change assumptions in its calculations of 0 and 1 per cent per annum. The CAS (1980) is even more optimistic, from the forester's point of view, in assuming real timber price increases from 1980 to 2025 between 1½ and 2 per cent per annum.

The planned level of forest production will reflect the planner's view as to the demand for timber at the end of the growing period, compared with the value of other products which could have been produced from the same land. However, when the forest has been planted there is still scope for varying the rate of production per hectare by adopting particular forestry practices such as fertilizer application, or modified cutting regimes. There is also some scope for varying the rate of output of timber in response to shorter term shifts in demand. For example, it is possible to fell trees when they are not quite mature or, if the market is depressed, they can be left to stand for a year or two more in hope that prices will improve.

The importance of the distribution of age classes within a forest in determining the demand for labour can be seen from the fact that there is a peak labour requirement at planting and at felling but very little demand in between. This point is well exemplified by reference to a model developed by Inglis (1977) to predict forest labour requirements in the Highlands of Scotland. He assumed basic labour requirements for silvicultural works over a 50-year rotation for a 58-hectare block, to be as follows:

Year		*Labour requirement (man-years)*
1	Site preparation	2.94
2	Planting	1.03
3	Beating up and weeding	0.78
22	Brashing and cleaning	1.06
26	Roading and fencing	2.07
27	Thinning and haulage	3.08
51	Clear felling and haulage	22.08

Thus, over a 50-year production cycle, more than two-thirds of all the employment generated, by initiation of new planting, will not appear until the final year. About one-seventh of the total employment arises in the first three years.

Inglis's model was then extended to a more operational situation where 50 separate blocks of 58 hectares each were developed, one per year. At the end of 50 years a continuously producing forest of even age, covering some 3000 hectares, is established, and a steady labour requirement results. Because the development period is so long it may be quite unrealistic to apply constant labour performance standards throughout the period. Accordingly he varied the initial requirements with two different assumed rates of change in productivity and the resulting total labour requirements are compared in Figure 5.1.

Since the harvesting operations require most labour we may take it that improvements in harvesting technique will be most likely to have an impact on forest labour requirements. Predicting the rate of technical change in any operation is hazardous and in timber felling and haulage this is particularly so, because major

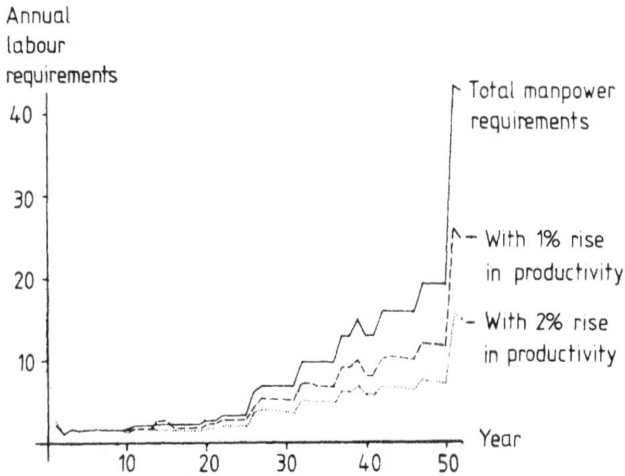

Figure 5.1 Total labour requirements

improvements in methods have only recently been introduced. In particular, the light-weight chain saw has revolutionized felling and the frame steering tractor has more recently speeded up the process of timber extraction. Large, multi-purpose harvesting machinery, such as timber processors, have also been developed. But such implements have not been particularly successful on uneven terrain or poorly drained soils. There may now be further scope for productivity growth based on extracting a greater proportion of the tree.

Table 5.1 shows the age class distribution of forests in Great Britain, as estimated in 1980.

Table 5.1 The age class distribution of forests in Great Britain, 1980

	Planting years						
	post-1970	*1961–1970*	*1951–1960*	*1941–1950*	*1931–1940*	*1901–1930*	*pre-1900*
			(thousand hectares)				
Conifers	383	362	325	113	100	53	12
Broad-leaves	13	14	25	16	15	55	183

Source: CAS (1980)

The large proportion of broad-leaved trees in the pre-1900 planting period emphasizes the long production period for broad-leaved trees, which explains the comparatively low priority given to commercial planting of broad-leaved forests in Britain. The age distribution of conifers, however, indicates both the shorter life-span to maturity of such trees and the changes of government policy with regard to planting. In Britain Forestry Commission planting only began in 1919, but it was not until the period from 1950 that substantial rates of planting were sustained. From this pattern of age classes and the proposed planting extensions, it can be seen that the demand for labour in forests will mainly reflect the rate of new planting over the next decade or two but thereafter the rate of felling will become important too, as the post World War II plantings mature. Thus within two decades the area of conifers in Britain will reach a more or less evenly distributed age structure and the demand for labour for all operations will be relatively steady, except in so far as labour requirements for different operations change at varying rates. Up to that point labour demand may be expected to grow as felling operations increase.

The rate of technical change in forestry is important, as it is in agriculture, in assessing labour requirements. In Britain foresters (Forestry Commission, 1977; CAS, 1980) seem currently to favour the assumption that the productivity of manual operations will increase at 2.5 per cent per annum. It cannot be denied that such assumptions can prove to be substantially wrong. Thus in the UK, after World War II, there was a widespread belief that forestry should be expanded, and to this end there was a massive increase in the training of foresters and some investment in housing for them. It was only a few years, however, before it became apparent that labour productivity was increasing so fast in forestry that the number of workers trained was in excess of those needed and that the planned construction of forestry villages was similarly excessive. Thus although it may be current practice to assume productivity change of this order it must be noted that the appeal of such assumptions can change drastically in a short time. Factors affecting forest productivity include the obvious ones of the rate at which new and more efficient machinery is introduced. Less obvious variables are the rate of extraction of timber, that is the proportion of the whole tree which is taken from the forest.

We may sum up the demand side of the forest labour market by saying that the demand for timber is expected to strengthen substantially, especially in the next century, but that the present view of productivity is that this will substantially check increases in the demand for labour. This view is represented in Table 5.2, which reproduces Commission forecasts of labour requirements in British forestry under various assumptions.

Table 5.2 Forecasts of labour requirements in UK forestry: traditional cutting regime

	Assumed rate of productivity change	*Labour requirements in thousand man-years*		
		1985	*2000*	*2025*
Forestry Labour				
Alternative 1				
No more planting	0	19.0	25.4	33.2
	+2.5%	14.8	13.7	9.7
	+4.0%	12.9	9.6	4.7
Alternative 2				
Planting another 1 million	0	22.3	30.2	47.7
hectares	+2.5%	17.4	16.3	13.9
	+4.0%	15.1	11.3	6.7
Alternative 3				
Planting another	0	23.6	33.0	55.7
1.8 million hectares	+2.5%	18.5	17.8	16.3
	+4.0%	16.0	12.4	7.8
Net job loss in agriculture				
Alternative 1		0	0	0
Alternative 2		0.6	1.0	0.7
Alternative 3		0.8	1.4	1.2

Source: Forestry Commission (1977)

The table compares three futures for British forestry: alternative 1 involving no increase in planting; alternative 2 involving a further million hectares of forestry and alternative 3, a further 1.8 million hectares. The implication of these different regimes for labour requirements in rural areas may be summarized in terms of the gain in forestry employment minus the jobs lost to agriculture, after allowing for replacement of farm production on the remaining agricultural area. Alternative 3, which represents a virtual doubling of the area under trees in the UK, is a fairly radical increase in production. It will be noticed however, that this does not add very many more new jobs to the rural labour market in Britain than alternative 2. The assumed rate of productivity increase is clearly vital here, as is the fact that extra felling labour requirements will not begin to affect total employment from new planting until after 2025. If we assume the labour requirements suggested by Inglis were to be applicable to the whole of the extra area planted then a further 33 million man-years is needed under alternative 2 and 59 million under alternative 3. However, productivity growth would reduce this drastically. If the labour requirements for harvesting fell at 2.5 per cent per annum the aggregate extra demand for harvesting would fall from 22 and 40 million to 6.2 and 15.6 million man-years respectively. It should be emphasized that these extra requirements would in fact be spread over a number of years, depending on the way in which the new plantings are phased. It is likely that even alternative 2 would need at least a decade to implement and the associated cutting requirements could be similarly distributed.

The last three rows of Table 5.2 indicate the net loss of agricultural jobs due to the various planting alternatives. This factor is important because most of the land planted in Britain is converted from extensive agricultural production. The estimated losses of agricultural employment are based on the assumption that the production lost from conversion of land to forestry will be made good by intensification on the remaining land. They are thus 'net' estimates of the loss of farm employment.

The distinction between the net effect on employment and the gross number of jobs is important in any context where the new jobs involve conversion of land from some other productive use. In many countries new forests are typically planted on unused land: but in Britain new plantings are generally on extensive farm land. Thus the number of jobs lost through withdrawal of land from agriculture could be important. One source which casts some light on this is a recent study by Mutch and Hutchinson (1980). These authors carried out a small number of case studies of the effect of private forest plantings on agricultural land in Scotland. These schemes mostly involved planting only part of the farms in question and it was found that conversion of about one-third of the area to forestry resulted in a small (10 per cent) drop in the number of farm employees. However, the new forest plantings drew in a substantial number of workers, equivalent to nearly 70 per cent of the initial farm work force, so the net effect of afforestation was to increase employment at the rate of roughly one man per 250 hectares. Because of the small size of sample here, these results should not be extrapolated to other situations without reservations. They do nevertheless roughly indicate the orders of magnitude of change in employment which may result from afforestation.

There is much less to be said on the supply side of the forest labour market. Here conditions are much the same as those for agriculture in that the work is often arduous and repetitive as well as being lonely and occasionally dangerous. One difference may be that forest workers are sometimes employed in greater numbers than farm workers because of the larger size of productive unit. However, this is true only of the larger Commission forests. Irving and Hilgendorf (1976) found that there are also many small units in the private sector which employ very few workers. In the largest Commission forests special forestry villages have been built, which have not been entirely successful. The main complaint seems to be, apart from the problems of forward planning mentioned above, that forestry villages tend to have most of the disadvantages of the 'company town' often combined with remoteness. Thus, there have been difficulties in persuading people to live in forestry villages because of these adverse conditions. With modern transport it is now easy to move gangs of forest workers from one location to another and the need for remote forestry villages has now virtually disappeared.

Employment in wood processing

The downstream increases in labour requirement which flow from the planting programmes compared in Table 5.2 are summarized in Table 5.3 where the Forestry Commission forecasts are reproduced. These are not precisely identical to those in Table 5.2 because the first year to which they relate is 1965 rather than 1985, and they include one central productivity assumption, namely an annual increase of 2.5 per cent.

The estimates emphasize that, even without any new planting, there will be a substantial increase in the rural processing requirement which follows from the increased rate of harvesting noted above. With no more planting, however, the requirement in processing begins to fall after the end of the century. By contrast, the second alternative of increasing planting by 1 million hectares would generate an increase in employment in the processing of 600 man-years which would be sustained to 2025; whilst planting of 1.8 million hectares would produce a further thousand man-years of employment in processing. These labour requirements in processing may seem modest but they relate to an industry which uses large-scale plant in some of which there is already substantial use of electronic control mechanisms. They also relate only to rural areas. They thus embody a locational assumption which is subject to a wide range of influences. Total processing demands are larger than those in Table 5.3 by a factor of three. Many of such processes could nevertheless be developed in rural small towns.

Table 5.3 Forecasts of employment in wood processing in rural areas assuming traditional cutting regime (thousand man-years)

	1975	*2000*	*2025*
Alternatives			
1. No more new planting	4.0	4.6	3.5
2. Plant another 1 million hectares	4.0	4.6	4.6
3. Plant another 1.8 million hectares	4.0	4.6	5.0

Source: Forestry Commission (1977)

These estimates contrast strongly with those for other countries, particularly because of the long production cycle in Britain. It is probably also important that forest management units are smaller in Britain so that 'leakages' from rural sub-regions to other areas may be larger. In Australia, for example, Reilly (1974) attributed the whole direct and indirect employment generated by softwood planting in Australia to rural regions. He estimated that if Australian forests increased from their 1971 area of 0.43 million hectares at the annual rate of 30,000 hectares, total employment would increase from 50,000 or so in 1980 to between 130,000 and 160,000 in the year 2000, from the 1.2 million hectares of softwood.

This comparatively rapid build-up of employment is possible because of the faster growth of timber in Australia. Employment estimates to the turn of the century thus include the substantial labour requirements for felling, whereas the UK estimates do not. It also appears that no improvements in technology have been assumed in the Australian projections.

Future options

Because a large share of forestry is state owned and much of the private sector is government directed, goals other than economic efficiency could be pursued through its employment policy. Thus the Forestry Commission could be encouraged to employ people who would otherwise find it difficult to obtain jobs, in the interests of reducing rural unemployment. Further, the wide variations in future employment with productivity indicate possible scope for policies to generate jobs. If labour costs are low due to persistent structural unemployment, then there may be a case for choosing technology (particularly through the machines introduced) which will employ more, rather than less workers. This policy option follows from the low social opportunity costs of labour in rural areas and has been discussed at some length by Price (1978).

We have seen above that forestry differs from other rural employers, notably agriculture, in important ways which suggest that its labour force may develop differently. Of major importance is the future evolution of demand for timber. Present assumptions indicate that demand will be increasingly strong through into the next century. One consequence of this would appear to be significant increases in the real price of forest products; however, such increases might encourage the development of substitutes for timber and to the extent that this occurs, the demand for timber may not be as strong as is now expected. Thus the uncertainty of such forecasts must be borne in mind in interpreting them. Meanwhile the sensitivity of the estimates of future employment in forestry to productivity assumptions underlines the possibility of varying the amount of employment in forests through technical innovation. These could be influenced by state forest policy if the generation of rural employment was thought sufficiently important.

6

RECREATION AND TOURISM

The growth of rural recreation and tourism, since World War II has been a notable phenomenon. In this chapter we review the economics of the 'recreation and tourism industry' following a similar sequence to that of previous chapters. After some introductory discussion, we examine the demand for the 'products' of this industry. Then we discuss the conditions of supply, and finally the potential employment in recreation and tourism.

Recreation and tourism are discussed together in this chapter because they relate to closely connected activities. However, there are important differences between them which are worth noting at this stage. Recreation essentially refers to physical activities undertaken for pleasure which are often linked with some form of sport. Tourism, by contrast, embraces both the concept of recreational activities and that of travel. Indeed, in tourism, travel may be the essential component and recreational activities may be relatively unimportant. However, because rural recreation often involves travel, due to the spatial distribution of population and recreational facilities, the distinction between recreation and tourism is not always clearly maintained.

An institutional difference between recreation and tourism is that the supply of recreational goods, particularly those for rural recreation, is often closely controlled and developed by government agencies. By contrast, tourism is usually much more clearly established as a private sector activity. There are exceptions to this generalization in that some forms of recreation are marketed as private goods and there are some aspects of the tourist industry which are public in nature. Nevertheless it remains generally true that recreation is more publicly controlled than tourism.

For their existence in rural areas both recreation and tourism require some particular physical attraction which provides a focus for participation. This will often be some natural feature – a lake, a mountain, a valley, cave or forest – which, either from its physical dimensions or from its historical associations, is perceived as a worthwhile location to visit. Such attractions may be tightly focused in one small area or diffused through a large tract of countryside. Where the focus is relatively precise and the attraction strong, there may be enough tourist demand to justify substantial private investment. Such investments often bring problems with them in that there may be a conflict between those wishing to develop an area for intensive commercial tourism and those who prefer to use it as a more lightly developed recreational resource. Such conflicts have become increasingly common in the developed world in the last two or three decades and have generated substantial government intervention.

Another reason for government intervention, particularly in the tourist industries, has been because of concern with international or inter-regional flows of income. Thus in Britain policies to develop tourism have been pursued through tourist boards which were established to promote tourism in Britain. Governmental enthusiasm for this activity was partly due to the thought that the balance of payments might be strengthened if foreign tourists could be encouraged to come to Britain and if domestic tourists could be persuaded to take their holidays within Britain. The vigour with which tourist boards have pursued their remit has brought them into confrontation with the environmental lobby in a number of instances.

A final introductory point is that unlike agriculture, forestry or manufacturing, tourism and recreation are essentially service industries. That is, they do not provide a physical good which can be bought and sold but a service which is often associated with a particular locality or region and which must be consumed *in situ*. Thus for both recreation and tourism it is essential to note that the consumer must be able to gain access to rural areas if he is to obtain the use of these services. Hence much of the growth of tourism and recreation is explainable in terms of the rapid spread of personal transport since World War II.

Demand

The least controversial aspect of tourism and recreation during the past three decades has been its rapid growth rate. The phenomenon has been reviewed by many authors in descriptive terms (for example Vickerman, 1975; Whitby and Willis, 1978) and in a more formal analytical mode by one or two official studies (ORRC, 1962; Economic Associates Ltd, 1967; Adams *et al.*, 1973) and by some individual researchers (for example Shucksmith, 1980; Stoakes, 1979). This section draws on the above sources to present a brief survey of findings: brief because recreational demand is relatively well understood and, compared to supply, less important in determining employment.

The growth in aggregate recreational participation in rural areas is difficult to measure because there are so many different forms of activity individuals may pursue, and very large samples are needed to obtain sound estimates from surveys. The study by Adams *et al.* in the USA was based on information collected from a sample of 4029 households in 1972. A similar survey for the UK, carried out in 1977 for the Countryside Commission, was based on home interviews with 5040 respondents (Fitton, 1978). These studies relate to a cross-section of the population in one year and therefore reveal little about trends.

Information on specific activities is also available. Visits to outdoor recreation sites are now being counted, and use of publicly provided camp-sites is being monitored. Membership of activity clubs – fishing and sailing for example, and broader groups such as the National Trusts in the UK is known. All of these data sources show a strong upward trend in participation since World War II. The explanation of this broad trend is generally accepted: the two main factors cited being the increased leisure time available to the individual and the growth in incomes. An associated cause is the spread of cheap personal transport. These three factors are worth considering separately before we attempt a summary of the development of demand.

The amount of leisure available for recreation might be roughly indicated by the average length of the working week. However, this would be only a very rough indication because less than half of the total population is in employment and, in any case, leisure tends to be a residual determined after the more basic requirements of earning a living and providing for a family have been met. Although the length of the working week in Britain has changed very little over several decades, the proportion of the labour force who are currently entitled to two weeks or more of annual holiday has grown from a mere 3 per cent in 1961 to very nearly 100 per cent now. In addition to this the number of Bank Holidays has been increased. The proportion of the population undergoing full-time education has grown as has the number and proportion of people on pensions. Such a development towards the extension of discrete concentrated leisure periods tend to promote expansion in recreation and tourism and they have been very strong trends during the post-war period. One more recent development which may have some impact on recreation, if not tourism, is the dramatic increase during the 1970s in the proportion of people unemployed. Unemployment in Britain has already exceeded 2 million and is expected to grow further (as noted in Chapter 1). Other developed countries have had similar experiences and it is at least worth asking whether such involuntary leisure will lead to an increase in the pressure on the cheaper forms of recreation.

For many recreational activities, changes in average income, as with the average working week, are only a first approximation of the real cause of growth. Particularly in rural recreation, the possession of a private car is almost a prerequisite, hence changes in the proportion of the population earning enough to own a car might predict the rate of recreational activity more closely than average incomes. Apart from such details, it is generally accepted that recreation and tourism are income elastic activities; that is, as income rises a more than proportional share of it will be spent on recreation and tourism. This means that the proportion of expenditure on these services will grow faster than *per capita* incomes. However, this does not mean that expenditure on all forms of recreation and tourism will grow at the same rate. Some activities will be more influenced by income than others which means that the pattern of demand for recreation will change as incomes grow.

The availability of cheap personal transport has already been mentioned as a determinant of recreational demand. However, participation in rural recreation, particularly, requires not only the ownership of a car, but the possibility of running it as well. Many studies of recreation have demonstrated an inverse relationship between participation at a particular site and travel costs. Since the main variable cost of car travel is petrol, expected increases in petrol prices have led to predictions of some decline in recreational participation, or at least some reduction in the rate of growth.

However, the deficiencies in data noted above, together with the range of possible activities and the even greater diversity of motivations for recreation, leaves this important question unresolved. In the UK, for example, Shucksmith (1980) has suggested that the high and rising elasticity of angling participation with respect to price, which he found at a particular reservoir, indicates some decline in the rate of participation during the 1970s in response to rising petrol prices. This view receives some support from the Countryside Commission's survey, referred to above (Fitton, 1978), where respondents were asked whether the increase in the price of petrol during the last two years (i.e. from 1975 to 1977) had led them to reduce their trips to the countryside. The results, analysed by income group show a strong inverse correlation between income in response to rising petrol prices: that is, the higher the income the smaller the proportion reducing trip-making. For the lowest income group (less than £1000 per annum) 51 per cent claimed they had reduced their rate of trip-making, whereas for the highest group (£8000 and above) only 9 per cent reported fewer trips. Such findings suggest that further increases in petrol prices may indeed reduce rural recreational participation. However, Stoakes (1979) takes a more optimistic view on the basis of an analysis of factors affecting rural recreation during the 1970s. He argues that the oil-price induced recession has been more important in reducing recreational participation than the price of petrol *per se*. Thus trips to countryside tourist attractions (wild-life parks, National Trust properties and the like), and trips involving large non-travel cost items (eating and drinking) will have been reduced more than informal recreation trips, according to Stoakes. The resolution of this particular argument cannot be attempted here, because it would involve very careful interpretation of the limited data available. Nevertheless it is important to note the argument because the Stoakes view, that high oil prices will reduce rural trip-making to some attractions, may have important employment implications for rural areas. Such attractions employ larger numbers of people on particular sites than informal recreational provision and, if their revenue is cut by high petrol prices, then rural employment will be reduced by more than it would be if informal trips were reduced in response to high petrol prices. The price elasticity of demand for recreation facilities is thus an important concept in recreation and tourist planning and firmer estimates of these elasticities would make for more accurate planning.

It should be recognized that the studies of recreational and tourist demand reviewed above have not been carried out with the intention of shedding light on employment creation. Consequently they do not discriminate between remote rural areas, where depopulation has made a potential case for jobs to be established, and the urban fringe, where there is no great pressure for generating employment. Perhaps the main conclusion from the discussion so far is that major overall determinants of demand for recreation are leisure and income. As far as depopulating and remote rural areas are concerned, the contribution of these activities to future development may be influenced adversely by increases in the cost of travelling to them. If the use of cars becomes very expensive, then those areas served by public transport will be well placed to attract participants away from places which can only be reached by car. However, such events depend upon the unknown evolution of petrol costs and it would be premature to forecast major swings in the fortunes of particular areas.

Supply

A theoretical explanation of the supply of recreational facilities would include the price of participation in activities, the cost of the inputs used and the technology available to combine them. However, in this particular sector two important types of physical constraint should also be noted. First, the majority of these activities can only be supplied for a limited season. Many activities are constrained to particular times of the year by law (fishing, shooting), by climate (skiing, swimming), or perhaps by custom (many field sports) as well as by the inclination of participants (visiting outdoor sites of all kinds). Secondly, the amount of some facilities which can be made available is physically restricted. There is a limit to the number of man-made or natural tourist attractions which can be supplied simply because the absolute number of such facilities is finite. However, this latter constraint is often reinforced by the pattern of asset ownership which enables exclusion of the public from some attractions. There is also a local constraint in terms of the carrying capacity of each facility.

These constraints on tourism and recreation supply partly explain the extent to which governments attempt to participate in managing it. In the UK there has been a very substantial effort to promote and regulate rural recreation by the establishment of national parks and various other institutions which administer subsidies and apply controls. A somewhat different aspect of tourist promotion has been in the establishment of tourist boards. These agencies, which are regional in their coverage, have been given the task of promoting growth of the tourist industry. They have largely done this through the transmission of information to potential tourists, but have also worked with subsidies to promote expansion of the supply of particular facilities. Advice to farmers wishing to enhance their income from tourism has also been available from the official Agricultural Development and Advisory Service for some years.

A related form of government intervention which is also important comes under the heading of planning. Where an area is subject to intense recreational and tourist pressure there may be sufficient concern generated to produce a public attempt to reduce or contain the pressure. A number of options are available to public authorities wishing to produce such an effect. They may seek to generate alternative recreational attractions in some other area which will perhaps draw off the pressure from the 'honey pot'. Alternatively they may resort to pricing, where the facility can be fenced off, and access to it can be controlled. Public authorities may buy a facility or gain control of it by agreement with its owner and may try to mitigate the effect of pressure by providing regulatory information and warden services. All of such approaches have been tried in the UK and they have been reviewed by Thomson and Whitby (1976) among others. Most developed countries have set up institutions to regulate rural recreation.

The supply of recreational and tourist facilities will be only partly a matter of the availability of particular scenic and historic resources in a given rural area. In addition to this there may be substantial man-made provision arising from various investment activities. This would include the provision of specific sporting and recreational facilities as well as building and providing accommodation for tourists who wish to stay in rural areas, and stimulating the local production of associated goods which tourists may wish to buy.

Amongst private sporting facilities in rural Britain the most exclusive are associated with shooting and fishing. The location of such facilities was initially determined by the location of game, but the possibility of introducing stocks, particularly of fish, has led to a substantial increase in fishing sites. Management of existing stocks is more important with shooting where an effective gamekeeper may make an essential contribution to potential supply.

Private provision also predominates in tourism as far as the supply of accommodation is concerned. Here the wide range, from the traditional hotel through guest houses, hired holiday cottages and caravans to youth hostels and camp-sites should be noted. Many of the lower cost facilities are provided by semi-public agencies such as the Youth Hostels Association. The UK Forestry Commission is a government agency which has also become involved in tourist provision in a variety of ways. For example, during the latter half of the 1970s its 35 or so camping and caravan sites supplied 1.5 million 'camper nights'. In addition it also provided 609 picnic places, 622 forest walks and nature trails, 29 visitor centres, 25 arboreta, 7 forest drives and 167 cabins and holiday houses in 1979 (Forestry Commission, 1980). Although revenue from timber sales is still growing to a steady annual amount, the Commission's financial accounts indicate that the revenue from recreational activities amounts to only a small share of its annual receipts.

Another form of private recreational supply arises where more or less exclusive clubs manage a resource. For example, sailing clubs are a common way of managing this use of open water. Such clubs are typically run by the participants in the sport although they may owe their initial establishment to the 'owners' of the water. In the UK (and other countries) water supply authorities have often taken the initiative in promoting recreational use of newly established facilities. Indeed, they are now encouraged (under the Water Act of 1973) to provide for recreational use in the design of water supply facilities.

Employment in tourism and recreation

From the diversity of data sources above it can be seen that measurement of total employment in recreation and tourist activities would be extremely difficult. The part-time nature of providing services for tourists, the seasonality of many recreational and tourist activities and the likelihood that many facilities will also be used for non-tourist purposes all suggest that precise identification of those employed in this sector will be costly.

The part-time aspect of tourism and recreation arises because, at a small scale of activity, such participation in the tourist industry can provide a supplement to the income of those who already live in scenic rural areas. There can be no general statements about the importance of such activities, but clearly the potential is there. Where a farmer's wife is willing to take in paying guests or to provide farmhouse teas during the summer season, this does enable further income to be earned. Some farms have also provided self-catering accommodation. In the UK this may take the form of short-term letting of former farm workers' cottages, or of more purpose-built chalets, or of permanent caravan sites. In other countries, where short-term seasonal labour is employed on farms, the accommodation provided for them can be used for recreational purposes. For example the shearers' quarters on New Zealand's farms and grazing properties are commonly hired out to temporary visitors. The importance of such activities is that they generate income in rural areas which is more likely to be spent there than the larger-scale facilities which may rely on migrant labour and 'imported' inputs.

The seasonality of rural recreational and tourist activities was noted above and can become important for the many recreational activities which are tied to more or less precise seasons – consider skiing, shooting, fishing, and perhaps hiking – so that their seasonality is highly predictable and well determined in advance. However, the greater spread of second and even third holidays for middle income tourists, together with increasing ingenuity in extending the seasonal availability of some activities (for example the use of artificial snow in ski-fields) tends to spread these seasonal peaks. Another approach to the problem of seasonality is for managers of recreation activities to offer cut-price facilities out of season. Thus winter skiing resorts may be used for conferences in the summer; summer resorts may be used for conferences in the winter. Many newly constructed facilities may be designed with such dual use in mind. The importance of seasonality is that it tends to restrict the employees available to the recreation industry to particular social groups. These may be those who are self-employed or people who reside in the area where the facility is located and are prepared to be employed for only part of the year. Alternatively, the facilities may be staffed by migrant labour, perhaps recruited from students or possibly workers in other industries which have complementary seasons. The use of migrant labour has obvious disadvantages from the point of view of the contribution of employment to the local economy. Migrant workers are likely to be trying to save money to spend elsewhere and will be less inclined to spend it where they earn it. They are unlikely to be at all interested in contributing to the local community life and may even occasionally form a dissident element within the area where they work.

The labour intensity of many tourists and recreational facilities varies considerably. Thus hotels and boarding houses may be substantial employers of manual labour, much of it unskilled labour. By contrast a ski-field will require the services of instructors and machinery operators as well as a range of more menial workers. Guides who conduct parties round scenic and historic sites are skilled in a very specific way although they may be able to acquire their skills in a fairly short space of time. The general tendency in the catering and hotel sector of developed countries has been towards the use of pre-prepared foods to a considerable extent, which, in the absence of local linkages, reduces the local employment generated by such industries.

Thus, for example, in the UK the British Tourist Authority claims that 1½ million people 'depend, directly or indirectly, upon tourism for their livelihoods' (BTA, 1980). It is important to note that this total includes both direct and indirect employment generated through tourism. That is, some sort of multiplier estimate has been used in arriving at the total (see Chapter 9). Furthermore, the fact that such a claim relates to the whole of the UK indicates that the majority of those included in this aggregate will be urban residents and therefore beyond the scope of this book. Such estimates, based on multipliers applied to rather weakly defined aggregate employment statistics, offer no means of assessing the level of rural employment. For Australia the data offer no more precision. Thus, Sinden (1977) points out that the 'amusement, hotel and restaurant' sector ranked fifth amongst Australian industries as an employer. The volume of annual sales of 'travel and tourism' was similarly large.

Local estimates exist for particular regions which show that some employment is generated by the existence of recreation and tourist attractions, but no aggregate estimates are available for rural areas as a whole. The local expenditure of tourists and recreationists in the regions they visit has been estimated by many workers. The volume of expenditure indicates the amount of primary employment generated and the expenditure resulting from this will then generate a smaller volume of secondary or indirect employment.

For example, Archer (1974) estimated that each £10,000 worth of tourist expenditure in the island of Anglesey generated 4.3 primary and 0.49 secondary jobs. Total primary and secondary jobs varied for different categories of tourist: hotel guests generated 4.9, static caravanners 4.0 and bed and breakfast users 3.6 jobs per £10,000. This compares well with general expenditure, which generated 1.9 direct and 0.49 indirect jobs per £10,000. Smith and Wilde (1977) have produced a similar study of the impact of tourism in Western Tasmania. The methodology of such impact studies is discussed in Chapter 9.

The focus of Archer's study above is on the various impacts of an increase in tourist expenditure. Another analytical viewpoint, taken by Brown and MacMillan (1977) starts from investment expenditure and distinguishes its impact during the capital investment process from its effect during the operational phase. These authors found, for the Interlake region of Manitoba in the 1970s, that capital expenditure of $1 million on outdoor recreation projects generated employment of 15.7 man-years annually over five years, compared with 11 man-years per year during the development phase. Notably these impacts were very much smaller than those resulting from various agricultural development schemes in the same region. On the basis of their analysis, which includes a substantial survey amongst visitors, they conclude that:

> The potential regional impacts of recreation development can be assessed relative to the achievement of the largest possible increase in the elements of a regional final demand vector. In the construction phase, the effect on final demand will be greater if more local people can be involved in construction and operation and if training is emphasised. Recreation sites can attract more additional visitors and expenditures to a region if care is exercised not to duplicate existing recreational opportunities. Regional impacts will increase if local businesses add services to meet the

needs of visitors and facilities are designed to increase stay length of visitors.

At a smaller scale of recreational provision is the farm-based supply of facilities. Two aspects, one private and one public, are important here. The private prospect of encouraging farmers to enhance their incomes by diversifying into tourism has already been mentioned. Indeed Archer's study found the single highest income multiplier impact of tourist expenditure, amongst hotels, caravans, tents and 'farmhouse and bed and breakfast' provision to be through the last category. That is, the small scale, labour intensive facilities seem to offer a substantial rate of impact per unit of tourist expenditure, with an expenditure multiplier of 1.76 compared with an average for tourist expenditure of 1.326. Nevertheless, it must be emphasized that farmhouse developments are likely to be very small and their absolute economic impact will not therefore be significant unless a high proportion of small farmers, say in a highly scenic area, provide facilities.

A few specific studies of the economics of farmhouse tourist facilities have now been completed in the UK and their results shed light on the employment potential here. Most recently Denman (1978) has published a study relating to Scotland which is based on a somewhat larger sample than the earlier study for England and Wales (Dartington Amenity Research Trust, 1974). Denman concludes that some 6100 private landholders (who may be the occupiers of crofts, farms, small-holdings or estates) were involved in some form of tourist or recreational provision in Scotland. This compares with a larger total for England and Wales, of 10,000–15,000 (Dartington Amenity Research Trust, 1974). Denman's study contains estimates of labour requirements, median size and number of enterprises in Scotland. These data are reproduced in Table 6.1, where they are combined to yield an estimate of total labour requirements.

The data were obtained by sample surveys, some of them postal. The number of holdings with given enterprises are listed first, showing the numerical importance of the relatively low labour intensity activities such as self-catering accommodation. Multiplying the second and third columns together gives the median labour requirement for each enterprise, shown in column 4. Only in the case of dinner, bed and breakfast and pony trekking does this amount to nearly a one man-year sized operation, underlining the essentially part-time status of tourism on farms. The author also estimates that, mainly because of the importance of caravan accommodation in Scotland and on farms, some 20 per cent of all holiday bed-nights are provided on private landholdings. The final column of Table 6.1, obtained as the product of the other columns divided by 220 (the notional number of man-days in a year) suggests a global total potential employment on Scottish landholdings. It must be emphasized that these estimates are very tentative, not least because of the uncertainty attached to the standard man-day requirement. Also it must be emphasized that, although total labour requirements amount to only 1400 or so man-years, nevertheless, because of the small scale of such enterprises many more actual people than this will have obtained some employment from tourism. Indeed a lower limit of the number actually obtaining some employment would be indicated by the total of the first column of the table, which is nearly 6000. This might be compared with total employment of full-time hired workers on Scottish farms of some 30,000.

The second aspect of the supply of farm-based tourism which is important in the economics of employment is the extent to which development is constrained by the physical resources available. This may be a question of the amount of suitable space, water, mountains, and other recreational features or of the extent to which other uses, such as agriculture, forestry, water gathering, conservation and defence, conflict with recreational land use. Such questions have been reviewed in Britain, at national level, by organizations such as the Institute of Terrestrial Ecology (1978), and the Countryside Commission (1974). More detailed local studies have also completed, for example by Feist *et al.* (1976) and others, such as Gibbs and Whitby (1975) and the Countryside Commission (1976), have focused on particular mechanisms of recreation provision. Gibbs and Whitby examined access agreements, whereby landholders and other interested parties allow recreational access to their land. In return they receive a financial consideration related to the amount of damage caused and are usually provided with a warden service which helps to regulate the recreational use. Such agreements are few in number and relate to low productivity land. The total exchequer cost involved in 1975 averaged £3.08 per hectare of land subject to agreement. Of this total some £2.05 was

Table 6.1 Number, size and labour requirements for tourist enterprises on landholdings in Scotland, 1975

Facilities (units)	*Number[a] of landholdings with facility*	*Median size of facility*	*Estimated[d] annual standard labour requirements SMD*		*Estimated[e] annual aggregate labour requirement in man-years*
			per unit	*per median facility*	
	(1)	(2)	(3)	(4)	(5)
Holiday cottages[b] (cottages)	1766	2.0	9.5	19.0	153
Static caravans (vans)	1026	2.5	4.2	10.5	49
Bed and breakfast (bed)	746	5.0	7.6	38.0	129
Dinner, bed and breakfast (bed)	840	10.0	16.8	168.0	641
Touring caravan site (pitch)	606	20.0	2.3	46.0	127
Camp site[c] (pitch)	606	20.0	2.3	46.0	127
Pony trekking (pony)	233	8.0	16.5	132.0	140
Total					1366

Source: Denman (1978)

Notes: a. Numbers obtained by applying percentages for all holdings by the total landholdings in Scotland reported by Denman as 46,640.
b. Including chalets, which are assumed to have the same size and labour requirements.
c. Assumed to have same size and labour requirements as touring caravan sites.
d. Standard man-days relate to a standard eight-hour day.
e. The product of the first three columns divided by an assumed 220 working days in the year.

devoted to provision of the warden service – most of it going on wages – and a further £0.89 to maintenance and administration. Thus the major share of expenditure through such programmes tends to increase rural employment.

This review of recreation and tourism highlights the dual nature of these industries in rural areas. Large-scale developments in particular localities may make a substantial contribution to employment while small-scale, part-time and seasonal activities will have a diffuse impact. Where they occur, the larger schemes will have a substantial local impact. On the other hand the aggregate contribution of the smaller schemes to rural employment may be as important.

7

RURAL INDUSTRIALIZATION

It is usually anticipated that industrial processes will, almost by definition, be located in urban areas. There they have access to the labour force, transport facilities and services which they require. Nevertheless, the establishment of industrial processes in rural areas is quite a common phenomenon. Traditionally, there have been two major reasons for this: firstly, the industries which are associated with agriculture, especially where they process agricultural products, have tended to be located in rural areas, and secondly, rural positions may be determined by the location of a necessary input or facility, such as mineral deposits or energy supplies. In this case, the scale of the operation can itself change a 'rural' location into an 'urban' one, such as has been the case in coal-mining villages. More recently, in seeking the development of rural areas, industrial activities which have no particular need to be located there have been encouraged to establish in order to replace the employment lost by declining primary industries.

The objective of this chapter is to consider the role which can be played by industrial processes in the development of rural regions and the various impacts which occur. We include in this both extractive and manufacturing industries. A wide range of industrial processes have the potential to be undertaken in rural areas. Those which are suitable in any one particular area will depend upon its characteristics and location relative to the necessary inputs and markets.

The successful establishment of industry anywhere is dependent upon a number of factors. Firstly, land must be available with appropriate planning consent for the erection of factory premises. It will be necessary for this land to have been, or at least have the potential to be, provided with services such as sewerage, electricity and telecommunications. The site must have access to transportation networks for the arrival of inputs and despatch of outputs and the local area must be able to supply the necessary labour force. There must also be housing for the incoming workers who will play a role in the initial establishment of the process. This group will expect the area to provide an acceptable range of services including schools, medical services and social and recreational facilities. Particular industries may have special requirements such as water supplies or harbour facilities.

We begin the chapter with a brief examination of two types of industrial process which have particular reasons for being located in rural areas: those dependent upon a specific deposit or facility at a particular location and those dependent upon rural products as a raw material. The major part of the chapter considers small- and medium-scale manufacturing industry in general, which has a range of location options open to it, both urban and rural. As such, it is of greatest interest to us in our consideration of the possibilities for rural employment. We therefore discuss the factors influencing the location of manufacturing activity, its impact in rural areas and policies to influence the extent of rural industrialization. We conclude with some thoughts as to the prospects for industry in rural areas.

Extractive industries and large-scale developments

Clearly the location of extractive industries is completely dominated by the availability of naturally occurring raw materials, and these are likely to be exploited on the basis of the quality of the raw material and its ease of extraction. These operations tend to be highly capital intensive and to require few locally produced inputs. They are operated with a limited time horizon, which could vary from a few years in the case of open-cast mines, to much longer periods for deep mining. While, in their operational phase, their impact on local economies may be quite small, they often have considerable effects on local populations and employment during their establishment phase. Furthermore, their environmental impact is often a cause of considerable concern.

Other large-scale industrial activities in rural areas are similarly likely to be attracted to some specific aspect of a particular area. For instance, the smelting of alumina in the production of aluminium requires a considerable input of electrical energy. This activity therefore tends to be established in locations where large supplies of electricity are available at low cost, such as near hydro-electric or nuclear power plants, and where transport facilities allow the movement of raw materials and of output. Locations with these necessary attributes are often in rural areas.

The location of extractive industries and large-scale development may be influenced by regional development objectives; for example, all of the three aluminium smelters established in the UK during the late 1960s were located in areas of high unemployment. However, because of the scale of the operation involved, such developments are unlikely to be suitable instruments for rural development, where the objective is to maintain the populations of small towns. We therefore generally exclude this type of development from the discussion in this chapter.

Processing of rural products

The increasing extent to which food is processed prior to final consumption and the availability of other raw materials, such as timber or wool, means that the processing of rural products provides an activity well suited to employment creation in rural areas. The types of activity included under this heading would include the canning and freezing of vegetables or meat, the production of dairy products or sugar, or the production of cloth or timber products. Processing rural products increases their value and can reduce their volume, although this will not be the case where elaborate packaging is used. Thus, the activity can make a contribution by raising local incomes as well as possibly reducing overall transportation costs. Doeksen and Schreiner (1972) quote research indicating that agricultural processing in the USA is less heavily concentrated than manufacturing as a whole and that at that time it was becoming more decentralized. Further, it was anticipated that employment in this sector would increase. This trend has encouraged a number of rural areas to examine the feasibility of establishing agricultural processing industries.

There are, however, limitations. The capital investment involved in processing often requires that equipment be operated throughout most of the year in order to achieve an acceptable return, while on the other hand a region particularly suited to the production of a single agricultural product is only likely to be able to supply this over a limited period. This may not be an important limitation for products which may be stored, such as timber or bulk frozen vegetables, and there are exceptions where the process is specific to a particular input, such as sugar, but it will restrict other activities to locations which can provide a variety of raw materials, such as fruits for canning. The demand for the output must also be considered. Where demand for processed agricultural products is increasing, then new areas may be expected to be able to develop these activities. However, when demand is static, new facilities are only likely to be viable if they can be operated at lower cost per unit of output or procure their inputs at lower cost than their competitors. A further qualification to the value of establishing an agricultural processing industry has been raised by Powell and Mandeville (1978). They point out the close interaction between agricultural processing plants and the agricultural enterprises from which they draw their supplies. Thus, where the rural sector is subject to instability, either due to variability in the volume of output or in its price, the processing industry will also be affected by this, with serious consequences for regions whose incomes are heavily dependent upon these two sources alone.

Finally, a potential benefit sometimes claimed for processing development, is that not only will employment be created directly in the processing plant but that it will also be encouraged in the rural sector supplying the raw materials. However, it appears that this is not necessarily the case. For instance, the increased production of vegetables following the establishment of processing in the Eastern Scottish Borders led to the substitution of peas for sugar beet and potatoes in crop rotations. Both of these latter crops have higher labour requirements than vining peas, which were by far the most commonly grown vegetable for processing (Hodge and Whitby, 1979). Given this lower labour requirement, it is probable that the overall level of employment on farms in the area will have fallen due to the introduction of vegetable production. This loss should therefore be balanced against gains in the processing industry itself.

When the raw materials are not already available in an area seeking to establish a processing industry, a complication arises in the need for the simultaneous introduction of the processing facility and the production of raw materials. This need for co-ordination may be overcome in a number of ways. Firstly, a development agency may identify the opportunities available and advise the various parties involved. However, it is probable that before any significant amounts of capital are committed, either in producing the primary product or in establishing the processing facility, firmer agreements will be required. This can be achieved through the establishment of a co-operative, whereby the growers themselves invest in the processing operation, so becoming financially committed to the venture's success; by the company establishing the processing plant, issuing contracts to growers with penalty clauses for failure to contribute the agreed quantities of raw material; or finally by complete vertical integration, whereby the raw material production and processing is undertaken by the same company. Co-ordination is likely to be difficult to achieve whichever approach is adopted and it seems likely that there will usually be a role to be played by a third party in bringing the various organizations together. In that processing activities do have flexibility in their location, often in terms of choosing between alternative rural areas, we may continue to bear them in mind in the remainder of the chapter as one example of a manufacturing process.

Small- and medium-scale manufacturing industry

The concept of manufacturing embraces a huge range of different activities, the majority of which could be undertaken in rural areas. On the whole, however, those which are likely to be operated there will tend to be those requiring a small work force and generally not requiring large quantities of bulky inputs, unless these are produced locally. Summers *et al.* (1976) have surveyed studies of industrial development in the non-metropolitan areas of the USA. While their study doubtless includes some areas which we would regard as urban, their results are of interest in this context. They present a summary of seventy-one case studies on which their work is based and many of these indicate the type of output of the various manufacturing plants. Table 7.1 shows a summary of the number of plants producing various categories of product.

As can be seen, a wide variety of products are produced in the 198 plants for which specific information on product type was available. Perhaps most notable is the lack of association with the traditional rural industries which service the agricultural sector. This variety too is reflected in the type of labour which is required by manufacturing companies. Many will seek to employ local unskilled

Table 7.1 Numbers of manufacturing plants producing products in various categories

Product group	*Number of plants*
Metal and metal products	36
Shoes and apparel	32
Wood products	14
Chemicals	12
Textiles and fibres	11
Electrical and electronic components	10
Transportation equipment	10
Farm equipment and supplies	9
Stone, clay and glass products	8
Paper and paper products	8
Furniture and domestic products	8
Machinery	7
Construction components	6
Sports and holiday equipment	6
Food	3
Others (where products were indicated)	18
Total plants indicating product group	198

Source: Derived from Summers *et al.* (1976)

labour which may be taught any necessary skills in the factories. Others, such as electronics companies, may demand at least some highly skilled employees who are likely to be attracted from outside the locality. The possible importance of differing qualities of labour in urban and rural locations is considered later.

The facilities which are required in an area in order to allow the establishment of manufacturing will be very largely determined by the type and scale of industry which is being considered. Those considered at the start of this chapter will be the basis of this, and specific enterprises may have other requirements, such as access to a river for the disposal of effluent. Manufacturing may be established in a relatively short time period and continue while demand for its output and its competitiveness is maintained. It is usually this last factor which will determine the success of enterprises; some of the factors influencing this are dealt with in the following section.

The location of industry

Decisions involving the location of manufacturing industry are almost exclusively made in mixed economies by private entrepreneurs. They will respond to the relative advantages and disadvantages of different locations, as they perceive them, in selecting sites for new industrial enterprises. It is therefore important to consider, at least briefly, some of the factors and objectives which are likely to influence these decisions, not only in order to understand the existing pattern of industrial location, but also in planning policies to influence this pattern. See, for instance, Richardson (1969) for an introduction to the theory of the location of the firm. The need for a company to select a new production location will occur when a completely new enterprise is planned, when an existing company seeks to expand and is unable or unwilling to do so in its present location, or when there is dissatisfaction with the present location and it is felt that conditions could be improved elsewhere.

In the theory of industrial location, it is generally assumed that producers will seek locations which maximize their profits. Because of the complexity of considering all the variables involved, models of site selection are often based on the principle of minimizing total transport costs, i.e. the costs of transporting both inputs and products. However, other costs too are likely to vary in alternative locations, such as the costs of labour or power. Many other factors will also influence profitability in alternative locations. For instance, it is not only the cost of labour, but also the quality and quantity available which is important. The public and private services which are available in alternative locations are important too. Thus there may be advantages in establishing close by major industrial centres where external economies can be exploited through the availability of skilled labour and industrial services. Finally, the pattern of demand may also be important. Factors which indirectly influence a firm's profitability may also have a bearing on the location decision. In this context, for example, a pleasant environment could assist in attracting high-quality staff while a highly congested environment could deter staff or lead to delays in deliveries or despatch of materials.

However, in practice it appears that firms rarely undertake a thorough search of all possible locations or apply strict financial criteria to the location decision. The evidence suggests (Stilwell, 1972) that the typical decision-making process has three features:

1 the location decision arises as a result of a near-crisis situation, such that a speedy decision is more important than an ideal decision;
2 there is no systematic consideration of costs and revenues in alternative sites;
3 the tendency is to seek something suitable close at hand, the implicit assumption being that the present location is probably optimal. The firm thereby searches outwards and accepts the nearest site which appears satisfactory.

Other factors more associated with the decision-maker's personal welfare than with company profitability have also been suggested as determining location decisions, such as the fabled preferences of the managing director's wife or the proximity of a good golf course. It may fairly be assumed, nevertheless, that on the whole firms will tend to select the more profitable locations in preference to others, and so it is pertinent to consider the possible economic advantages and disadvantages of selecting rural as opposed to urban locations.

It is often assumed that on balance for the majority of industrial processes the disadvantages of locating in rural areas outweigh the advantages. This belief is founded on the fact that distance from markets and raw materials will raise the overall transport costs and so render firms less competitive. Furthermore, inability to exploit the external economies which can be available to firms in urban locations may exacerbate this position. The fact that the majority of manufacturing plants choose to cluster in urban areas could also perhaps be claimed as supporting evidence.

Working against these factors are a number of features of rural areas which can be advantageous to some producers. First of all, raw materials are available to processes requiring the output of primary industry. We have already discussed the processing of rural products. Companies occupying factories in rural areas may expect that as a result of generally lower land prices, space will be available at a lower cost than would be the case elsewhere. This could be important in the manufacture and storage of relatively bulky products. Similarly, areas around factories are less likely to be congested so that plenty of space is available for parking and for delivery and despatch of goods. This absence of congestion could mean that the increased time spent in reaching more distant plants is cancelled out by the time avoided in queuing to reach busy urban locations. The extra space which is often available around factories may also be attractive to companies anticipating future expansion.

The quality of rural environments will also be important to those living in these areas. Cheaper land and opportunities for outdoor recreation may provide attractions to prospective staff, although weighed against this is the lack of cultural and entertainment opportunities which are available in the larger urban centres. On balance, the advantage appears to be with less urban locations. Hoch (1976), in comparing wages found in different cities, has found that wage rates for the same work increase with increasing city size. This differential has been persistent over time, indicating that it does not arise from disequilibrium in the labour market, which is in a process of adjustment. Rather, it appears to reflect a more or less permament monetary compensation for the costs, both in terms of money and in the quality of life, in the form of congestion and pollution, which employees bear as the size of city increases. More recent work (Hoch, 1979) suggests that this relationship also holds for rural settlements, that is to say that wages increase directly with settlement size, although there is some evidence that compensatory payments may be made to employees in the smallest settlements with populations of less than 10,000.

Finally, there is the question of the quality and availability of labour. The numbers of workers available in any location will depend on a number of factors. Generally, apart from the small absolute number of people resident within commuting distance anyway, large numbers are unlikely to be available in rural areas due to the tendency for unemployed people to seek work in alternative locations. The work force which is available in a rural area will typically not have had a tradition of industrial experience. This is sometimes considered an advantage when it is claimed that such workers will be more flexible due to their lack of unionization, and more conscientious. However, their lack of industrial training and the absence of local training institutions means that skilled workers may need to be brought into the area and potential production time lost in providing training for others. In an early comparison of the productivity of urban and rural labour, however, Harbury (1958) found no evidence to show that rural labour was less productive.

The factors influencing companies to locate in the more remote areas suggest their possible advantages. In a study of firms establishing in a mainly rural region, Devon and Cornwall in South West England, Spooner (1972) found that the factor most commonly indicated as being most important in the decision to locate in this region was that it was an attractive area for key workers and management. Oakeshott (1979) has recently described the attractions of small English towns for manufacturing enterprises. These include the attraction of their physical environment, easy access to the countryside and the lack of polarization by class which has occurred in the older, more traditional industrial areas. These are combined with the improved road system and generally lower volume of raw materials and outputs than in the past which reduce the extent to which remoter areas are placed at a disadvantage with respect to overall transport costs.

It is possible that if decisions concerning location are made on the basis of less than full knowledge of the costs and benefits associated with alternative locations, or in order to achieve objectives other than maximizing profits, or finally in response to government incentives which distort the market system, then there could be more systematic relationship between the type of environment and industrial productivity. Tweeten and Brinkman (1976) quote a study by Janssen (1974) which examined comparative profit rates by size of city in the USA. He found, for the most part, no statistically significant relationship between profit rate and the size of population of the communities among which the industries were located. This result conforms with the hypothesis that firms locate where profits are greatest and so push high rates down to the average rate in any particular location by additional firms being attracted there. However, Nicholson (1978) has presented a cross-sectional production function analysis of firms operating in the USA. He estimated separate functions for industries operating in 'rural' markets, defined where in a particular state 25 per cent or less of employment was in a Standard Metropolitan Statistical Area (SMSA), and 'urban' markets where more than 25 per cent of the state's employment was in a SMSA. On averaging parameters for the industries in common, he found that on the basis of the neutral efficiency parameter of the production function, overall 'urban' production efficiency was approximately 12 per cent above 'rural'. Although this result may not be significant overall, this does provide support for the hypothesis that external economies exist in urban areas.

These two results are not necessarily inconsistent. Companies in urban areas could be more 'efficient' than companies in rural areas and yet not make significantly different profits. Where efficiency is higher, more companies will establish so forcing product prices down and input prices, especially land, up. In fact it is likely that the value of any residual differences in profitability due to location will tend to be capitalized in land values and so accrue to landowners rather than company owners. Nevertheless, even if these results were accepted as evidence that on average industrial processes *are* more efficient in urban areas, it does not preclude the possibility that some types of activity could be more efficient in rural areas. Therefore, it is certainly not the case that encouraging industry to operate in rural locations will necessarily lead to less efficient industrial production. This issue is considered further in Chapter 10.

Local linkages

The introduction of new industrial processes in an area might stimulate the development of other related activities which either provide inputs for the new industry or process its outputs. The relationships between the two stimulated activities and the initially established industrial process are known respectively as backward and forward linkages. The impact of backward linkages would be included in the assessment of the multiplier effects of new activities, which we return to in Chapter 9. They are worthy of further consideration here, as different types of industrial process are likely to have differential linkages and consideration of these is of value in assessing the types of activity which are most suited to the achievement of local employment creation objectives.

When an industrial process is relocated to a new area, it has the choice of continuing to draw its raw materials from its traditional suppliers, or to seek new suppliers in its new location. Studies of firms moving to new areas have found that traditional suppliers are often maintained. For instance, migrant firms settling in East Anglia and the North of England mostly retained the linkages which they had used in their original location (Moseley and Townroe, 1973). In a study of twenty-four plants operating in West Central Scotland, Lever (1974) found that for the year 1970, only 20 per cent of their total expenditure was spent in the whole of Scotland, as compared to 20.5 per cent in South East England. It can thus be surmised that at least some firms do not need an established industrial base in the area in which they are located from which to draw supplies and are willing to maintain long linkages to relatively distant regions. However, the costs of transport are not negligible. Lever, on the basis of his study, pointed out that branch plants of non-Scottish companies had a tendency to retain links with suppliers and customers in their base region where this was less than approximately 300 miles from the Scottish branch plant, but that beyond this linkages were rarely retained. Similarly, mobile firms are unlikely to draw large quantities of inputs from the local economy, especially where this is relatively small and underdeveloped as is the case for rural areas. Where purchases are made locally, these are most likely to be in the form of local subcontracting and service provision, unless the plant has been established with the specific intention of making use of some locally available raw material.

In a study of newly established companies operating a rural area in the Eastern Scottish Borders (see Chapter 11), the authors (Hodge and Whitby, 1979) found that the two largest categories of local purchases were on local hauliers and other services, such as builders, electricians and hotels. For the seven companies for which full information was available, the estimated value of the contribution to local incomes resulting from local purchases per employee was calculated. It was found that for 1976, this figure varied between £50 and £500 per annum; the estimate for all the factories being £215. This figure appeared to be related to the type of work which was undertaken. Those companies undertaking the manufacture of small items for sale outside the area had least impact locally, while those companies either using local raw materials (even though the actual expenditure made on these had been excluded from this analysis) or providing a local service tended to lead to higher local incomes. However, the company making the highest contribution to local incomes sold practically none of its output in the area and did not use local raw materials or services. Its high contribution derived from a large expenditure on local haulage. In total it was estimated that 54 jobs had resulted from local purchases, equivalent to about 7 per cent of total employment in the factories studied. If the amount of local purchases was doubled the number of jobs in supplying local inputs was expected to rise to 125 or equivalent to 16 per cent of the factory employment.

Where the output of an industrial process represents an important input for other activities, then its establishment in an area can provide an incentive for the development of these other activities. Hirschman (1958) in the context of development in the LDCs has suggested three considerations which may make the domestic availability of a new product an effective spur to further development. These are that:

1 importing requires special skills and so may restrict the availability of suitable inputs for the development of these other activities;
2 production based largely on imports tends to be risky due to balance of payments difficulties or restrictions on international trade;
3 the producers themselves are likely to promote the domestic utilization of their product and so encourage the development of forward linkages.

None of these considerations are likely to be of importance when we have in mind the declining regions of a developed country, where products will be available elsewhere in the economy. However, it is possible that local availability will provide an opportunity to an entrepreneur who is looking for some suitable investment. Probably of greater importance is the development of mutually dependent activities, such as in the case discussed earlier of the establishment of an agricultural processing industry, where both activities are developed simultaneously.

The size of the induced activity is unlikely to exceed that of the initial process and an industry is unlikely to supply all the inputs or to purchase all the output. However, some types of activity will have greater associations with the local economy than others, and as such are to be preferred in employment creation policies.

The impact of industrial processes on employment and population

The impact of any particular industrial process on the overall level of employment and population in an area will depend upon its influence on the local labour market, its relationships with other local industries and the expenditure and behaviour patterns of those whose employment is affected by the change. Clearly, too, the type of employment provided will be determined by the nature of the industrial process. It has quite commonly been observed that a large proportion of the work forces of these enterprises are in the younger age groups (Summers *et al.*, 1976; Hodge and Whitby, 1979). This is probably due to the employment of school leavers and younger people who might have alternatively left the area, and as such has implications for the future growth of local populations.

The nature of an industrial process will influence the type of work which is available and hence the distribution of male and female employees. In the review of studies of rural industrialization by Summers *et al.* (1976) there appeared to be no overall trend towards a preponderance of either male or female employment. Typically, there are few women involved in the production of steel, bricks or in most metal-working plants. Alternatively, female employment was high in the manufacturing of apparel and electronic systems components. The balance of male and female employment which is created in an area may be expected to have implications for changes in the levels of population movement. If decisions involving migration are made on the basis of the employment prospects of the head of household, then a predominance of male employment will tend to have a greater impact on migration, while a predominance of female employment will have less impact on migration patterns, but will tend to raise average household income levels. However, in the absence of a full understanding of the migration process, it is difficult to predict accurately the consequences of employment change.

Once again, the question of which particular groups within a community benefit from an increase in industrial employment will depend on the type of process involved. Given that those members of the work force who can offer greater skills generally receive higher incomes, an industry which provides employment for higher skilled employees will be most immediately beneficial to higher income groups, although it might be argued that these benefits will ultimately spill over to be more widely experienced in the community. Conversely, where employment is provided for the unskilled it might generally be accepted that this will have greatest impact on the lowest income groups, including the unemployed. Where policies are aimed at improving incomes of the poor, the extent to which the policy may be regarded as successful will follow from the distribution of benefits between households within the community. This aspect of industrial development in rural areas is one which has received relatively limited attention. One study (Deaton and Landes, 1978) which was made of over 700 workers in firms which located in rural Tennessee between 1970 and 1973 found that new manufacturing jobs resulted in a shift towards equality of family incomes among these workers. However, as only a small proportion of these were considered to be in poverty prior to the introduction of employment, it suggests that industrialization cannot provide the complete solution to poverty problems. Clearly, an ability to participate in the labour force is a prerequisite to being able to achieve benefits directly from the introduction of new employment opportunities. Other benefits, resulting from an increased population and improved service provision, will be more widely shared within the community.

The introduction of new industrial processes to an area will be likely to have an impact on the existing activities there, other than those working through the effects of the multiplier. These will occur through the new activities competing for resources which are presently in local use, especially labour and land. In rural areas without a significant industrial base, the existing activities which are most likely to be affected are primary industries and the service sector. To the extent that an increase in local population and incomes will lead to an increase in the demand for most public and private services, it is the primary activities which appear most likely to be detrimentally affected. On the whole, manufacturing enterprises are unlikely to take a large land area out of agricultural or timber production, although other industrial processes, such as open-cast mining or large-scale activities could take significant amounts. Where this is the case, enterprises will either be taken out of production completely or will be reduced in scale. In some circumstances, in marginal farming areas, the disturbance resulting from the change of use of land could provide an opportunity for rationalizing farm structure into larger units which can then provide an adequate income for the operator.

Probably of more general significance is the impact of new industrial processes on the availability of labour to agricultural enterprises. This question has been studied in Western Ireland (Lucey and Kaldor, 1969) and in Wales (Jones, 1972). The study in Ireland examined the impact of two manufacturing plants which were established in rural communities. A number of the employees continued to be involved in farm work after their employment in the plants. This was the case for about 37 per cent of the total 308 workers who were employed. Of these, 32 were farm operators who did not change their farm work association subsequent to obtaining plant employment. The study included an examination of the changes in their farm businesses which took place as a direct result of their obtaining employment in the new plants. Not surprisingly, most spent less time on farm work, although in the majority of cases there was no reduction in the level of farm output. In fact, in many cases an increase in output was reported. This was achieved by operators giving up leisure time for farm work, increased work by other family members and increased use of machinery. These changes were complemented by greater farm investment from the increased household incomes in the form of the purchase of additional stock, heavier use of fertilizers and in some cases, purchase or renting of extra land. In general, there was a shift away from labour intensive enterprises, such as grain, root and green crops, and a corresponding increase in the area under grassland. The results suggest therefore that at least for these particular businesses, in the short run industrialization led to some increase in agricultural output. Another study in Ireland (Curry, 1972), however, found that the majority of farmers who took an off-farm job still retained a preference for farming as an occupation.

The study in Wales looked at the effects of the construction of a reservoir and power station in North Wales. In this example it appeared that workers from farms who took up employment on the new construction sites tended to sever their agricultural connections. There was evidence that those workers who moved from the larger farms in the area were replaced by workers moving from the marginal farms. However, it was found that on these farms, investment in relatively small amounts of machinery in association with the use of some casual labour and contracting, was adequate to make good the loss of labour and enabled most farmers to continue without having to reduce their stocking densities or to adjust their farming system. It was suggested therefore that the introduction of these industrial activities provided the final pressure to remove surplus labour, thus speeding up a process which was already taking place and so improving overall efficiency.

In conclusion, the available evidence suggests that the introduction of industrial processes to rural areas appears not to have detrimental effects on local agriculture, and can in fact, be beneficial. Industrial processes can conflict with recreation and tourism, particularly through their impact on the environment. This may often be the case for large-scale extractive industries, but rarely with the relatively small manufacturing establishments which are of most significance from a rural policy point of view.

While we are not primarily concerned with social aspects, they do at least bear mention in the context of industrialization. The introduction of new forms of work in an area requires new behaviour patterns and causes altered social interactions amongst the community. The immigration of industrial workers into rural communities, both those as key workers and others seeking employment opportunities, with different backgrounds and attitudes to the existing population may be expected to provide a further stimulus to social change. One immediate effect will be the increase in the size of a community receiving new industry, albeit in the context of a declining rural hinterland, and social changes will match those which have occurred with the growth of other settlements. Clearly the size of the development relative to the size of the existing community will be an important determinant of the scale of any such changes.

Other influences result from the introduction of a new, distinct social grouping into the area. Contradictory positions are sometimes held on this aspect of development. While in principle community leaders see the introduction of new industry and the creation of new employment opportunities as being beneficial, they do not desire the introduction of 'outsiders' into their community, who they see as taking jobs away from local people and perhaps even threatening their leadership. Thus while they want growth and development for their town, they do not want people moving into the town from outside.

In reviewing studies of rural industrialization in the USA, Summers *et al.* (1976) found that on the whole industrial development did not have dramatic effects on social organization. Any changes which do occur will be likely to take place over a long period and to be influenced by a wide range of variables. However, some trends were observed and, contrary to expectation, leadership was thought to have become more concentrated, with little displacement of established power groups. People felt that there had been little change in neighbourliness through the period of industrial development and the change was generally seen as being beneficial to rural communities. Conversely, a study of rural industrialization in Western Ireland (Cawley, 1979) found that social and economic cohesion was disrupted as polarization took place between the 'locals' and the 'newcomers'. Such effects are emphasized where recent immigrants have language or religious differences from the local population. They are likely to be of least significance when the immigrants are return migrants who had previously left the area because of the lack of employment opportunities.

Public policy and rural industrialization

Given the desire to raise the level of employment in certain rural areas and the potential for influencing the level and location of industrial employment, policies are followed which seek to promote the development of industrial processes, particularly manufacturing activities, in rural areas. Garbett-Edwards (1972) has listed a number of reasons for seeking to encourage the establishment of new industries in rural areas. These include the need to absorb labour which becomes available with the decline in employment in agriculture, the stemming of migration through the provision of more local employment opportunities, the easing of a local unemployment problem or the maintenance of the economy of a market or service centre in order to ensure that it continues to fulfil this function.

A range of strategies exist by which government can attempt to raise the level of industrial activities in rural areas. We shall discuss these under three categories, although the boundaries between them are not always clear cut and some strategies involve aspects of more than one category. They involve, firstly, the improvement of locations as sites for industrial development generally; secondly, the reduction of the relative costs to industrial activities in rural locations; and, thirdly, the augmentation and speeding up of information flows.

There are a large number of ways in which locations can be rendered more favourable for industrial development, and hence more attractive to mobile and newly establishing enterprises. One of the major disadvantages of rural locations stems from their relative remoteness from product and factor markets and so attention may firstly be directed towards improving communications between the area in question and its nearer centres of population. The nature of improvements will depend upon the location. It could involve the construction or improvement of road or rail links, the introduction of a regular air service or the development of public transport. Telecommunication links are becoming increasingly important and these too may be developed. The major effect of these improvements is that they reduce the costs of communications and hence the overall operating costs of enterprises in the area. Communications are also of importance within the area in question. In order to attract an adequate labour force where the population is widely dispersed, people may be required to travel long distances to work. The existence of a reasonable public transport network could give prospective employers confidence that enough labour can be attracted. However, because public transport in rural areas tends to be limited, companies often have to make their own provisions. The presence of good communications within an area could also influence employees' migration decisions. When a company establishes, it will require a factory with a variety of services available and a labour force, some of whom may need to be attracted into the area from elsewhere and others who will be employed in the local labour market. Efforts to make these factors available will enhance the relative attractions of an area to mobile industries.

One major instrument of rural employment policy is the construction of advance factories. These are factories built without any particular occupiers in mind and then let out to suitable tenants. The agency most involved in constructing advance factories in rural Britain is the Development Commission (which we mentioned in Chapter 3), although since 1976 its responsibility has been limited to rural England. Responsibilities for factory construction in Wales and Scotland have been taken over by the Welsh and Scottish Development Agencies. The Development Commission's involvement in factory construction goes back to 1947, although up to 1960 only a small number of factories were constructed, all of which were in Wales and Scotland. In the mid-1960s the Commission selected a limited number of 'Trigger Areas' for special assistance which were situated in regions experiencing depopulation, but which were centred around potential growth points where small industries could develop. These could help stem the depopulation and maintain the levels of services available. The construction of advance factories provided the central instrument of the policy. The first 'Trigger Areas' to be designated were in mid-Wales and in the

Eastern Borders. The policies operated in these areas have been studied in detail (Development Commission, 1972; Hodge and Whitby, 1979) (see Chapter 11), respectively. Schemes were subsequently established in other areas. While factories were funded from the Development Fund, they were actually constructed by the Industrial Estates Corporations in the Development Areas, where the occupants were eligible for special grants, and by the Council for Small Industries in Rural Areas (CoSIRA), which is an agent of the Development Commission (also funded from the Development Fund) elsewhere. Recently, similar schemes have been initiated more widely in Special Investment Areas, by the Development Commission in co-ordination with the relevant county councils.

The factories built are, on the whole, quite small, ranging from 'nursery' units of about 1500 square feet (140 square metres) up to larger factories of about 15,000 square feet (1400 square metres). They are constructed on fully serviced sites and space is available for future expansion. Table 7.2 shows the total numbers of factories approved by the Development Commission between 1959 and 1976. It should be noted that there can be considerable time lags between approval and construction and occupation. In England, over 70 per cent of the approvals on the basis of floor space and nearly 85 per cent on the basis of the number of units have been given since 1973, and just under 40 per cent of the floor space and over 50 per cent of the units between 1 April 1976 and 31 July 1976. These figures reflect the acceleration of activity and the tendency towards the construction of smaller units. This followed agreement from government in 1975 that the Development Commission should expand its activities. At that time proposals were prepared with a target of the creation of 1750 jobs per year. This was reached after consideration of an inter-departmental study on rural depopulation (HM Treasury, 1976), which suggested a need for about 2500 jobs per year over a ten-year period in order to achieve stable populations in the sparsely populated areas of Great Britain.

On the whole, the Development Commission has been successful in finding tenants for its factories. The position in mid-1976 was that the total factory space constructed since 1959 represented just over 50 per cent of the floor space approved and less than 10 per cent of it remained unallocated (Development Commission, 1976).

Since 1976 the Development Commission has only built factories in England, but at a dramatically increased rate. Up to the end of

Table 7.2 Development Commission factories approved for construction between 1959 and 1976

Location	*No. of units*	*Square footage*	*(Square metres)*
England	106	396,150	(36,800)
Wales	68	372,400	(34,600)
Scotland	29	148,000	(13,750)
Total	203	916,550	(85,150)

Source: Development Commission (1976)

March 1979, 689 factories had been approved covering nearly 2 million square feet. One hundred and sixty of the factories had been completed and a further 202 were under construction: together these would account for more than half the total floor space approved. Further, of the units completed only 20 per cent remained unlet. The Commission estimated that 1600 jobs had been created in the factories and that completion of all approvals would bring a further 6200 jobs (Development Commission, 1980). Multiplier effects will raise the impact of these factories on total employment, although not all of the original jobs in the factories will necessarily be new to the area. By any account, these figures are minute in the national context. However, their importance lies in their impacts on the small communities in which they are located.

The other major component of a company's needs, once it has premises and access to services is the availability of a suitably skilled labour force. The possible importance of public transport in this context has already been mentioned. If workers are already available in the area (and in rural areas potential employees rarely possess industrial skills), then opportunities for training may be important. This could involve the establishment of training courses in local technical colleges, although this is unlikely for a single firm. What is possible is that a number of companies specializing in one type of manufacturing, such as electronics, could be established in an area, and as a result adequate demand be created to justify specialist training courses as well as building up a base of skilled workers, providing attractions to further potential immigrants. Regional specialization in particular types of acitivity might be one approach to overcoming the lack of skills and expertise in industrial activities which predominates in most rural areas. Other immigrant companies will undertake the training of their work force themselves. For this, they will usually want to bring in a core of skilled workers. Grants to assist the movement of 'key' workers can be provided and receiving areas can also help by ensuring that housing and other services are available in convenient locations. With this objective, the Development Commission provides 'housing guarantees' to local councils, whereby the rents of local authority housing are made up by the Commission in the event that property is not let. This removes any risk that councils will fail to receive returns on their investments in property and means that a stock of available housing can be maintained.

One further policy bears mention in this context. This is the maintenance of a register of people wishing to move into an area, should suitable employment become available. When vacancies occur, those on the register with suitable skills and experience can be informed. Examples of these are the 'Counterdrift Register' maintained in the Scottish Highlands and Islands and the 'Borders Build-up Register' maintained in the Scottish Borders. Often, when particular skills are lacking in an area, employers have difficulty in locating and attracting suitable workers. Such registers provide an opportunity whereby those keen either to return to an area or those simply wishing to move there can be matched against employers' needs. However, the register needs to be large enough so that employers will be aware of it and feel that they have a reasonable chance of finding suitable employees, and those registering need genuinely to want to move, recognizing that the wages offered in rural areas will often be below those offered elsewhere.

The second of the categories which we introduced at the beginning of this section concerned the reduction of the relative costs of industrial activities. In selecting locations, producers will obviously favour areas where their relative costs are lower and if other factors are the same, their profitability is higher. Essentially, our first category also involved the reduction of costs, but these were achieved by improving the facilities in an area. We have in mind here the provision of specific financial assistance to individual companies operating in certain locations. Typical assistance available involves grants for new buildings and machinery, interest relief grants, assistance towards removal costs, rent free periods on advance factories and various tax advantages. This is a common approach to regional policy where areas are defined according to their relative priority and grants and subsidies allowed accordingly. It is less often applied to achieve specifically rural objectives. We may also include here the provision of capital by public agencies. This could either be available below market rates, so being equivalent to interest relief on private loans, or could involve loans made where funds are not forthcoming from private sources. By giving loans to higher risk projects a number of enterprises will be funded which otherwise would not be undertaken. On the assumption that some of these are successful, the level of employment can be raised. But, of course, the cost of a higher proportion of loans not being repaid must be faced.

Our final category involves efforts to improve the flow of information. When companies consider the possibility of a move or of expansion, they face a great deal of uncertainty about the opportunities available and about their relative merits. In selecting a new location, companies will require information about the facilities which areas can offer, about labour markets and about costs. Areas seeking to attract companies can collect and analyse the relevant data and pass it on to respective companies. In contemplating expansion, companies will require information about the extent of markets and the availability of inputs. Many firms, especially the smaller ones, may be uncertain as to how to undertake feasibility studies. This could mean either that they tend not to embark on expansion programmes while they could be profitable or that they do so when they are not. Either of these results leads to a loss of employment. Local development authorities can provide both local information and assistance with feasibility studies.

The value of information is not restricted to times when companies are making important policy decisions. Advice and assistance with accounting and management control procedures can also be of benefit. The Council for Small Industries in Rural Areas (CoSIRA) provides a range of assistance to small firms, including professional and technical advice on business management and marketing as well as advice on both modern and traditional rural industries. Like the Development Commission, CoSIRA now operates only within England. It is administered on a county basis through County Organizers and employs just under 300 staff. The Organizers make and maintain contact with local small firms and direct specialized assistance to them as required. A study of CoSIRA's activities has shown that over a period of seven years ending in 1972, the firms helped provided an extra 27,000 jobs, at an average cost per job (excluding repayable loans) of £130 (Development Commission, 1973). It is not possible to identify the numbers of these jobs which have been 'created' through CoSIRA's assistance, but the organization would appear to be making a valuable contribution to the growth of small firms in rural areas. As we suggest below, the development of indigenous companies is becoming of increasing significance.

Finally, when companies are moving or expanding they are faced by a mass of rules and regulations governing what they are and are not allowed to do, as well as to what grants they are entitled. The resultant bureaucracy causes delays and frustrations at a highly critical period in company development. Somebody with a detailed knowledge of the requirements and personalities involved can do much to expedite a company's progress through this maze. Such assistance is welcomed by the small company manager whose prime interest lies in operating his business.

Employment creation and public works

In our discussion of policies aimed at raising the level of employment in industrial processes, we should not neglect the more direct role which public authorities can play. They have the power to undertake public works programmes with the major objective of creating employment and incomes. They can advance such schemes, originally planned for the future, in times of high unemployment or undertake schemes which would not have been embarked upon at all under alternative conditions. Finally, they may provide the finance for such projects to be undertaken by other bodies. The basic element of such schemes is that they provide jobs over the relevant time period which would otherwise not be available. This is not always easy to ensure. It means that activities profitable to private entrepreneurs are not suitable. It is likely, therefore, that the output of such schemes will have the characteristics of a public good, i.e. while it is valued by society generally, no individual producer would be able to sell it through a market. Thus we find that such projects often involve environmental improvements and conservation. Other projects would not be undertaken because they fall into the scope of a public authority's activity anyway, such as construction of a public building or road, or alternatively because the recipients would be unable to pay for them, such as in personal social services. The project will increase the overall level of output in the economy, even though its output will often not be paid for by those benefiting from it.

The impact of these schemes on employment is usually only temporary in nature, although if they improve the quality of an area for industrial location, they may have longer-term implications for regional employment. The employment impact of this form of expenditure in the USA has been studied by Barrows and Bromley (1975). The long-term impact, however, is usually limited. In fact, Nabarro (1973) found that the impact of large public works in the uplands of Britain can in fact be negative in the longer term. Such schemes employ large numbers of people, but over a very brief period of time and from a relatively small area. During this period, labour is drawn out of local industries but is unable to return after the scheme is completed, so that unemployment in fact tends to rise. Because of the brevity of the boom, it is not worthwhile for local industry or public services to build up their capacity. Other, smaller-scale schemes could be appropriate to easing unemployment problems when they are particularly severe in specific settlements. The decision as to whether such schemes are worthwhile or not becomes quite difficult when the value of the output is not priced by the market and where the labour is alternatively unemployed. These issues are considered in some detail by Haveman (1978) and Kemper and Moss (1978).

Appropriate technology

The countries with which we are generally concerned have passed through the same process to reach the state which is described as 'developed'. A number of changes have taken place in their economies: increasing specialization in employment, increasing capital intensity of production, increasing complexity of technology, and increasing scale of industrial organizations. Such a process tends to work against the comparative advantage of rural areas which have a limited labour force and infrastructure. Further, there is a feeling that such trends have reduced the quality of life for society as a whole.

A wide range of problems are pointed to as deriving from the characteristics of the technology which has been developed in the quest for economic development (see, especially, Schumacher, 1973). These include the boring, repetitive and stressful nature of work, the unpleasant surroundings in which work is often undertaken, the high levels of unemployment, the inequitable distribution of incomes, the degradation of the environment and the excessive rate of exploitation of non-renewable resources. Perhaps at the root of these problems is the driving force of the process itself; namely the desire for an increased level of material consumption.

In response to these problems has been the advocacy of what is variously described as 'intermediate', 'alternative' or 'appropriate' technology. They are given somewhat different definitions but are all based on the idea that the value of new technology lies not only in its economic viability and technical soundness, but also in its adaptation to the local social and cultural environment (Jéquier, 1976). 'Appropriate' technology appears to be the most apt description in that it implies no necessary prejudgement as to what form it should take; even though in general usage it has come to take one. The objective is that technology can be applied so as to provide more creative and fulfilling work in the context of a sustainable society. This can be achieved through the establishment of small-scale enterprises, usually involving a low capital to labour ratio. The approach will expand the opportunities for individuals to gain status from their employment, i.e. an expansion of Hirsch's (1977) 'positional good' aspect of employment. The most obvious examples of activities which easily fit these criteria lie in craft activities, although similar principles could also be applied in manufacturing and energy production.

The objectives of such a movement are clearly regarded by most as worthwhile. What is uncertain is what needs to be given up in order to achieve them. Generally, large-scale, capital intensive industry has been regarded as a necessary condition for our present high standard of living: the use of small-scale techniques involving higher costs and hence lower real incomes. Lyons (1980) has recently provided estimates of minimum efficient plant sizes, in terms of employment, in UK manufacturing industries. Examining 118 industries (minimum list headings) on the basis of 1968 data, he found that 11 per cent had minimum efficient plant sizes of less than 50, and 42 per cent of less than 100. None were less than 25. The lowest values were found in consumer goods industries, especially clothing and some textiles. While plants of such sizes are quite feasible in rural areas, advocates of 'alternative' technology have in mind yet smaller enterprises. This implies, then, that under existing conditions and prices, at least some cost would be incurred in embracing small-scale enterprises across the board, although Lyons could say nothing about how much higher costs would be in firms operating below the minimum efficient plant size in practice. Two arguments could perhaps be raised against this. Firstly, the technology which is applied under existing conditions has been developed with urban, industrial applications in mind, so that little is known about the rural potential for small-scale production. The second point is that evidence of higher costs of small-scale solutions does not necessarily preclude their adoption. The benefits being sought are largely non-monetary in nature, so that some financial losses can be justified in their achievement.

In practice, few would advocate a complete shift to small-scale enterprises in all forms of activity. What is more realistic is the development of an alternative for those who place a relatively high value on the advantages and a relatively low value on material consumption. This means that those with the necessary commitment to make a success of the co-operation which is likely to be involved in such a venture can opt for this lifestyle, while others, the majority in the foreseeable future, can avoid this responsibility and follow more conventional forms of employment. Rural areas are likely to provide the most suitable environments for the development of small-scale technologies.

Opportunities for those wishing to follow such alternatives are very limited at present. Their development would involve efforts to make available through research and publicity the most appropriate technologies, which is an area to which public funds could be devoted. Furthermore, some institutional development would be required. This could stimulate the establishment of the sorts of communities in which small-scale applications could be adopted. Rural development agencies could fill this role. The issue of whether such initiatives are worthy of the investment of public funds requires an evaluation based on the principles which we consider in Chapter 10.

The future for industry in rural areas

Rural areas have tended to perform well in terms of manufacturing employment relative to other areas. Fothergill and Gudgin (1979) found a dramatic growth of manufacturing in rural areas of the UK between 1959 and 1975. Dispersion has been taking place away from the cities. The main process differentiating urban and rural areas appears to arise primarily from indigenous performance, i.e. from different growth among similar firms in different areas, rather than from firm movement or changes in industrial structure. Similarly, in the USA, manufacturing employment has tended to grow faster in rural areas (Whiting, 1974). Evidence suggests that at least in one region locally based firms and new firms are the most important source of growth (Rees, 1978). Nevertheless, while the growth rates tend to be higher, the actual numbers of jobs concerned are smaller.

The prospects for manufacturing employment in the future centres around the role of small firms in manufacturing employment and in the ability of rural areas to attract and retain manufacturing business. Debate has concerned the contribution which small firms make in the job generation process. Birch (1979) has found that in the USA between 1969 and 1976 firms employing less than twenty people generated 66 per cent of net new jobs. While there are difficulties involved in interpreting Birch's data, which were dominated by employment in non-manufacturing, evidence does appear to indicate that small firms are important in generating new employment in manufacturing, both in the USA and Britain (Storey, 1980).

Small firms are also likely to be more liable to closure, a fact which has significant implications for small communities with limited alternative employment opportunities. A continual source of new employment through plant openings and company growth is therefore necessary in order to maintain employment levels. For instance, Barkley and Paulsen (1979) found that in non-metropolitan Iowa an average of more than 4000 jobs was eliminated during each of the previous eleven years due to plant failures and out-migrations. Each year, then, this area would need to acquire 100 plants with 40 employees each in order to maintain its position. Debate has also surrounded the issue as to what type of plant is most liable to closure; particularly in the relative positions of branch plants and single plant companies. In times of recession, multi-plant companies have the opportunities of adjusting their production to reduced demand and lowering average costs by closing down branch plants. Single plant companies do not have this option. It also may be argued that the greater reserves of capital and expertise of larger companies, enable them to survive recessionary periods, while smaller companies are more likely to fail. Barkley and Paulsen (1979) found evidence for both these views. Between 1965 and 1975, both the out-migration and immigration rates of branch plants were higher than for locally owned single plant companies. This instability was greatest in the more peripheral areas and was related to the business cycle. Where single plant companies did close, it was more likely to be due to bankruptcy in times of severe recession than due to relocation. Plant ownership therefore influences the risk which a community faces from plant closure. Leaders in rural areas need to be prepared for the possibility that local employment may experience these cyclical variations.

The prospects for agencies seeking to raise the level of employment in rural areas under depressed economic conditions are as bleak as those with similar objectives elsewhere. Much regional policy has been based on the redistribution of growth towards disadvantaged areas through the provision of assistance to mobile companies. Efforts in rural areas have been similarly based. Under conditions of slow economic growth and higher unemployment, there are fewer mobile companies and more agencies angling for jobs. The result is that each one attempts to outbid its competitors through its offers of assistance and in the extent of its advertising. All of which does practically nothing to raise the amount of employment available. In particular, small rural areas with limited promotional expenditure are unlikely to be able to compete successfully with the superfluity of development agencies (Forester, 1979) which have evolved to promote employment at practically every decision-making level. Whilst the rate of economic growth may be influenced by macro-economic policies, at the local level efforts need to be concentrated on making the best use of resources available through the development of indigenous enterprise. This shift in emphasis is dramatically illustrated in our experience in the Eastern Borders (Hodge and Whitby, 1979). Of twelve companies occupying advance factories before early 1977, four had been operating within the area prior to occupation and it was estimated that a minimum of

25 per cent of their work force would have had employment locally if the factories had not been built. By late 1978, eight further companies had moved into factories, and of these, all but one had been located in the area before their move, and in the case of that one it had been allocated its factory in 1974, but construction of an extension and alterations had delayed the start of production. This means that none of these companies had made a decision to move to the area in the previous few years, and nearly 40 per cent of the jobs would have been available in the area in the absence of the factory programme. If the company which was allocated its factory in 1974 is excluded, this figure rises to 65 per cent. These figures highlight the folly of regarding the total numbers of jobs in advance factories as jobs 'created' by the factory programme, especially when many companies so housed were operating locally anyway. The contribution which these factories make to employment must be viewed in terms of the ability which they give to companies to expand to a size beyond that which they could have achieved otherwise. The expansion of local employment in periods of slow economic growth is both harder than under conditions of rapid economic growth and the results which are achieved may involve less real gain in employment than at first appears.

A range of factors will influence the more distant future potential for industrial processes in rural areas. Essentially, these will be the same as those influencing the pattern of economic development in general, although some have special significance for rural areas. The more important include the costs and availability of energy, the development and implementation of 'new' micro-electronic technologies, the evolution of international relations (about which we shall say no more, despite its undoubted importance) and general attitudes to living. These factors will influence the levels of incomes which individuals achieve and how they choose to consume them. The important features of rural areas as locations for industrial processes, as we have already suggested, are their distance from markets and the limitations on the scale of enterprises as a result of the restricted availability of labour and services. It is important, then, to consider how these factors are likely to be affected by possible changes.

The rising costs of energy will increase the extent of the locational disadvantage faced by rural manufacturers. Producers will, in general, tend to give greater priority to establishing at sites which minimize their transport costs. While, on the whole, this will mitigate against rural locations, those activities which reduce the volume of rural products, especially those processing primary products, may see greater advantage in rural locations. The likely effects of technological change, on the other hand, would seem to be working against this trend. The use of robots, as well as of less radical innovations, can allow greater flexibility in product runs, thus reducing the importance of economies of scale, and requiring a smaller labour input. Similarly, communications will become less dependent upon physical proximity, so reducing the need for companies to locate near to information sources. These factors would appear to increase the potential for small-scale manufacturing plants to be established in remoter regions, given an incentive to do so. They could thus enhance the feasibility of adopting 'alternative' technology, which, far from involving a move back to older, previously rejected methods, would involve the use of the most sophisticated techniques available. The introduction of 'new' communications technology will probably have a more immediate effect on the service sector. This is discussed in Chapter 8. On balance, then, these two elements of future change could cancel out, leaving the comparative advantage of rural areas largely unaffected. Changing attitudes to living, such as a desire to escape from intensive urban lifestyles, could provide the necessary incentive for at least some decentralization of manufacturing capacity. This would not need to be a mass movement. Indeed, if this was to be the case, it would face the danger of destroying the very attractions of rural areas upon which it is based. A relatively small number of people, especially those in management positions, could create a significant number of job opportunities in small rural settlements.

The future could hold some scope for new industrial processes in rural areas. The trends outlined above will create greater incentives for remoter regions to aim for self-sufficiency, especially in products with high transport costs and limited economies of scale. One area which has been the subject of considerable recent interest is that of energy production. Higher prices and interruptions in supply of petroleum products have stimulated a widespread search for alternatives. Ideally, these would be available locally so that supplies could be guaranteed and would be amenable to small-scale production. They should also, of course, be produced at a cost competitive to the existing sources. Two possibilities suggested for Australian conditions, but which might have wider application, are solar energy (Kaneff, 1979) and liquid fuels from biomass (Stewart *et al.*, 1979). Although the latter appears to be more expensive than some other alternatives at present, local energy production may be seen as providing other benefits, particularly in terms of jobs and as such also merits detailed evaluation along the lines discussed in Chapter 10. Detailed work is required in examining the alternative possibilities, and their most appropriate applications under alternative conditions.

8
EMPLOYMENT IN THE SERVICE SECTOR

In this chapter, we describe the position of the service, or tertiary sector. We begin with a general discussion of employment in the service sector in developed economies and then consider the factors influencing the location of service activities and the levels of service provision in rural areas. We next examine the potential role of both private and public services in rural development and possible public policies to encourage them. Finally, we briefly consider the prospects for rural services.

The service sector includes a wide variety of activities, which are hard to summarize within a single definition. It is perhaps most easily regarded as the residual of economic activity after primary and manufacturing activities have been excluded, thus including, for example, wholesale and retail trade, banking and finance, transport and communications, and government services and administration. The services which are produced do have common characteristics: they are not material, permanent objects; they are produced by people rather than machines and are consumable only at the instant of production. Goods also provide utility when they are used and a service may be an alternative means of supplying that, or a similar, utility. This would be the case in the choice between the use of an electric fan versus a punkah-wallah. In this chapter, we are concerned with employment in the provision of services. We do, however, exclude employment in recreation and tourism, which has been dealt with in Chapter 6. While much of the employment does result from providing services, such as accommodation or retail outlets, the underlying basis of the activity is in the quality of the natural environment which attracts visitors to the area. It has this dependence upon the natural resources of the area in common with primary industries.

Employment in the service sector represents the only important growth area in developed economies. The proportion of the labour force involved in the primary sector declined in all of the 19 major OECD countries between 1971 and 1975 (OECD, 1978), thus illustrating, as noted in Chapters 4 and 5, the persistence of this phenomenon at all levels of economic development. Similarly, the same source shows that for the same countries the part of employment in manufacturing employment declined for 14 of the 19. The exceptions were Japan, Austria, Finland, Portugal and Spain. In each of these growth was less than 1 per cent over that entire period. In the 13 major western economies for which data on employment in services are presented all experienced a growth in numbers employed between 1960 and 1970. The unweighted average annual rate of growth in service employment for those countries was 2.7 per cent. An increase in the percentage of total employment in the service sector was experienced in all of the original 19 countries between 1960 and 1971 and between 1971 and 1975. The highest proportion was reached by the USA, which had 67 per cent of its employment in the service sector in 1975, and 11 of the 19 countries had over 50 per cent. These figures reflect a well-known trend, which many sources view as being likely to continue in the future, although depressed rates of economic growth are retarding it at present.

The location of service activities

Services are, of course, produced by both the private and the public sectors. The private service sector operates to provide services for the general public, for example through retail outlets or transport facilities, for manufacturing activities such as finance or repairs and maintenance, or to other services such as accountancy or legal advice. Any particular service activity does not necessarily only service one sector. For instance, accountants serve all types of company as well as private individuals. Government services are provided at both national and local levels. Some are provided for private individuals, such as education, health or social security, while others are concerned with the organization of economic activities such as in pollution control or safety regulations.

The variety of the activities included within this sector, therefore, means that no single theory of location has been developed. Typically, service activities are located close to the industry or population with which they are linked. This is the case for those providing skills to particular industries and especially so for those directly serving the public, such as in retail outlets, schools and banks. However, many services are provided on a national or regional basis, so that they are unable to locate close to all of the activities or populations which they serve. When this is the case such services have traditionally tended to locate in capital cities or other major centres of population. This is usually the case, too, for government administration, which tends to be predominantly sited in the capital city of its respective administrative area. Location within large centres gives advantages in the form of ease of access and communication with other organizations. These factors are particularly important for services associated with such activities as international finance and trade or the stock market. These therefore tend to be located in the largest financial centres, and a variety of other organizations, such as company headquarters or government departments, may gain benefits from having convenient access to such a centre. The increasing importance of employment in the service sector has led to the growth of both national and regional service centres and the relative decline not only of agricultural areas, but also of areas dependent upon manufacturing employment, especially in the heavy industries.

Rural population and service provision

The bulk of service activity in rural areas directly serves the primary industries or the rural population. The reduction in primary employment, and hence population, has effects through the multiplier process on the level of employment in other sectors. Changes in the nature and location of the suppliers of agricultural inputs have exacerbated the shift of employment away from rural regions. The resultant decline in the levels of service provision operates in different ways in the private and in the public service sectors.

It is generally accepted that services can be provided at a lower *per capita* cost in areas of higher population density. This is to say that within an area there are economies of scale in service provision. This is a phenomenon common to most production processes; as the output of the process increases, it becomes possible to lower the average cost of production up to some point where costs begin to rise again. For instance, where a large number of households are being served within a given area, the amount of transport required per household served will be relatively low. This will be a significant factor for such activities as refuse collection, postal services or meter reading, which involve regular visits to houses. Another example occurs where inputs are indivisible, such as operating theatres or sporting facilities, and better use can be made of them within larger settlements, thus reducing the cost of making the service available to each member of the population. At very large scales, though, diseconomies of scale might be experienced. These could arise through increased travelling costs from a central base through the problems of managing large organizations, or through congestion. Thus it may be anticipated that the average cost of providing services would be high in small settlements and decline as the size of settlement increased, but rise again in the case of the largest settlements. However, it should be noted that Gilder (1979) has recently questioned this view as the basis for key settlement policies in rural areas.

In a mixed economy, a wide range of services are provided by the private sector, such as retail outlets, banks, insurance and taxis. Under a competitive system, resources will be invested in an area up to the point where the marginal return is equal to that achievable in other forms of investment. Thus, service facilities will be established in progressively smaller settlements until the cost of running the facility is not justified by the returns which are realized. This point is reached at different population levels for different services. Thus, for example, the largest settlements have theatres, medium settlements have banks and the smaller ones only have a general store, public house and a church. The very smallest will have no services at all. In the short run, changes in populations or changes in costs could lead to changes in the optimal pattern of resource allocation, but to which there may be no immediate response. Such a position may either be experienced where population has been expanded and new facilities have not been developed or where population has declined and where old facilities, such as village stores, continue to be operated even though they are no longer profitable. However, in the longer run where population declines, unless such services are subsidized, resources will not be reinvested or will be transferred to alternative uses, and there will be a consequent decline in the level of employment.

Public services are either provided by statutory authorities responsible for specific activities, such as telecommunications or electricity supply, or by a local government, which supplies a range of services. It is rarely, if ever, the case that the pricing policies for public services charge the consumer an amount equivalent to the marginal cost of production. Where charges are levied directly on the consumer at all, rather than the costs being met completely through taxation, they may either be subsidized from public funds or charged at a constant rate over large areas, often over a whole country, even though the costs of providing the service may vary from one area to another. Thus, for instance, the charge levied for supplying water to a remote dwelling is often the same as that paid in an urban location. The result of such pricing policies is that when individuals decide on where to live, they rarely do so on the basis of having to bear the full cost of that decision. When they choose to live in remote locations which still receive a range of services, the costs are shared widely within the community.

A number of studies have attempted to estimate the average cost curves for public services. However, the problem immediately encountered derives from the fact that there is often no satisfactory measure of the quantity of output from most services. For instance, what is a unit of output from planning control? Other services are somewhat less intractable. Education may be measured on the basis of numbers of pupils at various ages, or health may be measured by the numbers of patients treated. However, even these do not represent complete measures of output, to the extent that the quality of the service is not taken into account. Empirical studies have, of necessity, relied on such measures as are available. These have examined a variety of services in both urban and rural settings.

One service which has been widely studied is the provision of education. The majority of studies have estimated cost curves to find the extent of cost savings which can be achieved by increasing school size and the point up to which these occur. These indicate the existence of economies of scale which appear to be more marked in the provision of secondary education than in primary education. For instance, Keane (1978) quotes two studies which suggest economies of scale up to 4000 and 1675 pupils in secondary schools. In his study of elementary schools on Prince Edward Island in Canada, Keane found that economies of scale achieved by larger schools were not very significant. An Australian study of primary schools in rural areas (Hind, 1977), however, found quite significant economies of scale, but these were mostly exhausted by the 200 enrolment level. Generally, evidence of economies of scale has been found and attempts to achieve cost savings have been made through rural school consolidation. This has the disadvantage that pupils are forced to travel longer distances, which increases the costs of transport. Studies have therefore also examined the question of rural school consolidation on the basis of minimizing the sum of internal school costs and transportation costs. In one such study in the USA (Holland and Baritelle, 1975), it was concluded that while public schooling does seem to be characterized by economies of scale, consolidation cannot be counted on to provide large cost savings in sparsely populated rural areas. Thus, in areas of lower population density, pupils will need to be drawn from larger districts in order to achieve the scale necessary to minimize internal costs. This means that the size of school which minimizes total cost will be smaller in less densely populated areas. Any increases in the costs of transportation will emphasize this position.

However, little progress has been made in evaluating the quality of education provided by alternative size schools and studies have had to assume that there are no significant differences. This represents the present state of the debate. Efforts to close down rural schools in order to achieve cash savings are therefore resisted by those people who argue that the quality of the education provided is higher in smaller schools or that the transporting of pupils to more distant schools imposes external costs. Such arguments are accompanied by claims that schools in small communities provide a focus for community activity and so help to support rural populations. While the process of education is so poorly understood, it will be impossible to provide firm evidence about the quality of education supplied in alternative environments. Education generates a number of different types of benefit but these still need to be positively identified. The contribution which schools make to the stability of rural communities is also an element of the debate requiring careful analysis.

The example of education illustrates the process working towards the decline of public sector employment. Similar consolidation has occurred in such other services as health, and levels of service have been reduced in such amenities as transportation and refuse collection. The Standing Conference on Rural Community Councils

(1978) has attempted to document the decline of rural services in England.

Acting against this decline has been the rising level of service employment generally, which has affected both urban and rural areas. While this trend has had greater implications for urban employment, it may be expected to have placed some upward pressure on service employment in rural areas. The increase in the ratio of service employment to primary and manufacturing employment, at least since the 1950s, appears to be a widespread phenomenon. It has, for instance, been illustrated in Wagstaff's (1973) study of employment in rural Scotland and Davidson's (1976) study of regions in New South Wales, shown in Table 8.1.

Table 8.1 Ratio of employees in commerce and service industries to primary and manufacturing in farming regions of New South Wales

Farming zone	*1961*	*1966*	*1971*
Pastoral	0.7	0.9	1.0
Wheat and sheep	1.2	1.4	1.7
High rainfall sheep	1.4	1.7	2.0

Source: Davidson (1976)

The net effect of changes in primary or manufacturing employment (those industries regarded as being 'basic' in economic base theory), and the overall increase in services on the absolute numbers employed, therefore depends upon the relative magnitudes of these changes. Rapid declines in primary employment are likely to be accompanied by an absolute decline in the level of employment in the service sector, even though the proportion of employment in services will probably rise. As implied above, the decline in service employment will follow that in primary employment after some time lag. Neither the private nor the public sector will immediately respond to the change, although the actual time period involved is unknown. From the available evidence, Wagstaff has tentatively suggested that a lag of the order of five years occurs, over which time these changes could take place.

Service sector employment and rural development

Given the apparent dependence of service employment upon employment in the primary and manufacturing sectors, it is often assumed that it cannot contribute to the initiation of economic development. As a result of this, regional policy has concentrated on encouraging manufacturing industry to locate in depressed areas, with the anticipation that employment in services will flow from the increases in population and incomes which result. This view is based on the belief that the location of service employment is very largely determined by the location of primary and manufacturing employment. However, this is not necessarily the case: the outputs of some service activities are exchangeable between areas and the extent of such exchange seems likely to increase in the future. This exchangeability means, therefore, that there are options in the selection of locations for service activities and hence potential for service employment to play a part in regional development.

The nature of the output of service activities means that they can either be exchanged through direct, face-to-face contact or through some other form of communication. They can be exchanged between areas, then, either by residents travelling from one location to another, such as shopping trips to large cities, or by residents communicating by some remote form, traditionally through postal services, such as may be used for mail-order purchases. The opportunities for encouraging employment in rural areas, therefore, lie either in moving services used by rural residents from urban to rural locations or in moving services used by urban residents to rural locations. A final option lies in locating services which do not relate to specific populations at all in depressed areas, such as research stations or defence establishments. These possibilities are considered below, firstly in the context of private services and secondly in the context of context of public sector services.

Private sector services

The vast majority of private services located in rural areas are located there in order to serve local populations. However, not all the demands for services of rural populations are met from activities located in rural areas. Urban areas provide services, not only for urban populations but also for populations in a rural hinterland. Beyond such an area of influence, remoter areas are required to be more self-sufficient in service provision. Wagstaff (1973) has illustrated this trend by dividing the area of Scotland into three categories: cities and towns with a population of 50,000 or above; counties and parts of counties adjacent to urban areas; and rural counties. He found that in 1966 the ratio of primary and manufacturing employment to service employment was 1.27 for cities and large towns, 0.66 for adjacent counties and 0.97 for rural counties. Thus, the proportion of service employment tends to increase with remoteness from centres of population. It would therefore be expected that on average the introduction of new jobs in primary or manufacturing industry into remoter areas will lead to a greater overall increase in employment than would be the case in less remote areas. The converse is, of course, also true that a reduction in primary employment will be followed by an even steeper fall in service employment.

It is hard to estimate what potential there is for any shift in the location of service activities away from urban areas towards the rural populations which they service. In that more remote areas do appear to be more self-sufficient in service provision, then it is technically feasible, although it could only be achieved at some loss of efficiency. While the ratio of primary and manufacturing employment to service employment at 0.97 for rural counties was identical to that for Scotland as a whole, the range of services available in the rural counties would have been considerably more limited, i.e. the same proportion of people involved produces a more limited range of services. This is the case, regardless of the fact that urban areas would still provide a limited range of services for the rural areas such as in central government and administration. While any costs of relocating services must be weighed against the benefits to rural areas, an issue which we pursue in Chapter 10, there would appear to be limited scope for providing employment in rural areas by relocating activities which provide services for rural populations.

The position is somewhat different for service activities which do not require face-to-face contact with the populations which they serve. This is the case for a wide range of activities in the private sector, including insurance, finance and company head offices, although these latter could be classified under manufacturing. Goddard and Pye (1977) quote studies which indicate that communication is a major concern of managers responsible for office location decisions. Considerable research has been devoted to the question of the dispersal of office location from central London and it is suggested that the need to maintain personal contact with people in London is the principal reason why a large number of firms which consider relocation eventually decide against it. Similarly, a large majority of moves which were made were confined to the South East region.

The decision to relocate office activity clearly centres around the differences in costs in alternative locations. The savings which can be achieved by movement away from urban centres are primarily due to lower office rentals and clerical wages. The costs result from increased expenditure on communications which may be due to extra travel to urban centres or increased telecommunications. The position for individual companies will be considerably influenced by the nature and extent of the contacts which they make with other organizations and the extent to which these can be adapted to alternative locations. The opportunity to substitute telecommunication for travel will enhance the attractiveness of moves from urban areas. However, under present circumstances, telecommunication is not an effective substitute for all face-to-face contact. In the light of this, and the concentration of non-replaceable contacts in London, Goddard and Pye (1977) concluded that, on the basis of past experience, there is unlikely to be any widespread movement of office activity away from South East England. The development of telecommunications, such as networks of cheap teleconference equipment, would enable greater substitution for travel. This type of development is presently occurring and so presumably providing some incentive for decentralization, especially in economies which have their finance and administrative activities less concentrated in a single urban centre. The opportunity to choose from a wider range of locations could have important implications for some rural areas which can provide alternative attractions, especially in the form of a pleasant environment.

As with other types of enterprise, service activities will not locate in rural areas without being sure of being able to either take an adequate staff to a new location or of recruiting a suitably skilled work force there. This criterion could be hard to meet in many rural towns and so provides an important constraint on the dispersal of service employment to rural areas. Some smaller organizations, as used in computer programing or design, where often less than ten key members are involved, may be more flexible.

One further potential change resulting from improved communications lies in the reorganization of the location of functions within companies. Organizations whose function largely involves the processing and dissemination of information have the potential for dispersing their activities around a central data processing facility. This would then be linked to a number of work centres from which remote terminals could be operated. The ultimate form of organization would be where employees worked from their homes. Nilles *et al.* (1976) have studied the decentralization of an insurance company's operations in the Los Angeles region of the USA. They identified the potential benefits of establishing a number of remote office 'satellites', including reduced employee turnover and training, reduced salaries and fringe benefits which can be paid due to the more convenient location of work and reduced commuting, and a reduction in the numbers of staff owing to a higher calibre of staff and a better working environment. Costs were incurred in establishing the satellite offices and in their operation, for example in operating the telecommunication equipment and in the duplication of administrative tasks. On balance, it was found that decentralization by means of telecommuting represented a material reduction in the operating costs of the company.

Whether this potential flexibility in the location of a variety of service activities will lead to their establishment in rural areas is, as yet, unclear. One possibility is the development of suburban regional centres which can exploit the advantages of small town communities and easy access to rural recreation facilities, without losing access to the service and entertainment facilities which are likely to continue to be only available in larger urban centres. Such developments seem unlikely to offer salvation to the remote rural regions. Indeed, technological changes in service provision seem poised to further reduce the levels of employment necessary to provide services to the populations resident there. For instance, remote banking services could remove much of the need for any personal presence in small branches. However, improved telecommunications could, nevertheless, improve the quality of services which are available.

Public sector services

As with private services, the flexibility in the choice of locations for public services is determined by the nature of the service, and, more specifically, by the extent of face-to-face contact with the recipient population. In local government most services involve direct dealings with the public, so that easy access between the service location and population is a crucial consideration. The ease of access will be traded off against the cost of providing a large number of service outlets. One solution to this problem lies in taking the service itself to dispersed populations, as in mobile libraries or mobile citizens' advice services. The administrative sections of local governments may be less constrained in this respect, but will be most advantageously located near the largest concentration of other departments, i.e. in the population centre of the local government area. Any dispersal of functions from central locations is likely to incur added costs of travel and telecommunication, which may be offset against lower rental or wage costs, although such savings are unlikely to be very substantial in a move away from smaller urban centres.

The location of central government activities will be similarly determined, although there is likely to be less contact with the public. Instead, communications with other government departments are likely to be of importance and so provide an incentive for concentration within the capital city. Some activities will have other requirements which preclude a central urban location, such as agricultural research stations or defence establishments. Although most of these would have the potential for dispersal to remoter positions, again it would be at the expense of increased communications expenditures. Potential benefits from dispersal are likely to be greater than in the case of local government due to the considerably higher rentals and wages in national capital cities.

The impact of technological change is likely to be of as much importance in the location of public as private services. Large sections of many central government departments are involved in the collection, processing and dissemination of data, and as such may be amenable to relocation to remoter areas provided with the necessary telecommunications facilities. The negative impacts equally apply. Smaller numbers of personnel will be required to maintain the range of public services provided in rural regions. Information on job vacancies or planning proposals could be provided by means of remote terminals linked to central offices. In the most remote areas telecommunications could provide education facilities incorporating interactive instructional systems, which would be an improvement on the present type of techniques currently adopted in outback Australia, including specially designed courses both for school and tertiary education, or even 'telemedicine', where health care transactions can be made between less qualified personnel treating patients in remote areas and specialists elsewhere. This and less futuristic types of development will tend to reduce the requirements for face-to-face contacts with the general public, although at the same time increase the amount of information which can be provided. One factor which could work against such a change would be the demand for personal contacts in the provision of such services.

Public policy and the location of service activities

As mentioned earlier, the main impetus of regional policy tends to be directed towards influencing the location of manufacturing activities, with the resultant indirect impact on the service sector. Marquand (1979) has recently criticized this neglect of the service sector, arguing that services can make an equally great contribution to regional development. Some policies have, however, been implemented with the objective of encouraging the development of service activities in disadvantaged regions. A major example is the encouragement of activities associated with tourism. A recent report (OECD, 1978) has indicated three categories of measures intended to influence the location of service activities outside tourism. These are:

1 the application of investment incentives available in designated areas to service sector activities;
2 the application of restraints on development of certain activities (e.g. construction of offices) with a view to encouraging development in the designated regions;
3 the development of comprehensive location or dispersal policies for the institutions and organizations under government influence.

Incentives are provided in a number of countries in order to establish service activities in depressed areas. These will usually be those which have a choice of locations open to them, i.e. which have the potential for operating either in a prosperous or a depressed area. Encouragement is usually not aimed specifically at rural development, although rural areas may be eligible for grants. For example, in the UK assistance has been provided for establishment in intermediate areas, development areas and special development areas, at increasing rates respectively. However, the special development areas are to a greater extent centred around the larger depressed urban centres and there has not been any significant amount of office development in rural areas. The construction of offices has been used in order to attract service activities to rural areas in the same way that the construction of advanced factories has been used to attract manufacturing. Such development has been undertaken in Mid-Wales, although is not widespread. Probably such agencies attract more service employment as a multiplier effect of their other job-generating activities.

Restraint is exercised over office development in only three OECD countries, and these generally apply to limited areas. In the UK, decentralization of office employment from London was encouraged through the (now extinct) Location of Offices Bureau, although this agency had the more general objective of promoting a better distribution of office employment in England and Wales, paying particular attention to inner-city areas.

Both central and local governments have the power to directly influence the location of a substantial amount of service employment directly. A major example of this has been in the dispersal of central government activities from London, although the movement has been to a relatively small number of receiving locations. The need for this was emphasized by Hardman (1973) in his review of the possibility of dispersing government work. He notes general agreement that dispersal should take the form of the movement of reasonable numbers of staff to a few locations, rather than spreading out the same number of staff over a large number of locations. This would be inefficient in terms of the operation of departments, bad for the staff concerned in prospects of career management and of limited use in regional policy. Rural areas were not seen, therefore, as suitable locations for dispersal.

Local governments also have control over the location of their employees within their administrative areas. On the whole, however, rural development has not been viewed as a major determinant of the location of their activities. Some movement away from centres of population has occurred and the benefits of creating employment in small towns has been claimed. However, they have usually been the result of the reorganization of local authority boundaries, which has left the traditional administrative centres on the edges of new areas, or even outside the area completely. Given the need for the public to have access to most local authority functions, there is unlikely to be any significant movement away from population centres.

The future for rural services

The past role of service activities in rural areas has been very largely one of serving rural people and industries. Changes in the distribution of population and the pattern of resource use of primary industries have rendered much of this employment redundant. These trends seem set to continue and the pattern of technological change to reinforce them. However, this same pattern provides many services, especially those which have little face-to-face contact with the public or other organizations, with a broadened horizon when selecting locations. This is an area of potentially increasing employment, and rural areas which can provide cheaper land and attractive environments, especially where these are within reach of urban facilities, would appear to be well placed to receive footloose service activities. They will nevertheless need to provide a pool of labour and suitable accommodation and facilities for the incoming population. Towns which the process of depopulation has deprived of these assets are unlikely to be regarded as suitable locations unless managers can be persuaded of their imminent reintroduction. The more remote areas are not so well placed. Further improvements in technology which can increasingly allow the substitution of telecommunication for face-to-face contacts, together with a general acceptance of such methods of communication, would reduce constraints on the organization of the services sector and those with a taste for an Arcadian lifestyle could combine it with technologically sophisticated employment. Such a fringe could seek out undisturbed rural retreats. But any movement of this type, even if substantial, seems an unlikely base for a healthy future rural economy. More realistically, those remaining in remote rural areas will turn to new technologies to provide a substitute for, rather than a cause of, increased populations.

CONCLUSION TO PART II

The main findings of the preceding five chapters can now be summarized. As far as the rural land-using industries are concerned, we can see that the income elasticity of demand for their products may be an important determinant of their future rate of expansion. On these grounds we may expect agriculture to become less important over time whereas forestry may tend to increase in importance somewhat. Perhaps recreation and tourism, as a joint user of rural land with income elastic demand for its products, will also become increasingly important as an employer. Nevertheless it will be some decades before the present position of farmers as occupiers and owners of agricultural land is seriously eroded. Farmers will continue to be the predominant land users and their activities will affect the extent to which newer forms of land use can develop.

The scope for new industries in rural areas is closely linked to the level of economic growth and the relative costs experienced in rural locations. In the future, we may expect that transport costs will become an increasingly important element in the location decision, although against this technological developments may improve the relative position of rural areas. The development of service employment in rural areas will be partly a matter of the technology of service provision and the way in which new methods of providing services can be introduced, and partly of the policies pursued with regard to their provision by public authorities.

The general pattern of the development process, proceeding from an initial dependence on primary industries, through the evolution of secondary industries to a final concentration of tertiary industries, is reflected to some degree in the changes occurring in the rural areas of developed countries. The tertiary sector may then prove to be the most fruitful area in which new jobs will occur. The resource base, nevertheless, must remain the dominant influence for rural employment. The quality of the environment represents rural areas' greatest asset in the competition for jobs, either directly by encouraging recreation and tourism or indirectly by providing an attractive living environment for those working in secondary or tertiary activities. The revival of growth in many rural areas appears to a large extent to be a reflection of this.

Alternative patterns of development will result where governments intervene to stimulate the introduction of new industries in rural areas. All of the industries discussed in the preceding five chapters are subject to various levels of government intervention whether in the form of subsidies, tax concessions or regulatory controls. For this reason it is important to consider the way in which such intervention is carried out and the decisions which precede it. Accordingly, in Part III we turn to review the policy questions involved in attempting to stimulate rural employment.

PART III

Rural employment creation: assessment, planning and implementation

In the first part of this book we considered the processes of rural decline and the possible objectives of policy. In the second part, the actual and potential level of employment in the major rural industries was reviewed. Attention is now focused on the issue of promoting employment options in rural areas. Following an examination of the nature and impact of employment creation schemes, three chapters are devoted to various aspects of the question of assessing employment creation projects. The broader issues of placing projects in a regional context are then discussed. Finally, we relate employment creation policies to the broader institutional environment in which they are set.

9
CHARACTERISTICS AND IMPACT OF EMPLOYMENT CREATION

As we have considered earlier, a number of policies are operated which seek to raise the level of employment in rural areas. Indeed, with widespread high rates of unemployment, 'employment creation' generally has become an important objective of government actions (see for instance, Philip, 1978). In addition, the prominence given to employment in public debate suggests that it has itself come to be regarded as an important 'output' of economic activity.

Sen (1975) has distinguished three different aspects of employment, which he has called:

1 *the income aspect*, employment gives an income to the employed;
2 *the production aspect*, employment yields an output;
3 *the recognition aspect*, employment gives a person the recognition of being engaged in something worthwhile.

In wealthy societies, where incomes are provided for those unable to find employment, from an individual's point of view the recognition aspect represents an important motive for the achievement of a high level of employment. Thus, for many, work provides a role and status which they cannot achieve outside their work environment. This may be as an important figure in an organization or as one of a team at work. It may also confer the status of the provider to a family. The nature of the work and the conditions in which it is undertaken will be critical in determining whether employment is regarded as beneficial for its own sake. The improvement of working conditions and increase in the numbers engaged in non-repetitive occupations will further enhance the importance of the recognition aspect.

However, in the past, especially during periods of rapid economic growth, work has been viewed as a necessary evil. One of the major benefits of growth has been seen to be the opportunity for reducing the amount of work which has to be undertaken, so avoiding long periods of work in unpleasant surroundings. The current concern for increasing the level of employment is not quite the reversal which it might at first appear. What has come to be recognized is the importance of the *distribution* of leisure and work. Thus, while a reduction of the working week by 10 per cent is generally regarded as a benefit to all, the redundancy of 10 per cent of the labour force, when alternative opportunities are limited, provides benefit to nobody (unless it allows goods to be produced at lower cost). Clearly, the reverse is also true: a longer working week for all would not be seen as a popular objective and yet the provision of jobs for the unemployed is generally welcomed.

These apparent changes in people's views about work probably, though, derive more from an altered emphasis in what is said, than from any fundamental differences in individuals' valuations. When work was relatively plentiful, especially to the intellectual leaders in society, reduction in work was associated in most people's minds with a shorter working week. Under higher levels of unemployment, especially amongst those with professional qualifications, reduction in work has come to be associated with threats of redundancy, i.e. with certain individuals losing all of their work rather than most losing just a fraction of it.

Economic growth does not necessarily expand the level of employment. Indeed, there is currently widespread concern that it could lead to a reduction. While the monetary benefits of growth may be redistributed between the employed and unemployed, the losses of the recognition aspect of employment must be seen as a cost while present attitudes to status and employment persist. Even under conditions of full employment there are considerable restrictions on the extent to which these non-monetary benefits from employment may be expanded. The role of employment as a provider of status must be regarded as a 'positional good' (Hirsch, 1977) whose quantity, because it depends upon an individual's relative position within the work force, cannot be expanded through economic growth alone. Improvements in job satisfaction may, however, be achievable through restructuring responsibilities in the work force. New attitudes will be required to cope with any structural changes in the future and the resultant forced mobility of individuals within the social hierarchy. These will be associated with less reliance on employment in determining an individual's status and a consequent increase in willingness to move between high- and low-status activities.

The overall level of employment in the economy will be considerably influenced by macro-economic policies and international pressures. These elements of the debate are beyond the scope of this book. We are concerned with levels of employment within rural areas and take the macro-economic environment as given. This is not to deny the important relationships between national policy and rural employment. However, in advanced economies, where a relatively small part of the population is located in rural areas, national macro-economic policies are unlikely to be operated to achieve specifically rural objectives. We are, then, generally restricting our concern to local and regional differentials.

Employment creation programmes

The success of an employment creation programme tends, all too often, to be judged simply on the basis of the number of jobs with which it appears to be associated. This is sometimes viewed in relation to the cost which the exchequer has borne or by other measures of cost. The question of assessing the costs of such programmes is considered in Chapter 10.

The most immediately apparent difference between two programmes which bring, say, 100 jobs to a district, is in the composition of the work force. They may be male or female, full-time or part-time or skilled or unskilled. The value of employment for 100 unskilled females in an area suffering from a high level of male redundancy in a heavy industry is unlikely to be very high, while it could make an important contribution to rural incomes in an area of low male unemployment and low female activity rates.

A second qualitative aspect of an employment creation programme concerns the period over which work will be available. The establishment of an industry, especially where this is based on a locally available raw material, may be expected to provide employment over a long period, subject of course to variations in the pattern of demand or to technological change. Capital works schemes, on the other hand, can only be expected to provide employment over a short period of time, and so can only bring brief relief to unemployment problems.

Less immediately apparent are the changes which have brought about the employment. These can only be estimated on the basis of assumptions concerning the position in the absence of the programme. For instance, the provision of employment through government assistance in one location will often mean a reduction of employment elsewhere, especially when there is a high level of unemployment in the economy. There are six possible categories of change which can give rise to the appearance of employment 'creation' in a government programme.

1 Some of the employment associated with the programme might have been available in the same location in the absence of any policy. An example would be in the case of a policy of providing subsidies to a company so as to encourage it to establish in a particular area. While much of the employment which that company provides would not have been available in the absence of the policy, it is possible that the same or a similar operation would have been undertaken at a smaller scale, in which case the total number of jobs in the new enterprise exaggerates the extent of the employment created. Similarly, agencies operating public employment programmes may use employment creation funds to pay for employment which would otherwise have been paid for from other sources.
2 The numbers of persons employed in an area may be expanded without any expansion of the amount of work. This is the case of work sharing. A number of approaches might be taken to sharing the available work more widely (Basnett, 1978) including reduced overtime, increased holidays, increased part-time work, early retirement, a reduction in the basic working week, and an increase in the amount of training.
3 Policies with the objective of expanding employment in one area often achieve this by attracting mobile companies to establish in the preferred location. While from the point of view of the area in question, this represents 'new' employment, in national terms, employment has simply been relocated. Thus there will only be a benefit to the economy as a whole if the employment in the actual location is in some way more valuable than in its alternative. This may be associated with differential rates of unemployment in the two locations, so that the opportunity cost of employing labour could be reduced by

the establishment of production in areas with higher levels of unemployment. We return to this issue in the next chapter.

4 Differential investment subsidies and industrial opportunities offered by different nations will influence the location of economic activities between countries. These are likely to determine both where orders for production are placed, such as orders for shipbuilding, and where industrial plant is located, either by multinational corporations or by companies which are prepared to relocate their production facilities overseas. In effect, employment 'creation' by offering such subsidies represents a transfer of employment from one country to another. Subsidies for exports may also have the effect of competing with overseas employment.

5 Employment can also be 'created' by means of a change in the labour intensity of production. An alteration of the cost of labour relative to the cost of capital will usually encourage the selection of more labour intensive technologies. The effect of such a change is illustrated in Figure 4.1. Production takes place on the isoquant Q, which represents the various combinations of labour and capital which may be used to produce a given level of output (see for instance Lancaster (1969) for a more detailed explanation), at position A, with labour and capital used at L_1 and K_1. If the cost of labour is reduced, and the cost of capital is increased by an equivalent amount, so that total costs remain the same, and the isocost curve moves from ab to cd, then production will move to position B on the isoquant, using L_2 and K_2 of labour and capital respectively. This result is known as the substitution effect.
Subsidies for labour may either be paid to all labour used or only to new employment (i.e. on marginal employment). The Regional Employment Premium which has been paid on employment in the British development areas, is an example of the former. While this type of subsidy may be easier to operate, it is likely to have less impact than a subsidy which concentrates on firms which are making decisions about the type of technology to select for new production processes. A recent study (Layard and Nickell, 1980) has shown that a general scheme providing a subsidy to all new jobs, compares favourably with other possible policy approaches to creating employment.

6 Finally, employment may be associated with an increase in

overall output. Where there is an increase in demand for an industry's products, individual firms will expand their output and, given unchanged relative costs of labour and capital (and constant returns to scale[1]), greater quantities of labour and capital will be utilized in equal proportions. This is the basis of economic growth which is traditionally regarded as fundamental to the process of raising the levels of employment in an economy. The position is illustrated in Figure 4.2 where output expands from Q_1 to Q_2 and the consequent utilization of labour from L_1 to L_2.

The impact of a subsidy on a firm's costs will also have the effect of encouraging it to increase its level of output. An equal rate of subsidy on labour and capital will lead to the maintenance of the same factor proportions in production as shown in Figure 4.2. The effect of such a subsidy is to cause a movement of the isocost curve from ab to the parallel position cd, and production will expand from isoquant Q_1 to Q_2 at position B.

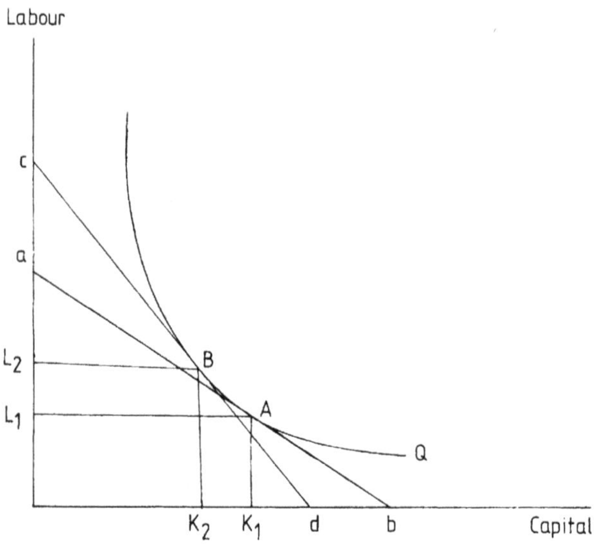

Figure 9.1 Substitution effect of a relative reduction in the cost of labour

1 Strictly speaking this assumption is unduly restrictive. We need only, in fact, assume a homothetic production function.

The impact which this subsidy has on the level of consumption of the product and on the other firms currently producing it, will be determined by its price elasticity of demand (i.e. the extent to which a fall in price leads to an increase in consumption). If other factors are constant, it is certain to place a downward pressure on prices and so place employment in other companies in this industry at risk. Efforts to avoid this type of effect have been associated with employment creation programmes which aim to produce output which would otherwise not be produced and therefore does not compete with employment in other locations.

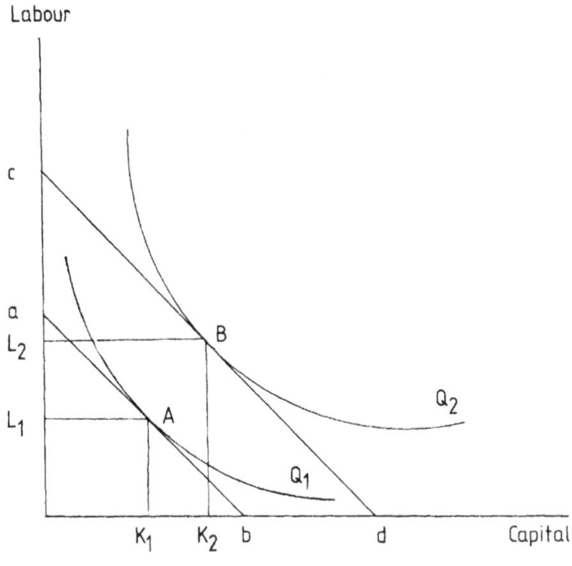

Figure 9.2 Output effect of an equal subsidy for labour and capital

Policies seeking to create employment will often involve a number of these effects. The contribution made by each to the final level of employment is extremely difficult to identify. For instance, a programme of forest planting may either result in the substitution of domestically produced wood for imported wood, or could alternatively have the effect of discouraging planting in alternative locations in the same country. Buck and Atkins (1976), in a study of the impact of regional investment subsidies on employment in Great Britain, concluded that they appeared to have a direct output effect which led to an increase in the demand for labour, but that they have also caused a non-negligible substitution effect against labour.

In terms of potential policies, then, there is a variety of approaches to expanding employment within a particular region. Given the objective of raising employment so as to raise incomes and to retain the populations of relatively poor regions, the approach of work sharing would seem to be unlikely to represent a suitable policy in this context. The approaches available, therefore, reduce to three categories: relocating employment, expanding output, and altering factor proportions. Under conditions of generally high unemployment, policies aiming to relocate employment are unlikely to be considered ideal or to be easy to operate. However, this *is* the option which is most often pursued. While the expansion of economic output is a desired objective, this falls largely into the realm of macro-economic policy, where competing objectives, especially reduced inflation, may conflict with employment objectives. As suggested earlier, the extent to which economic growth will lead to an expansion in employment is being increasingly, although perhaps excessively, questioned. This leaves the third option, that of altering the factor proportions employed in production processes. The question of employment is important in the debate over appropriate technology, which we discussed in Chapter 7. The potential exists for more intensive use of labour in a wide range of activities. However, the costs at market prices of such techniques are likely to exceed those of the alternatives. But we have argued that a high level of employment brings benefits beyond those reflected by wages in respect of the recognition aspect of employment. Should we not then, accept these higher costs by reducing the cost of labour relative to capital so as to achieve the social benefits? Many say that we should. The problem lies in the fact that in a relatively open economy consumers will not pay extra for goods produced by labour intensive techniques when the same goods are available at lower prices from overseas producers. The consequence of such a change therefore is not just to lead to increased costs, but also to cause a reduction in the level of domestic production. A unilateral substitution of labour for capital would therefore probably lead to an overall reduction in employment. Such a policy would need to either be applied only to items not traded internationally or be supported by tariff protection. Either way, the direct costs and consequent retardation of economic growth must be borne by consumers. The issue balances on the extra costs of production compared with the benefits of increased employment. Neither of these aspects is easily measured, with the result that widely differing opinions are retained as to the merits of such policies.

In assessing the impact of employment creation within an area, what is of most importance is to decide how many of the jobs which are associated with the scheme would in fact have been available there if it had not been undertaken. This requires a judgement on the basis of the nature of the employment created and the opportunities which would otherwise have been available. Having made this, it is then possible to estimate the overall contribution which the scheme has made to income, employment and population in the area under study.

Secondary impacts of projects

Employment creation programmes have effects beyond those directly associated with the specific industry which is encouraged. These effects arise from the impact which the changed level of economic activity has on local incomes and employment, and through these on the levels of migration to and from the area. This is simply a reversal of the process of rural decline described in Chapter 1. Such programmes are likely to make two types of direct impact on the local economy. Firstly, in the initial establishment stages of the project there may be construction works required such as in the erection of factories in an industrial project or hotels in a project to develop tourism. Secondly, during the operation of the project, there will be expenditure such as that on the good produced by the factories or by the tourists staying in the hotels. These impacts will lead to various sources of income being injected into the area. The construction phase of the project may require the purchase of local materials and labour, the wages paid to the employees in the economic activity which is being encouraged and the inputs purchased locally for this activity. Other local income could be generated, for instance through administrative expenses of the employment creation programme. Parts of these incomes will be spent locally, so increasing the other incomes of which part will be spent locally, and so on. At each stage of the process, various leakages will occur. These result largely from expenditure on goods imported to the region and transfers, such as taxation, out of the region. Clearly, the smaller the region under consideration, the higher the proportion of consumption made up by imports is likely to be, and so the smaller the overall increase in regional income which results from an initial injection. This relationship is given by the regional income multiplier which is usually measured by the ratio of the total income generated within the region to the direct income resulting from some injection.

A number of approaches may be taken in the estimation of the impact of a change in the level of economic activity in the area. These methods may be applied equally to both increases and decreases. The two most commonly used are input-output analysis and the application of a Keynesian regional income multiplier. Economic base models (e.g. Garrison, 1968; Wagstaff, 1973) have also been used. Input-output analysis is undertaken on the basis of a model which quantifies the linkages between the various sectors (industries, services, final demand) in the area being studied. This information is provided in the form of an input-output table which indicates the purchases made over a period of time by each sector and the sector from which they were made. Thus the impact of a change in the level of demand for the output from one sector on the outputs of all the other sectors in the area can be estimated. A fuller outline of input-output analysis is given by Whitby and Willis (1978). A number of studies of the impact of developments in rural areas using input-output analysis have been made, such as those by Sadler *et al.* (1973) and Mandeville and Jensen (1978).

While the input-output method has the advantage that it provides estimates of the impact of development on each individual sector, it has large data requirements which involve a substantial investment of time and resources. The development of non-survey techniques for the derivation of regional tables from national input-output tables and regional data has significantly reduced the effort required. For a description, see for instance Jensen *et al.* (1979). Furthermore, the production and maintenance of tables for standard planning regions can facilitate the use of input-output analysis with considerably reduced effort for estimating the impact of a variety of developments. However, in our concern for rural areas, we are seldom dealing with standard planning regions and will rarely have in existence the relevant tables. In this context, a less statistically demanding, although more 'rough and ready' approach to estimating the impacts of various changes in regional economies is possible through the application of a Keynesian regional income multiplier.

Brownrigg (1974) has suggested its basic formulation as

$$k_r = \frac{1}{1-c(1-t_d-u)\,(1-m-t_i)}$$

where k_r = regional income multiplier
c = marginal propensity to consume
t_d = marginal rate of direct taxation
u = decline in transfer payments associated with the increase in regional income
m = marginal propensity to import
t_i = indirect taxation associated with increased expenditure

The model identifies the leakages from expenditure on local goods and services which occur at each round, i.e. from income saved, direct taxation, reductions in transfer payments made to the region, such as reductions in unemployment benefits, expenditure on imports and indirect taxation. In a small rural region which produces a very small proportion of the goods it consumes, a high proportion of expenditure will leak from the region, and income remaining in it at each round will mostly be associated with payment for services and the margins charged on the sales of retail goods. Estimates of the magnitude of the coefficients of this type of model have been made for a number of regions and sub-regions (see for example Brown *et al.*, 1967; Brownrigg, 1974; Brownrigg and Greig, 1974; Archer, 1976; Hodge and Whitby, 1979). Typical values for a small region would be:

c = 0.9
t_d = 0.2
u = 0.15
m = 0.55
t_i = 0.15

These values would give a regional multiplier of 1.21. Other estimates have been made of multipliers for a small development area of 1.24 (Brown *et al.*, 1967); the Isle of Skye of 1.13 (Brownrigg and Greig, 1974); Mid Wales of 1.25 (Development Commission, 1972); and the Eastern Scottish Borders of 1.21 (Hodge and Whitby, 1979).

A number of problems are associated with the application of regional income multipliers. These arise from the assumptions and limitations of the model itself and the need to make accurate estimates of the coefficients. The model described above is implemented on the basis that any initial injection of income will result in the same increase in the level of regional income, regardless of where or to whom it accrues. This is unlikely to be the case in practice as different groups within the region are likely to save at different rates, spend any extra income which they receive in different ways and pay different amounts of taxes. Given detailed information concerning the nature of the injection whose impact is to be estimated and the expenditure patterns of the affected population, it would be possible to provide a more specific multiplier. However, such detailed data are rarely available and it is necessary to rely on averages of the relevant characteristics for the region. A further difficulty arises from the fact that the period of time over which an injection will expand the level of regional income by the extent of the multiplier is not known. It clearly cannot be instantaneous as a number of transactions need to be made in the various rounds, and thus the exact timing of the anticipated increment in regional income is not known. It is also possible that over this period changes may occur in the coefficients of the model themselves. The simple model, as presented here, has neglected several aspects which could be of importance in estimating the full impacts of changes in the level of economic activity in regional economies. For instance, there could be repercussions from inter-regional trade. Increased incomes in region A, which cause a rise in the level of imports, will stimulate higher incomes in other regions. These higher incomes could themselves generate an increase in the demand for exports from region A, and hence a further increase in its income. This effect is described by Steele (1969). However, in a small region relative to the rest of the economy, this effect is unlikely to be important.

Of more potential relevance in the context of employment creation is that, where the initial injection in a region is caused by a large flow of immigrant workers, investment would be induced by the immigrants' expenditure (Archibald, 1967). This adjustment appears to be less important where an employment creation programme has the effect of reducing the rate of depopulation. Greig (1971) has also adapted the basic model to take into account high levels of immigration. Because a high proportion of the population affected in his study were immigrants to the area, he used average propensities rather than marginal propensities in the first round.

Making estimates of the coefficients is a difficult exercise. Information on the patterns of expenditure and savings may be available, but, particularly in the context of estimating impacts on small regions, not necessarily for the specific area under study. Furthermore, it is usually the way in which individuals save or spend the increments to their incomes (i.e. their *marginal* propensities to save and import) that are of relevance, rather than their average propensities, for which data are most often available.

Accepting these limitations, the next stage in using a multiplier is to decide what it should be multiplied by, i.e. what should be the multiplicand. Brownrigg (1974) has generalized his basic model to

$$\Delta Y_r = k_r \, (J_1 + J_2 + \ldots + J_n)$$

where ΔY_r is the total change in regional income and the Js are the components of the multiplicand. These represent the various sources of income generation from the programme and are stated net of immediate leakages from the region. Thus, for instance, in a project to establish hotels in an area, regional income would be generated from the wages paid to hotel employees, the local purchases made by the hotels and the local expenditure component of their initial construction.

Having identified the likely change in the level of regional income, it is then possible to estimate the implications for employment in the various sectors which will be influenced by the development. To pursue the example of hotel construction, employment will increase in the hotels themselves, in the provision of supplies and services for the hotels and in the provision of services to the extra population now resident in the area. Increased tourism to the area is also likely to encourage expenditure and hence employment in the provision of other services directly to the tourists, but here we will concentrate on the impact of the expenditure to the hotels themselves. The actual numbers of jobs may be estimated on the basis of the total rise in income achieved by each of these activities, the proportion of this income which goes towards employment, and the costs of employing each person. It is likely that the average wages paid to various categories of employee will differ, and so, if it is assumed that the types of new employees hired will be in the same proportion as those already employed, then the amount of new employment in an activity (i) employing two categories of worker (a and b) will be given by

$$\Delta E_i = \frac{\Delta Y_i d_i}{(P_{ai}\, C_{ai} + P_{bi}\, C_{bi})}$$

where ΔE = change in employment
ΔY = change in income
d = proportion of income accruing to labour
P = proportion of employment in a category
C = cost of employing one person in a category
i = denotes the activity
a, b = denote employment categories

It is possible that some activities will have surplus capacity, so that increased demand will raise incomes of the existing employees without leading to the hiring of new ones. This may be accounted for by increasing the rise in income required to provide each extra job. The actual extent of any surplus capacity is quite difficult to measure.

Demographic impact of projects

The methodology described so far has, on the basis of a known change in the level of some activity in an area, provided estimates of the overall change in regional income and the employment which results from this. The final stage is to examine the demographic implications of these changes. This requires judgements as to the alternative situations of those who take up the jobs which became available. These people could either be engaged in some other employment or unemployed, either inside or outside the region which is being considered. The picture is further complicated by the fact that the withdrawal of a person from one position creates a further vacancy if he too was employed. It is the total impact of the new employment which is likely to be of interest and so an assessment needs to be made of the final impact on the labour market. Evans (1973) has suggested a Markovian approach to this problem.

If 100 jobs become available in an area, these would be filled by people moving from other jobs, people previously unemployed and people leaving school. If 60 per cent of those taking up the new employment left other jobs, then they would create 60 vacancies. If it is assumed that these are filled in the same proportion as the original vacancies, then the sources of employees for these jobs can be estimated, and so on. In considering the implications of employment creation in a small region, it is also important to consider the resultant movements of employees into the area and those out of the area which have been prevented. In a study of rural depopulation (HM Treasury, 1976), estimates have been provided of the sources of labour for incoming industry. These are shown for Wigtown in Scotland in Table 9.1. These are the initial sources. If it is assumed that the vacancies resulting from the reduction in local productive employment are filled in the same proportions as the initial vacancies, the final impact of 100 vacancies can be estimated on the basis of the method outlined above.

Table 9.1 Sources of labour for 100 jobs provided by incoming industry in Wigtown, Scotland

	Initial Impact		*Final Impact*	
Source	*Male*	*Female*	*Male*	*Female*
Reduction in local registered unemployment	55	30	73	50
Reduction in local unregistered unemployment	10	30	13	50
Reduction in local productive employment	25	40	—	—
Reduction in outward migration	10	0	13	0

Source: Derived from HM Treasury (1976)

These results assume that each set of vacancies created will be filled in the same proportions as the initial ones (i.e. constant transition probabilities). In a region with a small labour market, there could be limited numbers of people from some of these categories available for employment. Where this is the case, it is likely that vacancies will remain unfilled for longer periods or will not be filled at all. This can occur in remote areas when it becomes necessary to attract employees to move into the area, and may also be associated with increased wage rates. We consider the question of the costs which result from moving labour into new work in some detail in Chapter 10. Generally, because of the mismatch of skills and abilities which results from the relative immobility of labour, and because of the small size of the labour markets under consideration, we have to assume that some productive jobs will be lost, even under conditions of unemployment. When further information is available on the motivations and expectations of employees, it may be possible to use this in the construction of more likely alternative situations.

Another approach to this problem is through the estimation of relationships between regional levels of employment, unemployment and migration for the region under study. This approach was used in a study of the impact of factory construction in Mid-Wales (Development Commission, 1972) and is dependent upon these relationships remaining fixed throughout the period under consideration (i.e. other potentially influential factors remaining constant). Detailed annual estimates of the annual migration rates from the area under study are unlikely to be available, and this factor had to be treated as a residual in the Development Commission study.

Having identified the numbers of employees who would alternatively not have been in the region in the absence of the employment which has been made available, it is necessary to find their ages and the numbers of people who would have moved with them, so as to estimate the full present and future demographic impact. It might be assumed that they will be similar to previous emigrants from the area for which census data may be available, or data may be gathered directly from those who have moved, if they can be traced, or those who say that they would have moved. These data may be used to provide estimates of the present impact on the level of population in the region and the implications for future population growth.

In this chapter, we have examined the question of the differences which a certain number of new jobs in an area have made to overall regional employment and population. We have not considered the efforts which have been made to achieve these changes or whether they are worthwhile. We turn our attention to these issues in the following chapters.

10
THE EVALUATION OF PROJECTS

Public agencies may take initiatives to promote employment in rural areas by operating through a variety of activities in a variety of ways. In doing so they influence the manner and extent to which resources are used, such as in the construction of buildings, the use to which land is put or the occupations followed by workers. A particular form of initiative which is pursued in a particular area may be regarded as a project. As such, it should be capable of being analysed as an independent unit. In this chapter we are concerned with the principles behind the process of deciding whether to implement such projects.

The role of evaluation

An evaluation of a project is undertaken so as to provide information for decision-making in the design and implementation of new projects and in the management of existing ones. Generally, the most apparently favourable project will be subjected to an evaluation where the position with the project is compared with the position which would ensue if the project was not implemented. Then, if it meets the required standards, a decision will be taken to go ahead with it. Sometimes, though, it may not be clear as to which of the possible range of projects is, in fact, the most favourable. In such circumstances more than one project may be evaluated and the type or design of project which performs best will be adopted. Such appraisals, which are made in advance of a project being undertaken, are referred to as *ex ante* appraisals.

On other occasions, an evaluation may be undertaken after a project has been implemented and when its effects have already been experienced. In this case, the information may be used in deciding upon the future management of the project and in the implementation of further, similar, projects. Such analysis is referred to as *ex post* appraisal. While the principles involved in each of these cases are the same, the availability of data and the judgements which are required are somewhat different. After dealing with the principles involved in this chapter, we proceed to described an example of an *ex post* evaluation in the following chapter and of a hypothetical *ex ante* evaluation in Chapter 12.

The decision as to whether any particular project is worthwhile centres on a comparison of the positions with and without it. It is therefore necessary to identify the impact of any project and we begin this chapter with a consideration of the issues involved in this exercise. The decision which arises from such a comparison depends upon the objectives of the decision-maker, which determine which effects are taken into account and what importance is attached to them. Because these projects are pursued by public agencies with a view to promoting the public interest, the evaluation takes a somewhat different approach to that which would be taken by a private individual. We here describe two possibilities: firstly, we examine the implications for exchequer finances of the various costs and returns associated with projects, and secondly, we take into account the broad range of their impacts, both beneficial and detrimental, as they affect the way in which resources are used within the economy more generally. This takes us into the area of cost-benefit analysis. In the past few decades there have been many books on public project appraisal, or social cost-benefit analysis (from McKean (1958), Eckstein (1958), to Mishan (1971), Dasgupta and Pearce (1972) and Sugden and Williams (1978)), though few of them have much to say on employment creation policies. Those unfamiliar with the concepts involved may wish to consult a recent textbook on project appraisal.

The nature of evaluation

There are two aspects of the evaluation procedure which require quite different methodologies. First, the physical impact of the project on the sub-regional population must be assessed, and second, the resources devoted to the project and the benefits flowing from it must be estimated. Both aspects must be preceded by a clear-cut delineation of the economic boundaries of the project in both space and time.

The delineation of the project for assessment purposes involves defining the region in which it is set – that is the area over which employment created will be counted as beneficial. It is also necessary to establish the time dimensions of the project – the starting date and the period over which relevant benefits may be recorded. Various other accounting and methodological conventions will also have to be established. In particular, questions of the precise nature of financial or social costs and benefits have to be determined.

Having established the boundaries of the project, we then estimate how far it will take us towards its objectives. Possible objectives within a defined region might be:

- the direct establishment of new jobs
- the direct and indirect establishment of new jobs
- reduction of unemployment in the region
- achievement of a stated level of population
- reduction of outmigration of employees
- reduction of all outmigration
- generation of maximum cumulative person-years of employment over a stated period.

This list may seem formidable but it is by no means exhaustive.

In order to measure progress towards such objectives, it is necessary to estimate how the chosen variable would change, both with and without the project. This will require demographic data and analysis of the kind discussed in Chapters 2 and 9. Indeed, for some of the objectives, a good deal more information would be required.

The second aspect of the evaluation procedure is concerned with the costs and benefits which are associated with the physical impacts of the project. We devote the rest of this chapter to this aspect, considering first financial and then social evaluation.

Financial evaluation

For most projects a financial evaluation will be required at some stage of the decision-making process. It is not enough to know that the project creates a given number of jobs, agencies will also be concerned about the cost per job. Cost in this context would include the outlay of public agencies of all kinds which contribute to the project. Thus, we might expect site development and factory construction to be important costs in a rural industrial development project, land purchase and tree planting in a forestry project, or the payment of grants and subsidies to employers in other types of project seeking to encourage existing employers to maintain or expand their work force. Furthermore, such projects may result indirectly in greater payments being made by other sections of government, for example through more companies becoming eligible for existing regional grants or by increased exports being eligible for subsidies under a national scheme to encourage companies to export. We could then, add up these costs to provide a measure of the total costs to the exchequer of the project in question.

Against these costs, any project is also likely to raise the level of exchequer revenues. These may occur directly through the project, for instance from factory rentals or the sale of timber, or indirectly by means of the taxes paid on increased profits and incomes, or savings made in unemployment benefits and other public subsidies paid to those who are brought into employment as a consequence of the project. Again, as with the costs, these could be added and taken as a total measure of the returns received by the exchequer as a result of the project. Costs could then be subtracted from the returns to provide a net cost to the exchequer.

However, this procedure fails to take any account of the fact that the costs and revenues will occur at different points in time. In this discussion we ignore the effects of inflation and either assume that there is none, or that the costs and returns are measured in terms of the values of the units of currency ruling at one particular time. The latter is, of course, most likely.

Such projects almost inevitably involve a large initial outlay, with returns arising after an establishment phase. Typical flows of costs and returns are illustrated in Figure 10.1. The timing and scale of these flows in any particular project is, of course, dependent upon its individual characteristics and circumstances. Often the construction phase of a project will generate an immediate and relatively large increase in employment which might promote political support for it. However, such effects are likely to be of short duration compared with the lifetime of the project.

As can be seen from the figure, the issue as to whether the returns outweigh the costs is not quite so clear-cut as might at first have been imagined. We have to come to two decisions. Firstly, when is the project considered to be over, or over what *time horizon* is the project to be evaluated? In some circumstances the project will

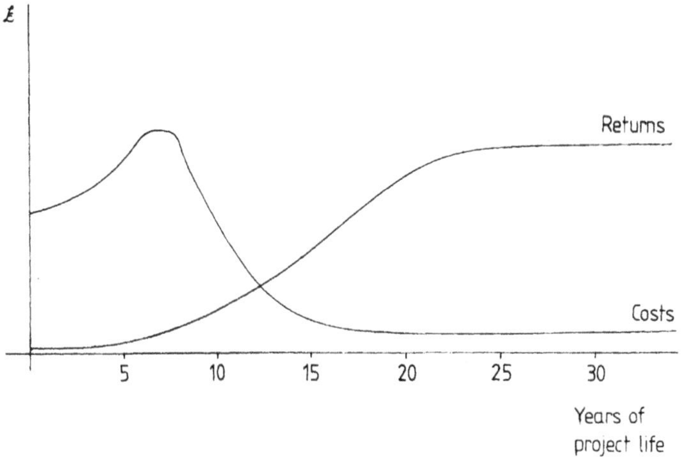

Figure 10.1 Typical flows of costs and returns in a development project

have a definite end, such as at harvesting time in timber production, or when some important capital item becomes worn out or obsolete. However, for other projects, as is the case in the figure, there is no obvious end, or at least, not in the near future and here we have to determine a somewhat arbitrary cut-off point.

This brings us to the second decision which we need to make. Can we treat the pounds of costs and returns as being equally important, regardless of whether they occur at an early or a later stage of the project? The commitment of funds to one particular project means that they cannot be used in an alternative elsewhere, in either the public or the private sectors. The benefits which they could generate in that alternative use are thereby foregone. The exchequer will therefore prefer to receive the returns earlier and to pay out costs later. This preference is taken into account by discounting the cash flows. That is to say that the actual figures are adjusted at a particular rate so as to take this opportunity cost of capital into account. The actual *discount rate* which is used will in fact depend upon a variety of factors, but generally reflects the rate of return which could be achieved by a project elsewhere which involves a similar degree of risk. Often governments will specify the rate which they believe should be achieved in public sector projects.

The discounting is undertaken by reducing the actual amounts by the rate of discount each year. Thus if R_1 is revenue in year 1, then this is equivalent to $R_1/(1 + r)$, in year o, or the *present value*, where

r is the discount rate (expressed as a decimal rather than as a percentage). Over the whole period of the project, we can calculate the present value of the revenues as

$$R_0 + \frac{R_1}{(1 + r)} + \frac{R_2}{(1 + r)^2} + \ldots + \frac{R_T}{(1 + r)^T} \quad (1)$$

where T is the time horizon of the project. This expression may be summarized as

$$PV_R = \sum_{t=0}^{T} \frac{R_t}{(1 + r)^t} \quad (2)$$

which represents the sum of the Rs where t takes the values between 0 and T. A similar operation may be undertaken in order to calculate the present value of the costs as

$$PV_C = \sum_{t=0}^{T} \frac{C_t}{(1 + r)^t} \quad (3)$$

where C represents the costs paid out in each year.

The issues of the time horizon and discounts rate are clearly interrelated. In general, extending the time horizon into the distant future will rarely make a critical difference to the result, in that the process of discounting will render the costs and benefits which occur in the distant future insignificant relative to those occurring in the present. For instance, a benefit of £1 in 50 years' time has a present value of £0.0085 at a 10 per cent discount rate. £1 in 25 years has a present value of £0.09. However, it could be important over short time horizons, especially when cash flows resemble those in Figure 10.1. Lower discount rates will give more importance to future events. In order to decide whether the returns outweigh the costs, we may then subtract the present value of the costs from the present value of the returns to give us the *net present value*.

$$NPV = PV_R - PV_C \quad (4)$$

Whether the net present value to the exchequer is positive or negative in the particular context of projects designed to create employment need not determine whether the project is worthwhile. It is quite likely that it will, in fact, be negative, especially over relatively short time horizons.

The list of possible specific project objectives earlier in the chapter suggests possible forms of criteria in terms of the cost of achieving a unit move towards an objective. Such cost-effectiveness criteria would be obtained by dividing the total effect of the project on, say, direct employment, into the Net Present Value to the exchequer over a given time horizon. In an *ex ante* situation it would perhaps be possible to clarify such questions as the appropriate time horizon and the objective to be pursued with decision-makers, hence reducing the relevance of calculating different criteria. In an *ex post* position, however, there may be uncertainty about such questions.

Individual studies can give rise to estimates of the costs of achieving public objectives by means of alternative projects. For instance, MacMillan and Lyon (1977) summarize the costs of creating employment through various activities undertaken in the Interlake area of Manitoba. These are reproduced in Table 10.1. Care is required in interpreting such statistics so as to identify the exact items of expenditure and returns which have been included. Furthermore, analysis would need to be undertaken in many rural regions before we could have confidence that the relative magnitudes of these effects are generally applicable.

The financial evaluation presented so far has suggested some yardsticks which might be used in comparing projects. However, it is vital to note that such analysis is of strictly limited prescriptive relevance. Indeed, it could produce some rather surprising results. For instance, while policies aimed at providing employment for people on low incomes would be considered favourably, due to the social security payments saved by the exchequer, so too would those aimed at further raising already high incomes, due to the high marginal tax rates paid by the recipients. Governments do not allocate their expenditures so as to maximize their returns. This is so because although exchequer funds available for job creation may be constrained, this does not provide the sole criterion for project selection in the public sector. The reasons behind this contention will be familiar to many readers. In essence they include the notion that public policies are justified in terms of the pursuit of broader goals. They have the objective of raising the level of social welfare, often giving special assistance to particular groups. This objective will be subject to constraints which will limit the extent of funds available, such as the need to avoid excessive distortion of the market system. The appraisal of policies, therefore, needs to examine their broader implications, such as may result from the fact that market prices may not be an appropriate reflection of what society is forced to give up by using particular resources, i.e. of *social opportunity costs*, or because the financial evaluation has

Table 10.1 Job creation per $1 million in alternative rural development programmes, Interlake region of Manitoba

	Man-years employment created per $1 million (1968 dollars)	*Timing of job impact*
1. Agricultural development[a]	160	Perpetual or life of drain
2. Food processing[b]	50	Perpetual
3. Education[c]	85	Annual expenditure required
4. Housing[d]	80	Annual expenditure required
5. Highways[e]	30	Annual expenditure required
6. Recreation (annual expenditure)[f]	60	Annual expenditure required
7. Manpower corps[g]	160	For the working life of trainees

Source: MacMillan and Lyon (1977)

Notes:

a. Estimated from analysis of agricultural development programs by Tung *et al.* (1976). Drainage, land clearing and farm management training, $8.4 million, generated 1.4 thousand man-years of employment.

b. A $1.4 million in DREE industrial incentives for a rapeseed processing plant is estimated to generate 47 plant jobs and 20 trade centre jobs (MacMillan *et al.*, 1974).

c. The 1968 Interlake education expenditures of $7.4 million create 635 jobs, 536 man-years of employment in the school system and 99 trade centre jobs (Molgat and MacMillan, 1972).

d. MacMillan and Nickel (1974).

e. Douglas and MacMillan (1972).

f. The job impact is calculated per $1 million of operating expenditures at Hecla Provincial Park, $700,000 in 1976. The capital cost of $5 million is excluded (Brown and MacMillan, 1977).

g. The $5 million Manpower Corps Expenditure 1967–76 increased wages from $82 to $219 per week and reduced the unemployment rate from 80 per cent to 20 per cent after training for 1300 trainees resulting in an investment of 160 jobs (Fernandez, 1977).

omitted some important items, such as the cost of extra services, which may or may not be provided by the market. We therefore turn to a social evaluation in the next section.

Social evaluation

Social evaluation is analogous to financial evaluation, but is broader in that it seeks to include all of the costs and benefits borne by and accruing to society as a result of a project. The project has the effect of causing resources in the economy to be used in a different way from that which would have ensued in its absence. The difference between these two positions therefore represents a measure of the value of the project itself. We refer to this difference as the *net social benefits* (NSB) of a project.

A methodology for assessing the NSB of a project which creates jobs in rural areas has been developed in a study by HM Treasury (1976). The main concept is that NSB comprise the difference between the value of the factors of production as used in a project and their social opportunity cost. (In fact the Treasury uses the term 'resource cost' where we use 'social opportunity cost'. Our terminology is preferred because it is somewhat less ambiguous than the Treasury's.) In algebraic form this becomes an annual series:

$$NSB = SB - SC = \sum_{j=1}^{n} Q_j (P_j - P^*_j) \qquad (5)$$

where j = factor of production ($j = 1, \ldots, n$)
SB = social benefits
SC = social costs
Q_j = the quantity of factor j used
P_j = the value of factor j in the project
P^*_j = the social opportunity cost of factor j

Under competitive conditions, where there are no externalities, and in the absence of government intervention, the market price of a factor will represent its value in the project. However, where subsidies or taxes are imposed on the use of factors, the price paid by employers and hence their valuation of them will not equal the market price. For instance, a subsidy on labour will mean that an employer will hire labour even when his own valuation is below the market wage. Each individual case therefore needs to be examined in order to decide whether the market valuation is an appropriate measure of the value of the factor in that use. If we find that the value of the factors in a project is equal to their social opportunity cost, then on the basis of this criterion we will be indifferent about whether this project is undertaken or not.

However, there are other consequences of establishing a project in rural areas, additional to those reflected in factor markets, which must also be brought into the reckoning. The most important of these will be the cost of providing public and private services to the extra population in the area generated by the project. We can also include in the evaluation the costs of migration and of the public administration of the project. Finally, we should in principle include any environmental consequences of a project and any changes in community welfare. This latter could be of importance in that projects such as we have in mind, which seek to create employment and to maintain declining communities, may produce benefits associated with the recognition aspects of employment and the quality of life for rural residents. However, because of the problems in quantifying these effects, we exclude them from this stage of the analysis.

Thus, for any particular year (t) the net social benefits is

$$NSB_t = \sum_{j=1}^{n} Q_{tj}(P_{tj} - P^*_{tj}) - K_t + M_t - A_t \tag{6}$$

Where the variables are as defined in (5), and

K = the aggregate net social cost of service provision
M = the value of saved moving costs due to reduced migration
A = the costs associated with the administration of the project

The annual flow of NSB is then discounted to the net present value as

$$PV(NSB) = \sum_{t=0}^{T} \frac{NSB_t}{(1+r)^t}$$

$$= \sum_{t=0}^{T} \frac{\left[\sum_{j=1}^{n} Q_{tj}(P_{tj} - P^*_{tj}) - K_t + M_t - A_t\right]}{(1+r)^t} \tag{7}$$

where variables are as defined above and

T = the time horizon ($t = 0, 1, \ldots, T$)
r = the social rate of discount

The next stage in the social evaluation is to place values on the items as identified in equation (7). Firstly, the expression $Q_{tj}(P_{tj} - P^*_{tj})$ is evaluated for labour, capital, and when appropriate, for land. Estimates are then made of the other items. We now consider each of these issues in turn.

The use of labour

In a perfectly competitive labour market, the price of labour, i.e. the market wage, would reflect the social opportunity cost of labour, i.e. the value of labour in its best alternative use. If the supply of labour increased, or the demand for it decreased, then wages would be forced downwards until all those who were seeking employment would be able to find it. However, this does not usually take place in practice. Involuntary unemployment can persist in an area as a result of the downward inflexibility of wages due to national wage bargaining procedures, strong labour unions, or unemployment benefits, as well as because of immobility of labour or the lack of particular skills. This situation can exist in some regions or occupations, even when national rates of unemployment are relatively low.

When there is involuntary unemployment in the area in which a project is being undertaken, it is likely that a certain proportion of those who take up employment in a new enterprise would have been unemployed had it not been introduced. Account should then be taken of the fact that the wages paid to the employees does not reflect the level of output which is given up as a result of this employment. This is to say that the social opportunity cost of labour is below the market wage. We therefore need to identify the extent of this divergence.

The market price of labour must first be determined for the project area. It is generally assumed that those employing labour will pay a wage equivalent to the value of its marginal product, so that the wage represents the value of the contribution to output made by an extra worker. The required information may be obtainable from published sources, directly or indirectly, or it may be necessary to conduct a survey to ascertain the present rates of earnings. In either case there is unlikely to be information as to the way present rates may be expected to change in the future. As the calculations are to be carried out in constant real prices the task of forecasting wage rates resolves in questions as to whether the area will see a *real* increase in wage rates relative to other prices. Having established the pattern of market wage rates we then turn to the problem of the social opportunity cost of labour.

In essence this is estimated as the weighted average value of the marginal product of all workers where an employment state has been changed as a consequence of the project. This may be calculated from

$$W^* = \sum_{i=1}^{n} P_i \, Y_i \tag{8}$$

where W^* = the social opportunity cost
P_i = the probability that a worker would alternatively be in employment state i
Y_i = the value of the worker's marginal product in state i
n = the number of employment states

This can take into account several possible alternative employment states. Some people would have been employed anyway, earning a similar wage to that achieved in project employment. Others would have been unemployed. These are not assumed to be totally unproductive; they may work in their own homes and gardens, or perhaps as part of the 'black economy'. Either way it seems reasonable to impute some value to their time. We might also include a category of 'concealed' unemployment. By this we have in mind people who are formally in employment, but who, if they left, would not be replaced. This indicates that the value of their marginal product in that activity is below the market wage. This position can arise where changes take place in the firm for which they work or in the labour market, and where the employer is reluctant to actually dismiss them.

Values can then be imputed for the probabilities and the value of the alternative marginal products in equation (8) and hence the social opportunity cost of labour estimated. This may then be expressed as a percentage of the market wage. This relates to the situation ruling at the time at which the evaluation is being undertaken. We then face the much more difficult question of whether the long-run social opportunity cost is changing over time. Assumptions need to be made about the likely future nature of the labour market in the project area. The project itself will, if successful, be an important factor. But also account should be taken of other factors, both local and national. Estimates of the social opportunity cost of labour applying in the project area over the entire time horizon of the appraisal are then made.

The use of capital

Capital may be defined simply as the result of past productive effort which is an input into the present or future production. The implementation of the project may involve the use of a wide variety of forms of capital, such as buildings, machinery, seeds, roads and so on. It is therefore less easy to generalize about the evaluation of the use of capital in employment creation projects. We may usually assume that the market price of capital items will reflect their social opportunity cost. They are usually bought and sold under competitive conditions without the institutional restrictions which play an important role in the labour market.

Potential inefficiencies in the use of capital in a project appear most likely to result from deliberate efforts to influence the market system by public agencies who can make capital items available to producers at artificially low prices. For instance, subsidies may be provided either directly or by means of favourable tax treatment for machinery purchase in agriculture in order to encourage agricultural development, or to manufacturing activities willing to establish production in particular areas. Mention was made in Chapter 9 of the idea that if subsidies are paid which influence the relative costs of resources, there is likely to be a change in the proportions in which the factors of production are combined in a production process. If the prices paid as a consequence no longer reflect their respective social opportunity costs then allocative inefficiency will be introduced. However, estimating the extent of this loss would present considerable measurement difficulties, particularly in the case of small projects being undertaken under unique circumstances.

Perhaps of greater consequence in our present context are the potential losses arising from the encouragement of enterprises to locate in what could be sub-optimal locations. In Chapter 7 we considered the advantages and disadvantages facing companies operating in rural areas. The evidence is unclear as to whether rural companies in general are likely to achieve lower rates of return on capital than would be the case in alternative locations. However, if grants and subsidies are provided so as to encourage companies to establish in rural areas, the possibility must be faced that they will achieve lower rates of return than otherwise. If this is so, this loss of efficiency must be included as a social cost of the project. In order to assess the magnitude of this cost, we need to consider the use to which the capital involved in the project would have been put in its absence, and its productivity in this alternative use.

The nature of this alternative position requires careful consideration, especially in terms of how government policies might have been different. Our concern with rural areas and essentially small-scale projects leads us to the assumption that other government actions would not be influenced by the presence or absence of rural employment policies, i.e. that other government involvement in regional or macro-economic policy would have been unchanged. This partial analysis is defensible where the project is small scale in national terms. It would be less readily acceptable in the analysis of larger projects, such as national regional policy, or where rural employment policies comprise a significant component of national economic activity. In such examples, governments would be expected to make macro-economic adjustments so as to maintain the level of demand in the regions from which the economic activity has been drawn (Rhodes and Moore, 1973). However, this is unlikely to be the case in the examples which we have in mind. For instance, assistance to development in the Eastern Borders (see Chapter 11) in 1974–5 represented some 0.05 per cent of total UK expenditure on regional policy.

Against this background, we may then consider what position the enterprises providing employment would have been in had the project not been undertaken. Firstly, for mobile companies this is likely to involve a similar activity being undertaken in an alternative location. Other companies could be operating in the same or similar locations but at a smaller scale. Finally, the companies might not have been established at all. For the first of these possibilities, a net social cost results from any difference in return in the alternative region and the actual return achieved, net of any subsidies paid. For the second and third of these possibilities the cost derives from any differences in return associated with the incremental local investment or with the total investment in its actual and its alternative use. These are difficult items to measure. One possible approach suggests a maximum extent of this differential. The extra level of grants and subsidies paid to these companies which leads to the extra investment in these particular activities in this particular location cannot exceed the losses incurred by so doing. In fact, assuming rational decision-making, the differential must be less than these government payments, but by an unknown amount.

Some companies so assisted may, nevertheless, be seen to have good reason for operating in the locality. Some will draw on local raw materials; others will supply local markets. For these we may assume that there is no significant net social cost resulting from their location. Further, some companies will have been previously operating in areas which suffer from similar potential disadvantages. Where this is the case, we may trust in the manager's wisdom and assume therefore that these are not of significance in this particular case. For the remainder, the extent of funds provided as an incentive to establish production in this area may be taken as a maximum measure of the net social cost associated with the project.

Other types of project will include other forms of capital cost. For instance, agricultural projects may involve the provision of infrastructure in the form of dams and water distribution systems as one initial investment, the benefits of which are shared amongst many producers. Others will incur initial investments, such as tree planting and road building in a forestry scheme or extension work in a project designed to improve the management skills of a particular group of farmers. These investments are generally unique to and inseparable from their particular projects, so that their value can only be assessed in the context of a cost-benefit study of the entire project.

The use of land

The third category of resource with which we may be concerned is land. In assessing the loss involved in taking land out of agricultural production so as to raise the level of employment in a region through, for instance, planting forests, the market price paid for land does not necessarily reflect its social opportunity cost. In fact, it often exceeds it. One major reason for this is that the support commonly given to the agricultural sectors of developed countries tends to become capitalized in the values of rural land. When land is taken out of agricultural production, all that society loses is the contribution which it makes to farm output so that its social opportunity cost may more appropriately be measured by the present value, discounted in perpetuity, of its net agricultural production. The opportunity cost of land is unlikely to be of significance in industrial development programmes, but may be important in forestry and other land-using activities.

Costs of service provision

Apart from possible benefits from the promotion of service activities as a means of generating employment, the cost of servicing larger rural populations must be included in project assessment. There are two aspects of measuring such costs. First, the number of extra people demanding services must be assessed. The change in the demand for services will depend partly on the total increase in the number of people in the area and partly on the age distribution of the new population. A preponderance of young families will demand more in the way of education and so on.

Second, the capital costs and the operating costs of providing services need to be estimated. One argument which is sometimes proposed in favour of retaining populations in rural areas concerns the fact that declining areas are likely to have surplus capacity in social capital, such as schools, hospitals and the various forms of infrastructure. By holding population in these areas, and therefore reducing the rate of growth of population in other, more congested areas, the overall capital costs of providing public services can be reduced. The extent to which this occurs will depend upon where the increase in population occurs within the rural area and where this population would have been in the absence of the project. In rural areas, population loss tends to occur throughout the region, while population growth tends to be centred within the larger settlements which provide the new employment opportunities. Within these settlements, therefore, new facilities may well be required. This means that potential savings from the utilization of surplus social capital may not be as large as anticipated. However, this is an issue which should be taken into account in assessing the costs of service provision.

The operating costs must also be included. If these two types of cost are taken together and long-run costs are considered, we need to estimate the marginal costs of providing services, i.e. the cost of providing the last unit of any particular service. For each type of service in each type of location, it could be argued that the service should be supplied to each individual up to the point where the marginal benefit derived from it, i.e. the benefit gained from the last unit supplied, is equal to the marginal cost of its provision. This position is illustrated in Figure 10.2.

As the level of service provision increases, the benefit from an extra unit of consumption (MB), decreases. Over this range of production, the marginal cost (MC) is increasing, so that the optimal level of production is at Q*. Service provision beyond this point will incur costs beyond the benefits. In reality, of course, it is unlikely that the curves would be as smooth as those illustrated. As indicated already, studies have shown that the unit costs of providing services in areas with greater population densities are likely to

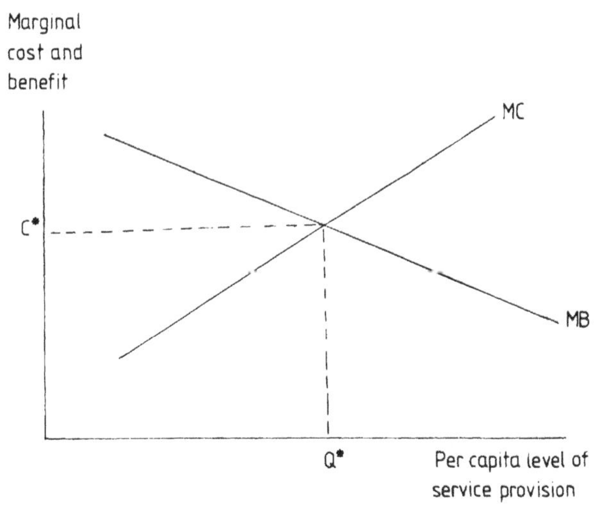

Figure 10.2 Optimal level of *per capita* service provision

be lower than in sparsely populated areas. This position is illustrated in Figure 10.3, where two marginal cost curves are shown; MC_R represents the marginal cost of providing services in a less densely populated (rural) area and MC_U represents the marginal cost of providing services in a more densely populated (urban) area.

Thus the implication is that an optimal level of service provision in less densely populated areas will be below that provided in other areas ($Q_R < Q_U$), and that the unit cost will be higher ($C_R > C_u$). Whether or not total expenditure on providing the service is higher or lower in less densely populated areas will be determined by the relative positions of the curves. Some scope is available for altering the type of environment within which the services are provided. This typically involves changes in the administrative areas by which the

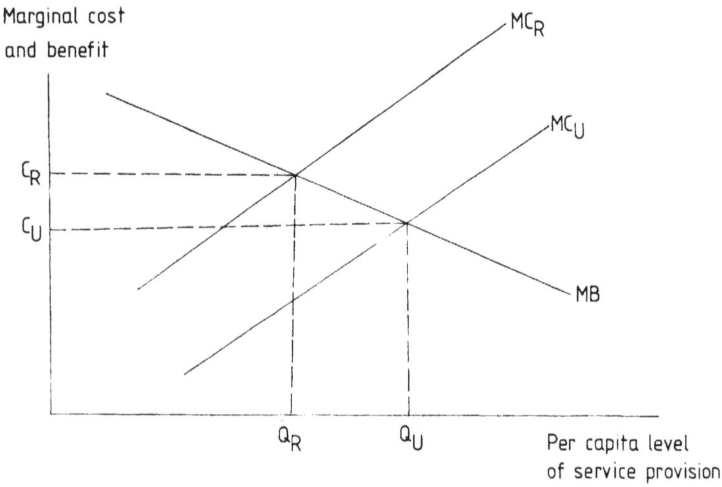

Figure 10.3 Optimal level of *per capita* service provision in urban and rural areas

supply of services is organized or policies which influence the numbers of people resident in such areas.

Clearly, in the absence of satisfactory measures of the quantity and quality of the output of many service activities – a problem which we referred to in Chapter 8 – it is not possible to identify the marginal benefits curve or the optimal level of provision. Under these circumstances, decisions are made against an objective of minimizing costs, subject to the constraint of achieving a certain 'acceptable' quality of service. In some cases, the level of the service to be provided may be easily agreed upon. For instance, dustbins should be emptied once a week; all homes should have water and electricity supply. In others there is usually some qualification, such as that all people should have reasonable access to a hospital or police protection. Under these circumstances, decisions about the level of service will be made in relation to the remoteness of the area in question, i.e. in relation to the cost of provision; even though this is likely to remain unquantified. For each service, therefore, there will be a certain settlement size which will allow full exploitation of the potential economies of scale. While this is likely to be different for each service, the aggregate cost curve would indicate the optimal settlement size from the point of view of service provision. Such a curve is likely to be stepped, leading to certain thresholds, where costs will rapidly change through a small population increase (Whitby and Willis, 1978). However, the shape of this aggregate cost curve has not been adequately identified in practice.

Service provision in the private sector We have discussed the process by which changes take place in the level of private sector service provision in rural areas in Chapter 8. This pattern will conform in the longer term to the ideal, illustrated in Figure 10.2, provided that the price received for the service represents a true measure of its benefit and that the full cost is met by the producer. While it may be regretted that there is not a wider range of services available in small settlements, the reason is most likely to be that the benefit of the service, as valued by the price paid, is less than the cost, and so investment in extra facilities would be less valuable than alternative forms of investment. In the short run, responses to changes in populations or changes in costs may not occur immediately, although adjustments will take place in the longer run. Therefore, because resources can ultimately move to their most productive use, we do not include any social cost of resource use in private sector service provision.

Service provision in the public sector We also suggested in Chapter 8 that public sector agencies tend to levy standard charges for the services which they provide, irrespective of their marginal costs of provision. When this is the case, individuals who decide to continue to live in remoter areas, or to move to them, will make this choice without bearing the full cost. Nevertheless, these costs must be borne. Therefore, if we wish to assess the full social cost of policies seeking to promote the survival of small rural communities, it will be necessary to estimate the relevant marginal costs.

We face a large number of problems in formally estimating the net social costs of providing services to populations retained in sparsely populated areas. Primarily, as we have already mentioned, we are often unable to compare the quality of services provided in different environments. Furthermore, we do not know where the population retained in the aréa would alternatively have been living. We can make two simplifying assumptions in order to get around these difficulties. Firstly, that the levels of services provided in the area in question are the same as in 'average' areas and, secondly, that the extra population in the area would alternatively have been living in an 'average' area. This first assumption is clearly less acceptable, the more remote is the area in which the project is undertaken. This reduces the problem to that illustrated in Figure 10.4. MC_A represents the marginal cost of providing services in an 'average' area, and Q is the level of service provided in both areas. The net social cost may now be defined as the expenditure which is required to produce the standard level of service provision in the remoter area, beyond that required in the 'average' area. Thus the net social cost for a particular project is

$$NSC = \Delta P(C_R Q - C_A Q) \qquad (9)$$

where ΔP is the change in the level of population, and C_R, C_A and Q are as in Figure 10.4.

In practice, even estimating this cost is no easy task, given the large numbers of services and the problems of evaluating marginal costs. However, it will usually be feasible to approach the service agencies for advice. Such advice can probably be translated into financial terms without too much difficulty. A comparison can then be made of costs within the project area and either national or regional averages or costs in an area of 'average' population density.

Moving costs

The costs of movements arise because the pattern of migration will

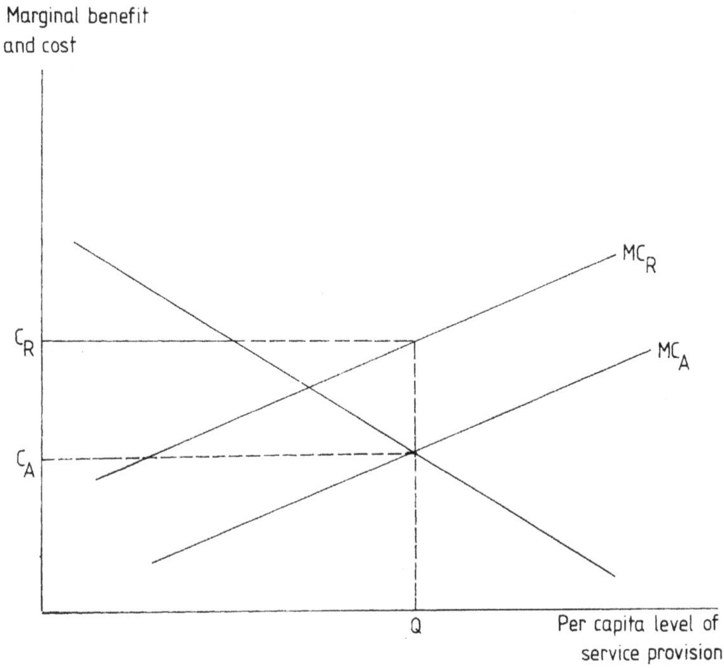

Figure 10.4 *Per capita* service provision with fixed standards

be changed by the project. Some people will move into the project area and others who would otherwise have left, will in fact stay. The net saving or loss in movement costs associated with the project may be estimated as the average social cost of moving, multiplied by the number who would have left, minus the number who did move into the area. The numbers of movements stimulated and prevented will have been estimated at an earlier stage of the evaluation.

Administration of the project

The implementation of the project will involve a variety of administrative costs, such as the employment of people to oversee and organize it, costs of giving publicity to the opportunities, and so on. While these costs are unlikely to represent a large proportion of the total, in that they are necessary costs of achieving the objectives of the project, they should be accounted for.

Environmental costs and community welfare changes

Environmental costs are rarely easy to evaluate, but at least the source of any such costs should be noted in a full appraisal. They might arise from the physical production process itself – perhaps the noise, smell, visual intrusion of the plant in an otherwise non-industrial landscape. In other cases they might be more directly measurable if the development destroys a particular facility which has to be replaced. Under such circumstances the replacement cost would provide a direct measure of the environmental cost of the project.

There may, equally, be additions to community welfare as a result of the project which could be brought into the assessment. For example, where unemployment is reduced significantly the community may be more peaceful and there could be savings in police costs. However, it must be acknowledged that such benefits are likely to be impossible to measure, as are environmental costs, and it may be that the analyst will have to be content with providing a list of factors not brought into the calculations.

Investment appraisal

Having assembled the data for evaluation, it may then be summarized in the form of investment criteria. From the preceding pages we are now in a position to calculate the present value of net social benefits (NSB) as in equation (7) on page 168. The procedure is the same as that described in the earlier section on financial evaluation. Firstly, the costs and benefits occurring in each year are calculated, and these are brought to present values by applying the social rate of discount over a particular time horizon. The debate as to how a social rate of discount should be calculated remains unresolved and we will not air the various issues involved here. Those wishing to pursue this may like to consult one of the texts on public project appraisal which were mentioned at the beginning of this chapter. The considerations raised about the time horizon in our discussion of financial evaluation apply here too. In principle, a social evaluation would tend to give more weight to the future than a private one, and this would be reflected in a lower discount rate and longer time horizon. In practice the rate applied will often be one recommended by the government and the process of discounting will render the costs and benefits which occur in the distant future relatively unimportant so that the time horizon is unlikely to be a critical decision.

A final stage of the evaluation is to compute measures of social cost-effectiveness. These may be produced by dividing the NSB by denominators representing the objectives of the project, such as numbers of jobs provided. The list of possible objectives of the project at the beginning of this chapter illustrates the range of possible denominators. This enables comparison of different projects with the same objects so as to examine which are the most preferred. Alternatively, NSB may be divided by the level of exchequer expenditure to produce measures of the level of benefits per £1 of exchequer expenditure. Such criteria may be attractive as a means of comparing different methods of allocating public expenditure. They are broader in their applicability than cost-effectiveness ratios. They must nevertheless be interpreted with some caution because of the number of assumptions which have had to be made in their calculation. Generally, the more different the form of public project they are being compared with, the greater should be the caution.

Conclusions

The methodology outlined here does not produce a decision for the decision-maker. Rather, it is a way of analysing and presenting the available data to him. Some aspects of the project will not be quantified and these need to be weighed against those that are. Judgements still need to be made about the relative importance attributed to costs and benefits incurred by different groups within the community. However, the process of evaluation represents a systematic consideration of the issues involved and provides an opportunity for open, rational decision-making.

11
AN ASSESSMENT OF EMPLOYMENT CREATION IN THE EASTERN BORDERS[1]

So far, we have described the approach to assessing projects seeking to expand employment in rural areas. In this chapter, we provide a summary of such an evaluation which was undertaken of the construction of advance factory units in rural towns in the eastern area of the English-Scottish Borders. The general location of the area is shown in Figure 11.1, which also identifies the area which was defined as the 'Eastern Borders' for the purposes of promoting regional development.

While the Borders area in general is quite well known for its textile industry, this is almost exclusively concentrated outside the Eastern Borders, which has traditionally been heavily dependent on agriculture for its income. As a consequence, there has been a lack of alternative occupations for those leaving agriculture and substantial emigration from the area. The total population of the Eastern Borders declined steadily for over a century, so that by 1971 the population represented about 60 per cent of that in the area in 1851. Since that time, the net decline for the whole area has slowed down and there has even been a net increase in some of the larger settlements. The area includes five towns, which comprise about 40

Table 11.1 Size of population centres in the Eastern Borders, 1971

Berwick upon Tweed	11,647
Kelso	4,852
Eyemouth	2,530
Duns	1,768
Coldstream	1,278
Total for Eastern Borders	54,850

1 This chapter is based on our study of the Eastern Borders which was carried out over the period 1976–9. All of the tables in the chapter are adapted from our published report (Hodge and Whitby, 1979); all values are in 1976 prices.

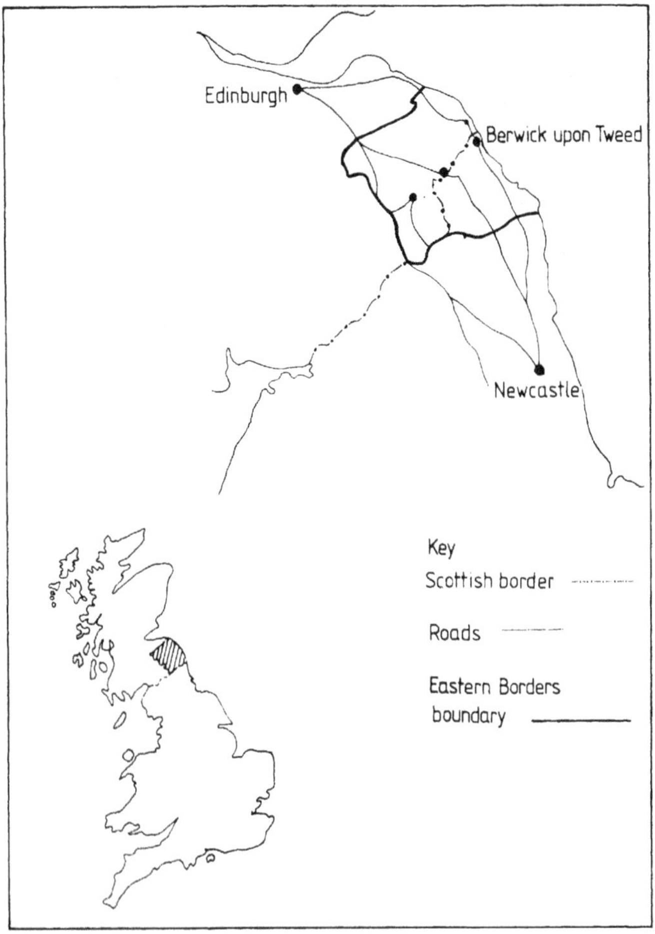

Figure 11.1 Location of the Eastern Borders

per cent of the total population, as illustrated in Table 11.1.

As a result of these long-run trends, the region exhibits the classic symptoms of rural depopulation in terms of the population's age structure, the availability of services and employment opportunities. Assistance was therefore sought for the area in order to promote development and stem the population decline. Since 1966, the Development Commission has provided funds for the construction of advance factories in each of the five small towns. By 1977, twelve of these (4 in Berwick, 3 in Duns, 2 in Kelso, 2 in Eyemouth and 1 in Coldstream) had been occupied involving a direct total employment of 788 people. Four of the companies were involved in food processing, the others being concerned with a variety of small-scale manufacturing activities, including motor vehicle components, printing and electronics. The total capital expenditure on factory construction and site development up to 1977 was some £2.2 million.

The study was undertaken *ex post*, in the absence of any formal *ex ante* evaluation and this raises a number of obstacles (Haveman, 1972). The approaches taken for the identification of suitable areas for advance factory construction have changed since the selection of the Eastern Borders. The objectives credited to the factory programme now could be different from those in 1966; for instance it is likely that a higher priority would be given to the creation of employment opportunities. Nevertheless, it is felt that the study of such policies can provide some guidance in the formulation of future policies. We turn our attention to *ex ante* evaluation in the following chapter.

The impact of the factory programme

Any appraisal must begin with an assessment of the impact of the project on employment, incomes and population. There is a need, therefore, both to identify the position with the project in operation, as well as the alternative which would have occurred in the absence of any policy intervention. The predictions of how events would have progressed from the initial position without the policy represents a significant area of uncertainty, but it is generally not acceptable to assume that nothing would have changed. The methodology adopted here followed that described in Chapter 9 and the various elements involved in estimating the local impact of the factory programme are illustrated in Figure 11.2.

Data were collected in the Eastern Borders, including interviews with factory managers and a survey of employees. The employees in the factories were asked both what they had been doing prior to their employment in the factories and what they believed that they would have been doing if factory employment had not been available. Neither of these could be taken as representing the actual position in the absence of the factory programme. In particular, some people would have changed their occupation anyway, especially those previously at school, and employees could not be

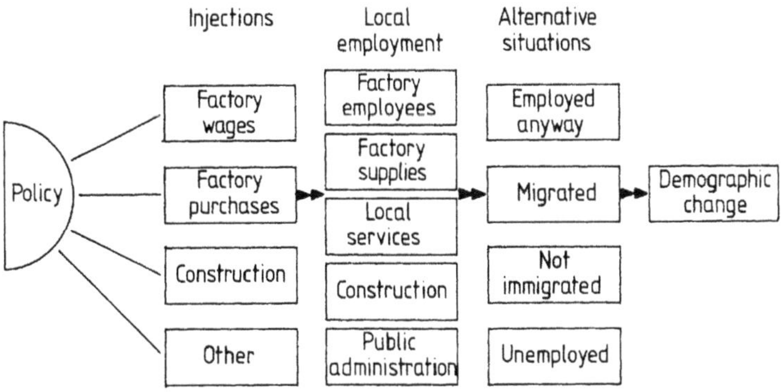

Figure 11.2 The impact of factories in the Eastern Borders

expected to know what implications the factories had had on the local labour market. Thus, while a high proportion indicated that they would have found an alternative occupation locally in the event of their not being engaged in factory employment, in practice they would not have been able to.

It was estimated that a minimum of one-quarter of the jobs would have been provided in the area by the companies occupying the factories in alternative premises without the factory construction programme. A number of employees indicated that they would have remained in their old jobs if ones had not been available in the factories. These movements have been ignored on the basis that where these were productive jobs, they would have been replaced and so by not leaving them they would simply force different individuals to be seeking employment. However, a proportion of the vacancies created would not have been filled, i.e. these would have represented 'concealed' unemployment. It was assumed that those who said that they would have left the area would have done so and that those previously unemployed (or the equivalent number) would have remained so. It was known how many employees had moved into the area. This enabled account to be taken of the impact of most jobs; those not accounted for were distributed between unemployment, emigration and retirement according to the same proportion indicated in the survey of employees. The estimates made of the distribution of employees' situations in the absence of the policy are shown in Table 11.2. It should be emphasized that this table relates to all those who have changed their employment state as a result of factory construction, rather than to a simple description of how the factory employees specifically would have been occupied.

Table 11.2 Distribution of employees' situations in the absence of policy

	Male	*Female*
Registered unemployed in the Eastern Borders	75	50
Unregistered unemployed in the Eastern Borders	7	116
'Concealed' unemployed	11	29
People not immigrated	79	45
People emigrated	105	58
Retired	4	12
Employment available anyway	94	103
Total	375	413

The factory wages, the purchases made by the companies, the construction of the factories and other local expenditures will all have made contributions to increasing local incomes and employ-

Table 11.3 Local expenditures and incomes due to the factory programme

	Estimated expenditure past financial year £	*Proportion of expenditure represented by local value-added LVA*	*Contribution to local incomes £*
Wages (adjusted for tax and National Insurance)	1,202,000	1.00	1,202,000
Electricity	39,000	0.08	3,120
Oil and fuels	50,000	0.09	4,500
Telephone and telex	27,000	0.36	9,720
Postages	6,000	0.58	3,480
Vehicle operating costs	45,000	0.17	7,650
Local hauliers	142,000	0.50	71,000
Other local services	120,000	0.50	60,000
Locally purchased materials excluding primary products	51,000	0.20	10,200
Rates and water	23,000	1.00	23,000
Total purchases	503,000		192,670
Construction	185,000	0.275	51,000
Other	41,000	0.35	14,300

ment. Leakages from the original expenditures were examined separately and the resulting local incomes raised by the regional multiplier. Table 11.3 shows the estimates made of the local expenditures and resultant local incomes.

The implications of these injections for regional income were then estimated on the basis of a Keynesian regional income multiplier, such as that discussed in Chapter 9. This was constructed on the basis of regional data and previous studies. A figure of 1.21 was arrived at which is similar to other small area regional income multipliers which have been derived from the UK. Lack of time and resources precluded the construction of input-output tables for the area. The implications of regional income changes for employment were pursued following a procedure similar to that adopted by Greig (1971). It was assumed that employment would also be increased in public administration, to maintain the same proportion to that already existing in the region. The total employment associated with the operation of the factories is shown in Table 11.4.

Table 11.4 Total employment associated with the factories

	Male	*Female*	*Total*
Factory employees	375	413	788
Local services and distribution	46	57	103
Factory supplies and services	27	27	54
Construction	15	—	15
Public administration	47	15	62
Total	510	512	1022

Due to the impracticality of identifying individuals whose employment was dependent upon factory programme expenditures, but not within the factories themselves, the alternative situations of these people were assumed to be in the same proportions as those of the factory employees. These estimates were then combined with details of the marital status, numbers of children and ages of the factory employees (non-factory employees being assumed to have similar characteristics) so that the demographic implications of the factory programme could be examined. These gave the results shown in Table 11.5.

Table 11.5 The effects of the factory programme

	Male	*Female*
Direct employment in the factories	375	413
Direct employment otherwise not available in the Eastern Borders	281	310
Numbers who would otherwise be unemployed in the Eastern Borders	112	204
Net increase in the population in the Eastern Borders (excluding children estimated to be over 15 years old) (up to 1977)	486	420
Total annual employment over 10-year period (person-years)	3119	
Increase in the level of regional income (annual estimate for 1976/7)	£1.3 million	

The effectiveness of exchequer expenditure

The exchequer has committed funds to the purchase and development of land and the construction of factories in the area. Through existing arrangements, companies establishing in such areas were eligible for two-year rent-free periods as well as removal grants and capital subsidies. One approach to assessing the effectiveness of the project, therefore, lies in a comparison of the level of public expenditure and the extent to which the objectives have been achieved. However, if the project is successful, it will lead to an increase in exchequer revenue through reduced unemployment and other benefits paid out, taxes on the new incomes earned and taxes on incomes which have been increased. The exchequer will also benefit from rentals paid for the factories. Thus a more appropriate measure of exchequer burden lies in the net cost, measured over some period. Expenditure in the Eastern Borders was high up to the end of the period of factory construction, after which expenditure was only associated with the payment of grants on further capital purchases. The returns to the exchequer were directly related to the level of employment in the factories and this rose steadily as the factories were occupied and was assumed to continue to increase as the companies reached their full potential. Estimates of the costs and returns to the exchequer as a result of the factory programme were made on the basis of known costs, anticipated changes in employment and the associated taxes received and benefits paid out by the exchequer. These indicated that over a ten-year period and at a ten per cent discount rate, the exchequer would incur a net loss (£–1.27 million), but that over a longer period of about twenty-five years or more, there would be a net gain to the exchequer. It is hard to select an appropriate time horizon for viewing exchequer returns. It could range from a long term such as might be seen as appropriate from the point of view of society as a whole, to the very short term reflecting potential political gains. Table 11.6 illustrates some measures of the exchequer cost-effectiveness of the Eastern Borders' factory programme over a ten-year period.

Table 11.6 Exchequer cost-effectiveness of the factory programme (ten-year time horizon at 10 per cent discount rate)

Total exchequer cost per	£
Direct factory job	1607
Direct and indirect job	1240
Direct factory job otherwise not available	2145
Person otherwise unemployed in the Eastern Borders	3998
Employee otherwise outside the Easern Borders	3353
Extra person in the Eastern Borders	1251
Person-year of employment over ten-year period	406

However, as already noted, the measure of exchequer expenditure provides a limited assessment of the cost borne by society in achieving the various benefits. Pursuance of a policy aimed at minimizing exchequer costs per job created need not lead to optimal policies. Information on the exchequer cost-effectiveness of expenditure on regional development can provide assistance to policy-makers towards the achievement of specific objectives subject to a budget constraint, but is of limited value in comparing regional development programmes with alternative forms of public expenditure. This latter form of assessment can only be achieved through a broader study of the costs and benefits of the programme. We therefore proceeded to examine the social costs and benefits.

Net social benefits of the factory programme

The assistance provided for the establishment of industry in the Eastern Borders has influenced the pattern of resource use in the economy. However, for a variety of reasons, the private profit of the companies operating in the factories does not necessarily represent the net social benefit associated with their activities. This is the case, both because the prices paid for factors may not represent their social opportunity costs and because of government objectives in providing relatively equal access to public services regardless of cost. The important factors in this context are labour and capital. The net social benefit of the project may be defined as the difference between the market value of the factors of production and their social opportunity cost.

This may then be adjusted for the real resource implications of the pursuance of government policies. These include the extra resources which may be required in the provision of public services as the government generally accepts responsibility for the provision of a minimum level of services in remoter areas, the full costs of which are seldom met by the recipients. Also included is the use of resources in the movement of people and equipment caused or prevented as a result of the policy and the costs of administration.

This figure may be calculated on the basis of the position in each year of the project's operation and then discounted back to a present value. The components of the net social benefit of the programme are now considered in turn. We exclude therefore any evaluation of the environental consequences of the project, which appear to be unlikely to be of importance, or of any increases in welfare arising from the higher population level.

The provision of job opportunities in the Eastern Borders has led to the employment of people who would otherwise have been unemployed. Thus the opportunity cost of this labour will be below the market wage, and the increase in output which has resulted from the increased employment represents a benefit of the project. The extent of this benefit was derived from the difference between the costs of employment (market cost) which is assumed to represent labour's contribution to output and the output lost (social opportunity cost) as a result of the factory employment. This was based on the estimated alternative situations of employees and the changes in earnings on taking up factory employment as indicated by respondents to the survey. The net social benefit resulting from the factory programme employment for both factory employees and for those whose employment was dependent upon them, was estimated for the position in each year from its initiation and projected into the future. The calculated social opportunity cost of labour is reported in Table 11.7.

Table 11.7 Calculated social opportunity cost of labour

	Full-time	
	Males	*Females*
	£	£
Gross annual income, 100 workers	314,012	287,143
Losses in output without factories attributable to		
registered unemployment	66,750	40,080
unregistered unemployment	9,750	94,320
'concealed' unemployment	1,950	3,880
migration from Eastern Borders	11,220	1,930
non-migration into Eastern Borders	14,050	0
	103,720	140,210
Social opportunity cost, 100 workers	210,292	146,933
Social opportunity as per cent of market cost	67.0	51.2

We are here only taking limited account of the effects of employment creation outside the area. In that those moving to the area may vacate productive jobs which could lead to further labour market adjustments in the areas from which they have moved, we could in principle attempt to assess these more distant consequences of the project. However, due to the uncertainties involved and the necessary time lag for such full adjustments to take place, we are restricting the analysis to the immediate impacts of migration. Parallel considerations would apply to those people alternatively leaving the area. On the other hand, we have assumed that full adjustments occur immediately within the region and that there is no loss of productive employment. These two simplifications would cancel out, at least to some extent.

Table 11.7 shows that the social opportunity cost of full-time males is estimated to be 67 per cent of the market cost and that of females to be 51 per cent. These estimates relate to the conditions prevailing during the 1970s and therefore must be adjusted to the anticipated long-run social opportunity cost. This involves a judgement as to the likely future conditions of the local labour market. The objective of creating employment in the area will have the effect, if it is successful, of raising the social opportunity cost of labour, and this should be taken into account. However, relatively high levels of unemployment appear to be likely to prevail generally in the economy, at least in the immediate future. On balance a small upward adjustment was felt to be required and the final estimates of the social opportunity cost of labour were 70 per cent of the market cost of full-time males and 55 per cent of the cost of full-time females.

The encouragement of companies to establish in less preferred locations may be expected to lead to a reduction in the productivity of capital, largely through increased transport costs. However, for some of the companies, the Eastern Borders was a logical location and some had in fact been operating in the area prior to the programme. This was the case for those companies which relied upon a local raw material, such as locally caught fish or locally grown vegetables, and those which sold a high proportion of their output locally. Others had been attracted to the area by the availability of the advance factory and the grants. However, it seems unlikely that these companies would have made the move if the reduction in productivity was greater than the extra grants received above those available in urban locations, which were provided in order to encourage the move. This differential was, therefore, used as a measure of the maximum reduction in capital productivity caused by the factory programme.

Of the twelve companies involved, four had moved into the area, four had moved within the area and four were established as new companies. The fact that four managers had previously chosen to establish in the area without any special encouragements implies that they perceived no particular disadvantages, and so no loss of productivity was assumed to be involved. Of the other eight companies, three made use of a local raw material, justifying their location in this particular area. The other five were presumed to have been attracted to the area by the incentives which were available. The net contribution made to these companies by the Development Commission was therefore brought to an equivalent annual amount over the life of the factories and taken as an indication of the maximum potential loss of productivity associated with their location in the Eastern Borders.

There are two aspects of the cost of providing services to populations in remote rural areas which might be expected, at least to some extent, to offset each other. Firstly, the fact that the population of the area has been declining means that there could be surplus social capital available which could provide services to the increased population. However, in the recent past, while the population overall has been declining, the population of the towns in the Eastern Borders has been static or increasing, so that the population increase resulting from the factory programme which is located in these towns will need to be provided with new facilities, similar to those required outside the region if the process of depopulation had been allowed to continue. This argument was therefore ignored. Secondly, the cost of the provision of services to a population in a remote area may be expected to be higher than would be the case if people had continued to migrate to less remote areas. This differential would, of course, have been higher if the retained population had been located in the rural parts of the area. Estimates were made for the range of public services, of the extra costs of providing services to the population in the Eastern Borders' towns compared with national and regional averages. The results are summarized in Table 11.8. These were aggregated to provide an annual figure per extra person living in the area and then calculated for each year of the programme's operation.

Table 11.8 Net social opportunity cost of service provision

Type of service	*Estimate of cost per person per annum* £
All local authority services	8.60
Electricity supplies	5.40
Gas supplies	2.20
Postal services	2.00
Telecommunications	0.25
Health services	0.13
Water supply	—
Sewerage	—
Broadcasting	—
Total cost	18.60

Finally, it was estimated that on balance, the programme had reduced the numbers of movements made (i.e. immigration stimulated was less than emigration prevented) and an approximate figure for the savings was included. An allowance was also incorporated for administrative costs in the establishment of the programme.

These items of social costs and benefits were then assembled in the form of annual cash flows and their net present value at the beginning of the programme calculated. This was undertaken at various discount rates and over various time horizons. Two alternatives are evaluated; a high and a low cost one. The low cost estimate assumes that there is no loss of capital productivity due to the factory programme. The high cost alternative includes the estimate which we have described above. The results are shown at 10 per cent discount rate and over three different time horizons.

Table 11.9 Present value of net social benefits (at 10 per cent discount rate) by discount period

Time horizon (years)	*Present value in £ million for cash flows*	
	Low cost	*High cost*
10	1.625	1.151
25	4.679	3.923
50	5.584	4.792

These results may also be presented in terms of the denominators which we applied earlier to the measures of exchequer cost-effectiveness. We show this in Table 11.10. This has the advantage of putting them into a form which is potentially comparable with evaluations of other programmes with similar objectives.

Table 11.10 Social cost-effectiveness of the factory programme (twenty-five-year discount period at 10 per cent discount rate)

Net social benefits per	*Low cost*	*High cost*
	£	£
Direct factory job	+4,578	+3,839
Direct factory job otherwise not available	+6,100	+5,115
Person otherwise unemployed in the Eastern Borders	+10,610	+8,896
Extra person in the Eastern Borders	+3,321	+2,784
Person-year of employment over discount period	+246	+206

Finally, net social benefits may be compared with exchequer costs. The expenditure on factory construction, land acquisition and site development (factory cost) was £2.17 million and total expenditure (total cost), including regional grants and other payments, was £2.78 million. The measures of net social benefit may be divided by these figures to provide estimates of net social benefit per £1 of exchequer cost. These are shown in Table 11.11.

Table 11.11 Net social benefits per £ of exchequer cost

Discount period (years)	*Cash flow*	*Net social benefit per £ of total cost*	*Net social benefit per £ of factory cost*
10	Low cost	0.58	0.75
10	High cost	0.41	0.53
25	Low cost	1.68	2.16
25	High cost	1.41	1.81
50	Low cost	2.01	2.57
50	High cost	1.72	2.21

Thus, when benefits are measured over a ten-year period, they are less than the initial outlay made by the exchequer, although this is not the case over the longer periods. These results do not of themselves either justify or condemn the factory programme. Rather they provide an opportunity for comparison with other forms of expenditure.

Conclusions

The analysis suggests that the project is a worthwhile one, both from the point of view of the exchequer, which over twenty-five years gains returns sufficient to pay for the factory programme using a 10 per cent discount rate, and from the point of view of social benefits exceeding social costs. This result is heavily dependent upon the relatively high rates of unemployment which have been experienced while the factory programme has expanded. In that these rates were probably not anticipated when the project was initiated, then the benefits of the scheme may be regarded as somewhat fortuitous.

The relative remoteness of the Eastern Borders has tended to increase the social costs of the scheme through the higher costs of services in the area and the likely loss of capital productivity. If the project had been undertaken in an area with an equivalent level of unemployment, but without the regional disadvantages, then it would have looked more favourable on the basis of the criteria applied here. However, in that the project was established with the primary objective of encouraging development in an area suffering the consequences of its relative remoteness, then these costs may be regarded as the price that must be paid. In fact this cost is relatively modest due to the fact that by world standards the region is not especially distant from large population centres, because the developments were able to make use of locally produced raw materials and because of the factories themselves were established within settlements which already offer the range of necessary services.

In the context of future decision-making, the critical assumptions concern the levels of unemployment which will be experienced and the numbers of jobs which can be created which would otherwise not have been available. We turn our attention to *ex ante* analysis in the following chapter.

12
ASSESSING OPTIONS FOR THE FUTURE OF POVERDALE

In Chapter 2 we introduced the imaginary depopulating rural region, Poverdale, and recounted its demographic development over half a century to 1980. In this chapter, we explore the options open to those responsible for planning the future of Poverdale, first in demographic terms, and then by applying the principles of project evaluation which were discussed in Chapter 10. The important difference between this and the case study of the Eastern Borders in the previous chapter is that here we are assessing the options for the future, whereas there we made a retrospective appraisal of a project which had already been under way for some time. We are here, therefore, considering an *ex ante* appraisal rather than an *ex post* one. Our purpose in once again raising the various issues which are involved is to examine the procedures and data requirements of an *ex ante* evaluation. It is at this stage that the most important decisions are made and consequently when efforts to achieve effective decision-making may be most rewarded.

Demographic projections

Our first requirement is to examine the likely future development of Poverdale, in the absence of any deliberate intervention. This provides us with a bench-mark, against which we then can measure the probable impacts of any policy initiatives. In order to project the population into the future we must first decide upon the values of the main demographic variables to be used. In essence this means assessing whether there is any reason why birth, death and migration rates may be expected to change over the forecast period. In a real world example there might well be reasons for inserting different, or changing, birth and death rates, as noted in Chapter 2. However, here, the same rates as were applied over the period

1930–80 have been retained in the projections to 2005. Migration has been handled differently because it is capable of changing rapidly under the influence of economic and policy variables. Three rates of out-migration have been tested in order to demonstrate a range of possible results. The central value chosen is the same as the 'actual' rate in the base period (see Table 2.2); on either side of this, a zero and a high rate (twice 'actual') have also been tested in the projections. In order to explore possible policies, some 'once-and-for-all' immigrations have been assumed to occur in the base year of the projection period. Such immigrations would correspond to the establishment of a project which created a fixed number of jobs in one year. Again, this variable has been given three levels – zero, medium (about 200) and high (about 400) – and these have been inserted in the projection model, giving us a total of nine alternative migration assumptions. The assumed age distributions corresponding with the two positive rates of immigration are recorded in Table 12.1. These have been assumed to be the same as the distributions found of immigrants to the Eastern Borders.

Table 12.1 Age and sex distribution of immigrants to Poverdale

	Rate of immigration			
	Medium		*High*	
Age	*Male*	*Female*	*Male*	*Female*
0–4	12	10	23	20
5–14	20	17	40	35
15–24	17	15	34	31
25–34	28	24	59	48
35–44	22	19	44	38
45–54	5	6	11	12
55–64	1	2	3	3
65+	0	0	0	0
Total	105	93	214	187
Grand total	198		401	

Source: Derived from Hodge and Whitby (1979)

The resulting projections are displayed in Table 12.2, where it can be seen that only two of the chosen migration assumptions (1 and 2) actually yield an increase in population at the end of the projection period. In two cases (1 and 5) immigration virtually succeeds in maintaining the 1980 population to the end of the period, but in the other six cases there is some substantial net decline in population. As in Chapter 2, the qualitative effects of population decline can be summarized in the terminal dependency ratios. These show that immigration serves to reduce the ratios within any given rate of emigration. Also, for a given rate of immigration, the ratio rises directly with the rate of emigration.

Table 12.2 Population projections for Poverdale, to 2005, by various migration assumptions

Projection number	*Emigration*	*Immigration*	*1980*	*2005*	*Net change*	*Terminal dependency ratio*
0	Zero	Zero	1589	1383	−206	0.364
1	Zero	Medium	1589	1646	+57	0.354
2	Zero	High	1589	1828	+239	0.348
3	Medium	Zero	1589	1133	−456	0.379
4	Medium	Medium	1589	1344	−245	0.368
5	Medium	High	1589	1559	−30	0.359
6	High	Zero	1589	949	−640	0.397
7	High	Medium	1589	1107	−482	0.389
8	High	High	1589	1297	−292	0.375

The time path of demographic change was also projected, at five-year intervals. The actual trend of population in the base period is plotted in Figure 12.1, together with projections 0, 1, 2, 3, 5 and 6, as shown in Table 12.2, to the year 2005.

From Figure 12.1, there are two ways in which the success of a policy seeking to retain population might be measured. The first of these would simply record the vertical distance between the lines with and without a population injection. But this distance varies through time it and may be hard to decide the particular time at which this represents the most appropriate measure of success. An alternative approach might be to measure the area between the lines, (i.e. the number of person-years by which the population has been raised), which incorporates the idea that there is virtue in both increasing the population of Poverdale in 1980 and in retaining it at a higher level. This, however, introduces a further complication, namely that it may be possible to choose between boosting the population immediately and allowing it then to decline or achieving a slower, but sustainable increase in population. These two patterns could achieve an equal area between the lines, but might not represent equally attractive alternatives.

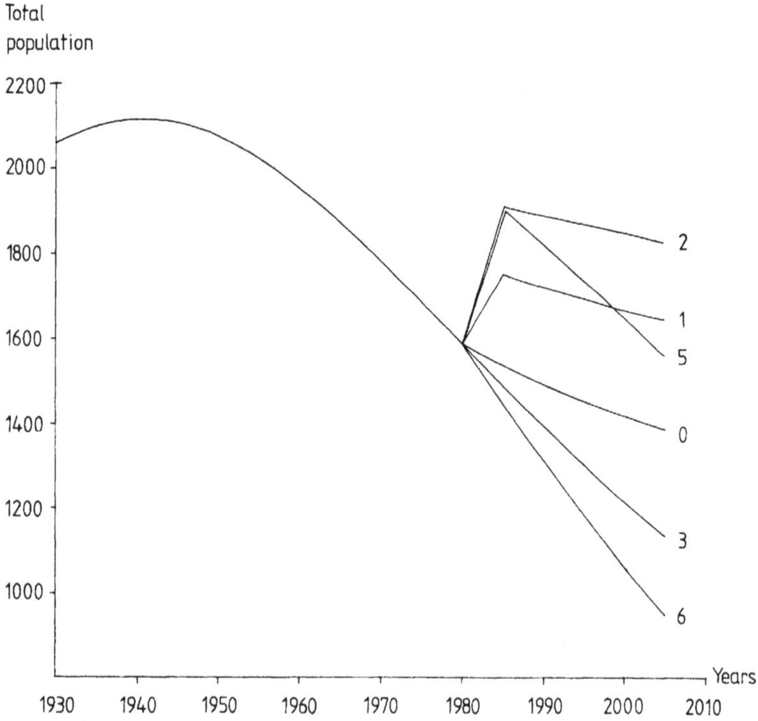

Figure 12.1 Trend of population of Poverdale, 1930–80, and projections to 2005

Furthermore, we should note that the projections have been carried out as if the rates of immigration and emigration were independent. Thus, under most assumptions, the population by 2005 has fallen below its 1980 level. However, it is a common assumption that the creation of employment will lead to the development of settlements which are in some sense more viable than they would otherwise be; that they can provide a wider range of opportunities and thereby stem population loss. It is as if the aim was to achieve a certain critical threshold, above which the population of the sub-region would sustain itself. But this is an area in which we have very little knowledge, so that we must remain uncertain as to the actual changes in Poverdale's population.

Policy objectives

In the light of the projected population levels in Poverdale, we may consider the possible policy initiatives which may be taken in order to improve the situation. If the policy objective was to stabilize the population, that is to halt its continued decline over the 25-year period, then a project which increased immigration in 1980 by at least 198 (the medium level of immigration) would produce the desired result given zero emigration as would increasing immigration in 1980 by 401 (the high level), given the medium rate of emigration. However, we hope that the increase in population and economic activity would lead to at least some fall in the emigration rate, so that the high increase in immigration would not be required so as to achieve the objective. Indeed, to hope to raise a population of about 1500 by 400 in the short term would seem to be unduly optimistic. We will therefore concentrate on the objective of an increase of 198 in the population, which of itself would be no mean achievement, and which will require further increments to the population in order to account for population losses over the 25-year period. If the migration did continue at the medium level, this would involve over 200 people.

The assumed age and sex distribution of the 198 immigrants has already been set out in Table 12.1. It will be noticed that the immigrants include no persons over 65 and, indeed, very few over the age of 45. There is a substantial proportion of children aged 14 and less. It would be important to consider what proportion of those of an age to join the labour force would, in fact, join it from this stream of immigrants. Generally, activity rates (defined as the number in or actively seeking work as a percentage of those of working age) amongst men are high, whereas amongst women, activity rates may be low. Furthermore, activity rates would be particularly high for men in a stream of immigrants who are assumed to have moved to a rural area in the expectation of employment. Accordingly, a 95 per cent activity rate is assumed for men in this stream and a 50 per cent activity rate for women. Application of these activity rates of the 198 immigrants would give an addition to the work force of 70 males and 33 females; 103 in total. Because of the secondary employment which will result from a development project, it will not be necessary to provide all these jobs directly in the project itself. The actual number of direct jobs will be found by dividing this by the relevant regional employment multiplier (the extent to which a given increase in employment raises the total regional employment). If this is taken as 1.2, then 86 direct jobs would be required, which we assume to include 58 males and 28 females.

But, for a given number of jobs created, only a certain proportion will be taken by people who would otherwise be resident outside the area. Some will be drawn from unemployment and others from 'concealed' unemployment. If we are to achieve the desired increase in local population therefore, it will be necessary to create a larger number of jobs overall. Just how many more depends on the alternative situations of the prospective employees. This is clearly a particularly difficult issue to resolve in an *ex ante* appraisal. Guidance may be drawn from the results of studies of past developments in rural areas, such as were reported in the previous chapter, and from the experience of people closely concerned with the local labour market, such as employment service managers.

We may draw some conclusions about the likely alternative situations of employees from the information which we have already presented. This may be supplemented with some further details about Poverdale, which would be available to those undertaking a real-life appraisal. We therefore make the following assumptions about the labour market in Poverdale:

Activity rates	– Male	90
	– Female	40
Per cent unemployment	– Male	5
(registered)	– Female	3½

From this we may infer the size of the pool of unemployed from which new employment may be drawn. From Table 2.1 we find that there are 555 males of working age and 449 females (assuming that they work up to the age of 64). Applying the activity rates to these figures we have 500 economically active males and 180 females. Of these, 25 males and 6 females are assumed to be registered unemployed. It is unlikely that all of these males will have the skills or motivation to be drawn into the work force; so we will assume that of the total, 20 males and all 6 females do. We are not concerned here whether these people directly take the new jobs or whether they fill the vacancies which result from other people taking them.

We also have knowledge of the likely pattern of migration from the area. If we assume that the introduction of new employment can deter all emigrants over a five-year period, then we can also estimate the maximum number of people who would alternatively have emigrated. It is clearly improbable that this maximum would be achieved, in that a certain number will be likely to leave the area to follow education or employment activities which are not possible in Poverdale. Nevertheless, on the other side, the impact of employment could deter emigrants over a longer period. In the five-year period 16 males and 21 females are assumed to emigrate in the absence of the employment creation.

We further assume that the industrial structure of Poverdale is similar to that of the Eastern Borders and therefore that the alternative situations of employees are also similar. These are then adjusted on the basis of the above discussion to give estimates of the alternative work situations which result from 100 new jobs for males and females in Poverdale. They are shown in Table 12.3.

Table 12.3 Percentage distribution of employees by alternative employment states in Poverdale

	Males		*Females*	
	First 100 jobs	*Further jobs*	*First 100 jobs*	*Further jobs*
	%	%	%	%
Registered unemployment	20	5	6	0
Unregistered unemployment	2	5	25	21
'Concealed' unemployment	3	2	7	5
People not immigrated	33	47	19	25
People emigrated	16	0	15	6
Retired	1	1	3	3
Employment available anyway	25	40	25	40

It is clearly not possible that, every time 100 new jobs are introduced, the alternative work situations will remain the same. We therefore assume a different distribution for any further employment creation. Fewer will be drawn from unemployment, and the increasing difficulties involved in establishing new activities to the area mean that a higher proportion of jobs would have been available anyway. These tendencies are also shown in Table 12.3.

We are now in a position to return to the question of how many new jobs are required in Poverdale in order to achieve the population objective. It was concluded above that direct jobs for 58 males and 28 females, who would otherwise be outside the area, would be needed. From Table 12.3 it can be seen that, if we regard the objective solely in terms of overall population, i.e. that we are indifferent between immigration stimulated and emigration prevented, so that the total numbers immigrating and not emigrating sums to 58 and 28, then it will be necessary to provide 119 jobs for males and 82 jobs for females. The actual distribution of direct employees by alternative work situation is detailed in Table 12.4.

Table 12.4 Actual distribution of alternative employment states due to new jobs in Poverdale

	Males		*Females*	
		%		%
Registered unemployment	21	18	5	6
Unregistered unemployment	3	3	21	26
'Concealed' unemployment	3	3	6	7
People not immigrated	42	35	16	20
People emigrated	16	13	12	15
Retired	1	1	2	2
Employment available anyway	33	28	20	24
Total	119	100	82	100

Note: Figures adjusted to sum to desired totals. Percentages may not total 100 due to rounding.

The apparent precision of this exercise is not intended to give the impression that planners can have confidence in the exact estimates which result. Even in an *ex post* study, the lack of data and the number of necessary assumptions mean that it is not possible to be sure how close to the truth any estimates may be. In an *ex ante* study, where it is uncertain even whether the desired level of employment can be achieved at all, our objectives must be much more modest. The purpose here is to illustrate the issues involved and to identify the orders of magnitude of the relevant figures.

Employment creation in Poverdale

The next stage is to formulate a project which will, it is hoped, achieve the population objective. This could involve a wide variety of activities such as have already been considered and the most promising alternatives will need to be identified. For convenience, the project in Poverdale will be the same as the one which was evaluated in the previous chapter. It will, therefore, involve the construction of advance factories, which will be let to companies on favourable terms in order to encourage the establishment of small-scale manufacturing activities in the area. At this stage of the evaluation, the analyst obviously does not know what sort of companies will be attracted and what actual employment will be achieved. But it will be necessary to make some assumptions about these in the light of local knowledge, and of experience in similar projects elsewhere. We will assume that the factories in Poverdale do provide the required level of employment exactly.

Again, in practice, a host of details will need to be considered. What land with the necessary access and service facilities is available? What size and design of factories should be constructed? How are potential occupants to be identified and encouraged to locate in the area? What assistance will they require in moving to and establishing in a new area? And so on. This stage in the analysis needs to consider not only what can be attempted, but also what can be achieved. The analyst should have confidence that the proposed project is at least technically feasible. However, rather than invent hypothetical answers to hypothetical questions which are not necessary to this exposition, we shall presume such questions to have been answered and proceed to the evaluation.

The appraisal of this project will follow the same pattern as in the previous two chapters. First, a financial evaluation will be undertaken. This will then be followed by a social evaluation.

Financial evaluation

The approach to a financial evaluation has already been described in Chapter 10. Suppose that, in the interests of simplicity, the average cost of establishing jobs in factories in Poverdale is the same as in the Eastern Borders. This means that the net present value to the exchequer, discounted at 10 per cent over a ten-year time horizon would be £323,041. From this we may calculate the various cost-effectiveness ratios, and the results are shown in Table 12.5.

Table 12.5 Exchequer cost-effectiveness of Poverdale project (ten-year time horizon at 10 per cent discount rate)

Total exchequer cost per	*£ (1976)*
Direct factory job	1607
Direct and indirect job	1340
Direct job otherwise not available	2183
Person otherwise unemployed in Poverdale	6461
Employee otherwise outside Poverdale	3136
Extra person in Poverdale	1632

These figures are expressed in terms of 1976 prices, and may therefore be compared with the results found for the Eastern Borders. The fact that most of the cost-effectiveness ratios for Poverdale are higher, other than the cost per direct factory job of course, has resulted from the assumptions concerning the smaller size of Poverdale compared with the settlements in the Eastern Borders. We have assumed a smaller regional multiplier leading to fewer indirect jobs and the size of the labour market has limited the numbers of people leaving unemployment in the area. This feature has, however, had the favourable consequence of reducing costs per employee otherwise outside the area. But, in practice, this characteristic would make the attraction of the necessary labour force harder and tend to discourage potential employers from establishing in Poverdale; perhaps placing the project itself at risk.

Social evaluation

Continuing the pattern of the previous two chapters, we move on to the social evaluation of the Poverdale project, considering each of the issues in turn.

Labour

From the analysis of the labour market, and the impact of the factory programme, we can estimate the probabilities of there being an employee in each of the possible alternative situations for each extra job which is created. First, the percentages are re-calculated excluding those for whom employment would have been available anyway as they have not led to any changes in the labour market. The percentages are then divided by 100 so that they reflect probabilities.

Table 12.6 Estimated probabilities of employees being in alternative employment states and their respective productivities, Poverdale, 1980

	Probabilities		*Productivities*	
	Male	*Female*	*Male*	*Female*
'With the project'			£	£
Market wage	1.000	1.000	4000	3500
'Without the project'				
Registered unemployed	0.244	0.081	1000	1000
Unregistered unemployed	0.035	0.339	1000	1000
'Concealed' unemployed	0.035	0.097	3400	3200
Not immigrated	0.488	0.258	3500	3500
Emigrated	0.186	0.193	3800	3400
Retired	0.012	0.032	0	0

The productivity of labour in the project is assumed to be reflected in gross incomes. Other productivities could be established in the same way as the market wage by survey, or, more cheaply, they could be estimated from *a priori* assumptions as to their relationship with the market wage. The estimates of productivities in Table 12.6 have been derived from Eastern Borders data and adapted to reflect conditions in the tighter labour market of Poverdale. Because of the importance of this information in determining social opportunity costs, it is worth explaining how the assumptions have been arrived at. As noted in Chapter 10, some value is imputed to the value to the time of the unemployed, in this case £1000. The 'concealed' unemployed men and women are assumed to have been producing something less than the market wage. This is unlikely to be substantially less, otherwise they could not have remained in this employment. It is assumed that those not migrating into the region would alternatively have produced £500 less than average, whereas the productivity of women not migrating would remain unchanged without the project. This would be consistent with male immigrants being 'key workers' who must be persuaded to move by financial incentives whereas the women who move with them would not necessarily expect to earn more. Those deterred from emigrating by the project would, it is assumed, earn £200 extra as a result; this is taken to be the minimum premium required to retain them in the region. Applying these values, as described in the previous chapters, gives the following estimates for men and women:

	Annual social opportunity cost	*As percentage of market wage*
	£	
Men	2812.8	70.3
Women	2289.6	65.4

These relate to the conditions in the labour market found in 1980. But the project in Poverdale is yet to be undertaken, and then is to be evaluated over a period of, say, twenty-five years into the future. How should these rates be adjusted to reflect likely future conditions? If we assume that the project is successful in improving employment conditions in the area and that there is no dramatic loss of jobs from any other local industry, then we should raise the social opportunity cost of labour somewhat. In a small region such as Poverdale, the direct and indirect employment associated with the project will account for a substantial share of the total labour force. Accordingly, the initial estimates could be adjusted upwards, say to 75 per cent of the market wage for men and to 70 per cent for women. However, in the light of the uncertainty faced, the analysis could be undertaken with a range of assumptions. In this example, we will therefore regard this estimate as a 'low cost' one. Because of the high level of immigration which is required in order to provide the labour force for the project, it could lead to a loss of productive employment in the area, especially in the shorter term. We therefore include a 'high cost' estimate of 90 per cent for men and 85 per cent for women.

Capital

Following on from our earlier discussions of the social opportunity cost of capital, the position in Poverdale is now considered. We assume that the only source of a net social cost arises from the possible sub-optimal location of the companies providing the employment. In parallel with the Eastern Borders project, we can suppose the total exchequer investment associated with the project to be £1,136,000 in 1980 prices. We assume that one-half of this investment is devoted to companies which have strong local linkages, so that there is no social cost of capital involved. The rental revenue resulting from the other half of the investment is £33,410 per annum. We then turn the initial exchequer investment in this half into an annual cost over a 25-year period at a 10 per cent discount rate. This becomes £62,576 per annum. We can therefore take the difference between these two amounts, being the net contribution made by the exchequer to the companies to achieve their relocation, as our measure of the net social cost of the use of capital in the project. This is £29,166 per annum. As a high cost alternative we assume that no companies have strong local linkages, so that all of the net contribution is counted as a subsidy to induce relocation, reflecting the social cost. The social cost of capital would then be twice the above amount; £58,333 per annum.

Costs of service provision

The objective of the project in Poverdale is actually to achieve an increase in the size of the population, returning it to what it had been about ten years earlier. It thus seems unlikely that there will be any significant savings in the capital costs of service provision resulting from the utilization of surplus social capital, especially in view of the differences in age structure between the immigrants and the existing population.

However, annual costs of service provision may be expected to be higher than would be the case if the extra population had alternatively been living in a less remote area. In an area with such a small population, we would expect these costs to exceed those found in the Eastern Borders. The extent of this difference would be influenced by its distance from other major settlements. The estimate of the net social cost of service provision in the Eastern Borders mounted to some £30 in 1980 prices. Our picture of Poverdale suggests much higher service costs and on this basis, a figure of £100 has been assumed as the 'low cost' and £150 as the 'high cost' estimate.

Moving costs

The analysis indicates that 42 men and 16 women are expected to move into the area as a result of the project, and that 16 men and 12 women are assumed to have been prevented from moving out. In this example, we have assumed that all of these movements would take place in the first year of the project; in practice it is likely that these effects would be spread over a number of years. If we assume that half of the movements of women are part of families which are moving anyway, we have 50 families moving into the area and 22 families being prevented from moving out. On the further assumption that moves in either direction cost the same amount, namely £500, we find a net cost as a result of movements of £14,000.

Administration

The project will require some administration and control. In that it is quite a small project, we will assume that it will be undertaken by one person over a five-year period. In practice this work could be shared by a number of people in different government departments. We shall assume that this person has particular skills which could otherwise be used in an alternative occupation and therefore include a cost to the project of £4000 per annum over the first five years.

Environmental costs and community welfare changes

While no costs or benefits are included in the analysis for environmental or community welfare changes, it would be hoped, of course, that a successful project would lead to an improved economic and social environment for the people of Poverdale. Environmental impacts are less likely to be of consequence.

Investment appraisal

We now bring together the various issues which we have considered. The costs and benefits occurring in each year may be calculated as follows:

	(Market wage-social opportunity cost)	*Net social benefit*
Labour	£	£
Low cost assumption		
Male	(4000–3000)	+103,000
Female	(3500–2450)	+77,700
High cost assumption		
Male	(4000–3600)	+41,200
Female	(3500–2975)	+38,850
Capital		
Net annual social opportunity cost (as calculated above)		
Low cost assumption		−29,166
High cost assumption		−58,333
Service costs		
Extra population in Poverdale × annual net social cost		
Low cost (£100 per person per annum)		−19,800
High cost (£150 per person per annum)		−29,700
Moving costs (initial year only)		−14,000
Public administration (first five years only)		−4000

These figures give the following streams of net social benefits:

	Low cost	*High cost*
	£	£
Year 0	113,734	−25,983
Year 1	127,734	−11,983
2	127,734	−11,983
3	127,734	−11,983
4	127,734	−11,983
5	131,734	−7938
et seq.	131,734	−7983

These streams may then be discounted to present values. The results are shown for two time horizons, ten and twenty-five years at a 10 per cent discount rate. The respective present values are:

	10 years	*25 years*
Low Cost	£859,712	£1,284,652
High Cost	−£84,637	−£110,389

From these we could also calculate measures of cost-effectiveness and net social benefit per £1 of exchequer expenditure, as in the Eastern Borders example, which could provide a basis for comparison with other projects and other forms of public expenditure.

In order to demonstrate the relative importance of the various items within the net present values, we also show the present values of the individual items. These are shown in Table 12.7.

Table 12.7 Present values of the components of the net social benefits calculation (twenty-five-year time horizon at 10 per cent discount rate)

	Low cost	*High cost*
	£	£
Male labour	+1,028,430	+411,371
Female labour	+775,815	+387,907
Capital	−291,215	−582,440
Service provision	−197,698	−296,547
Moving costs	−14,000	−14,000
Administration	−16,680	−16,680

Clearly the critical, indeed, in this case the only, quantified benefits derive from bringing labour into productive employment. Against this, significant costs arise from losses in capital productivity and from the costs of providing services in small and remote settlements. In the high cost example, these two items just outweigh the benefits from labour utilization. This illustrates the crucial importance of the environment within which the project is to be undertaken. The attributes of rural areas work against the viability of relatively large projects seeking to provide employment opportunities. Smaller projects, taking a proportionately higher number of people out of unemployment, concentrating on activities with strong local linkages and seeking to maintain rather than raise rural populations, may be expected to perform better according to these criteria.

In this case, the results do imply a greater than 50 per cent probability of achieving a positive net benefit from the project. Further analysis could be undertaken to identify the probabilities associated with the various possible outcomes. Nevertheless, the computation of a negative net social benefit does not necessarily rule out a project from being undertaken. To the extent that account has not been taken of some possible benefits, especially improvements in community welfare, then it could be decided that the evaluated costs are worth bearing so as to be able to achieve the unevaluated benefits. What the analysis has achieved under those circumstances is the identification of the magnitude of those costs.

Conclusions

In this, and in the preceding chapters, we have dealt, at some length, with the evaluation of projects. At this stage, it is worth considering whether, and under what circumstances, such detailed and laborious calculations are worthwhile. This must be partly a matter of what credence can be placed on the results, but also partly of the insight gained from carrying out the analysis. Data may be gathered on a range of issues, such as the state of the labour market, costs of constructing factories or of individuals' expenditure patterns. Judgements are required on the likely impacts of the project, particularly in terms of population and labour market changes. More detailed information can improve these judgements, and the analysis can identify the areas of uncertainty and importance where further information would be of greatest value. However, in the final analysis the political process must be the arbiter of the claims of one form of public investment against the others. Where calculations such as these are not routinely undertaken in public expenditure analysis in general, it will be difficult to assess their impact on the effectiveness of public decisions.

13
A REGIONAL APPROACH TO EMPLOYMENT PLANNING

Up to this point, each rural employment activity and its evaluation has been considered in isolation. However, the problems of depopulation are identified on a regional basis as a result of a number of changes. Given the regional nature of the problem, efforts are made to find regional solutions, which may involve the development of employment in more than one activity. To the extent that there are interactions between these activities, then planning needs to be undertaken on a regional, rather than on an individual activity basis, although the organization of functions within the public sector often impedes this.

This chapter addresses a number of regional issues. First of all, the question of the nature of problem rural areas is considered in the context of which criteria are most appropriate for the identification and selection of rural regions for developmental assistance. The next stage is to consider the potential for employment and the constraints against which this operates, in view of regional resource endowments and demand. Finally, on the basis of such data, some possible approaches to integrating and co-ordinating alternative employment creation activities are discussed.

Selecting rural areas for assistance

In allocating scarce public resources between alternative areas, it is necessary to identify the relative priorities which should be attached to them. The actual number of areas to which development initiatives are directed will depend on the relative importance which is acredited to rural employment as compared with all other demands which are made upon public funds. However, the allocation between areas depends upon their internal characteristics.

In establishing a general regional policy, it is common practice to direct assistance towards those areas suffering from the highest rates of registered unemployment. In urban areas, where this represents a fair indication of the proportion of those seeking work who are unable to find it, this makes good sense. As shown in previous chapters, the introduction of people to the work force who would otherwise be unemployed can bring substantial social benefits and where regional problems are directly related to unemployment, then such a policy is clearly tackling the root of the problem. However, as has already been indicated, the problems of depressed rural areas are somewhat different. Most fundamentally, this difference derives from the propensity of people to migrate from such areas when they are unable to find suitable employment. This means that rural problems are, to some extent at least, reflected in urban unemployment statistics, and rural unemployment is that much lower. Secondly, people in rural areas, especially women, tend not to register as unemployed. Thus while registered unemployment rates can be quite low, activity rates can also be low. Finally, changes in population and their impact on the levels and costs of service provision are also an element of the 'rural problem'. While emigration from urban areas is unlikely to have a significant impact on the general level of access to services for those remaining, even though it may affect the ability of the area to raise funds for service provision, this is not the case in rural areas. For all these reasons then, the proportion of the work force which is registered as unemployed is unlikely to represent an adequate single statistic for identifying the most 'deserving' rural areas. It is possible that some other statistic could serve this purpose.

In Chapter 3, we considered the possible objectives of public policy in rural areas. Clearly, the selection of areas must flow directly from these objectives and the nature of the assistance offered. Efforts to improve the general level of welfare in rural areas are usually associated with raising the incomes of particular groups, maintaining population levels or improving access to public and private services. In the context of developing employment, we are most directly concerned with the first two of these. It may be anticipated that the position of the last will be improved through the first two. Thus we can anticipate that areas with low average incomes, high unemployment and low activity rates, and high emigration rates will be the most 'deserving'. Any of these provides a potential indicator of rural 'need'. In a study of alternative criteria for guiding the selection of economically depressed areas for special funding, Horne *et al.* (1974) examined the relationships between possible criteria. A number of measures were included: under-employment, unemployment, median income, poverty, population change and rurality. The estimates of percentage under-employed were calculated on the basis of the relationship between the county actual median income' and the county's 'median earning capacity' which was derived from the ratio of the county actual median income to the national median income, adjusted for (a) age/colour mix, (b) educational status (c) labour force status and (d) employment factor of the labour force. The procedure is detailed by Kampe and Lindamoud (1969). The measure of rurality was the percentage of the population classified as rural.

Any of these measures, except rurality, provides a rationale for an area deserving special assistance, with regard to the objectives of rural policy which have been identified. Correlation coefficients were estimated for all 404 counties in six states of the USA. This included urban counties. Their results are shown in Table 13.1.

Table 13.1 Simple correlation matrix for 404 counties of five selected states,* 1960

	Under-employment	*Unemployment*	*Median income*	*Poverty (income less than $3000)*	*Population change 1950–60*	*Rurality*
Under-employment	1.000	−0.097	−0.776	0.739	−0.363	0.575
Unemployment	−0.097	1.000	−0.192	0.169	−0.186	0.117
Median income	−0.776	−0.192	1.000	−0.957	0.539	−0.600
Poverty (income less than $3000)	0.739	0.169	−0.957	1.000	−0.483	0.546
Population change 1950–60	−0.363	−0.186	0.539	−0.483	1.000	−0.418
Rurality	0.575	0.117	−0.600	0.546	−0.418	1.000

*Arizona, Idaho, North Carolina, Oklahoma, Pennsylvania
Source: Horne *et al.* (1974)

The figures show reasonably close correlation among the variables other than unemployment, which appears to stand out as being different from the others. The negative correlation between unemployment and under-employment is surprising, notwithstanding the problems associated with the latter's measurement. The explanation of the relative isolation of unemployment lies in its association with the most urbanized counties. The implication is then, that the allocation of funds on the basis of unemployment data alone, as has already been suggested, is most likely to lead to depressed rural areas, with supplies of under-utilized labour, receiving a relatively small share. The emphasis by the Economic Development Administration on unemployment levels is suggested as an explanation of why the south of the USA, with its substantial need, had a disproportionately small number of counties designated for special funding. Other criteria would provide a more satisfactory means of identifying rural areas for special assistance. Horne *et al.* suggest under-employment as the most appropriate.

There is clearly some interrelationship between each of these variables associated with rurality and so it may be expected that decisions should be made on the basis of some combination of variables associated with rural depression. Cloke (1977) has developed an 'index of rurality' for local authorities in England and Wales, for 1961 and 1971. The index was created from a number of variables associated with rurality, including population density, population change, occupational structure, distance from an urban centre and migration. These were combined by means of principal components analysis by which they were weighted so achieve a maximum discrimination between the least and the most rural areas. Index scores for each local authority were calculated by substituting the individual authority values into the principal component equation. The ten extreme non-rural and extreme rural authorities for 1971 are shown in Table 13.2 where it can be seen that eight of the ten extreme rural districts are located in Wales.

Cloke (1978) has also examined the changes in his index of rurality between 1961 and 1971. Perhaps this dynamic aspect of rural change provides a more appropriate indicator of areas deserving assistance, especially in the form of new employment opportunities. The fact that areas are very rural, i.e. that they have low population densities or high dependence upon primary industries does not, of itself, provide any case for public intervention. If such areas have low average incomes, then appropriate policy measures are most likely to involve assistance to agriculture or direct income transfers. One exception could be in attempting to raise household

Table 13.2 Extreme rural and non-rural districts, England and Wales, 1971

Extreme non-rural	*Extreme rural*
Whiston	Newcastle Emlyn
Meriden	New Radnor
Warrington	Painscastle
Workingham	Reeth
Highworth	Machynlleth
Hartley Wintney	Knighton
Easthampsted	Lleyn
Grimsby	Llanfyllin
Wigan	Penllyn
Blaby	Kington

Source: Cloke (1977)

incomes by providing employment for women, when there is evidence of low female activity rates. Probably more often public policy seeks to stem rural decline. This type of change, declining employment in traditional industries, and hence declining average incomes, and declining levels of service provision, is most likely to be a cause of distress. Furthermore, efforts to use new employment opportunities to maintain populations, income levels and access to services seems to have the highest chance of success. It is considerably easier to provide a labour force through reducing emigration than it is through encouraging movement back to a rural area. Good prospects of recovery and growth are likely to be an important criterion applied in allocating funds for rural development.

Cloke divided the districts on a quartile basis between extreme rural, intermediate rural, intermediate non-rural and extreme non-rural districts. Concentrating on the extreme rural, then those areas experiencing the most rapid increase in rurality may be regarded as those most deserving assistance. Of the ten shown in Table 13.2, all had become more rural between 1961 and 1971, except Knighton, which became very slightly less rural. However, other districts have experienced more significant shifts towards rurality. Many of these were non-rural on the basis of the 1961 index, although some, such as New Radnor, Painscastle, and Newcastle Emlyn all of which are, incidentally, in Wales, were defined as rural.

However, an index in which the relative weights are calculated on a mechanistic basis, without reference to public policy objectives cannot provide an optimal approach to resource allocation. The relative importance of the various indicators of rural depression need to be imputed on the basis of a social welfare function (see, for instance, Whitby and Willis, 1978), which indicates the relative weights for benefits provided to various individuals or groups in society. An index, such as that produced by Cloke, or any single variable, can, however, provide a broad screening device so that more detailed examination of regional policies against public objectives may be made against those likely to be awarded assistance. An attempt has been made by McGuire and Garn (1969) to surmount this problem by selecting weights explicitly to relate equity and efficiency objectives in public project selection, which would then be validated through the political system. They took levels of unemployment and of incomes as the two indicators of area need or marginal utility, and constructed a function for deriving a single index from these. The parameters of this function could be set to reflect different value judgements about the trade-off between these two variables. These values would be explicitly selected to reflect the decision-maker's preferences. Their approach was criticized by Mathur (1971) who suggested that administrators are probably unaware of, or unable to cope with, the complexities of the explicit weighting method. This seems likely to be true, and the method is further confounded by the fact that politicians may see advantage in a certain degree of obfuscation in the process of giving preference to individual areas, such as might be the case in giving assistance to marginal constituencies.

In practice then, areas will tend to be selected through some more obscure process. Some single, screening, variable may be used for the identification of a broad range of eligible areas, such as rates of depopulation, beyond which a range of issues may be involved. For instance, in designating areas for special assistance, the Development Commission bases its decision on action plans, which are drawn up by local authorities in these areas and cover the background to the need for assistance and the specific proposals for regeneration. It is then able to judge each on the basis of the information provided against any criteria which it sees to be appropriate.

Identifying regional potential

We now shift emphasis from comparisons between regions to the examination of intra-regional policy. Having identified the areas for assistance, then how can potential initiatives be defined and implemented? As the previous chapters have shown, a range of activities may present suitable avenues for the development of employment. However, for any individual region, some will represent stronger possibilities than others and those with the highest chance of success need to be selected. Further to this, some indication of the potential level of employment which these activities can generate will be required.

The first stage in designing a scheme for regional regeneration must involve a study of the region's resources. Their availability will determine both the nature and scale of potential employment growth. Clearly, our immediate concern is with the availability of labour and a study of potential may well begin by examining the nature and size of the labour force which is available. As we have already seen, a number of statistics are relevant in this context. The information sought is the number of people who could be available for work in the area if it was available. First of all, the number of people registered as seeking work provides a starting point, but not the full picture. Indeed, some would claim that many of these are, in fact, not interested in actually working at all. Further sources of labour lie in an increase in activity rates, reduced emigration, increased immigration or a withdrawal of labour from other activities. Available statistics relating to the relevant labour market need to be collected, and interpreted. This will provide information on only some of the important variables. For instance, a census will show how many people there are, within a reasonable commuting distance of a proposed growth centre, who are not working. A comparison with the levels of employment in other areas, with greater employment opportunities, can suggest the potential for growth of the existing labour force. However, other components of the potential labour force, especially those associated with changes in migration patterns, can only be tentatively estimated in the light of local knowledge and experience of change in other areas. They will not only be influenced by the present position of the area, but also by the type of employment which is developed, especially the levels of skills required and the wage rates paid. Without knowledge of these, it is clearly impossible to specify labour availability. It remains extremely difficult even with such information. The potential of the labour force may be enhanced along a different dimension through education and training. While some employers prefer to take on people without industrial experience who can be trained to their own particular work patterns, the development of special skills in the work force not only provides an attraction to potential employers, but also enhances local earning capacity.

Beyond labour, different activities have a variety of requirements. The development of agriculture and forestry involves the use of large areas of land, although not necessarily their availability for purchase. Agricultural development is almost invariably achieved through some relatively minor changes in the farming systems of existing producers. This is in contrast to development in poor countries where land reform is often an important component in achieving the appropriate conditions for development. In identifying potential agricultural developments, then data concerning the quality of the physical environment, including soil quality, climate and topography, will be required. This may already be available through past surveys. But information will also be required on a range of other factors affecting the economic viability of potential enterprises, such as distances to markets, availability of management skills and motivations, and prices. It is not adequate simply to identify the physical potential of an area as this needs to be placed in its economic and social context. Forestry development is less sensitive to the availability of high quality land but, in that it is often undertaken by a large organization moving into an area, whether it be publicly owned or not, land will need to be available for purchase. Widespread compulsory acquisition of land is unlikely to be an acceptable approach. While other activities self-evidently require less land, the lack of suitable sites can present a surprisingly significant impediment to development. The problems of acquiring sites for the Development Commission's factory developments in Great Britain have led to lengthy delays in factory construction. For instance, in Northumberland between 1969 and 1971, six factory projects were approved, but, due to difficulties in finding suitable sites, progress could only be made at one location. As a result, in 1972, the county council embarked upon a policy of compulsory purchase (Development Commission, 1976). Clearly, it is not a physical shortage of space which prevents factory construction in rural areas, but an unwillingness of local landowners to sell, perhaps, due to modest valuations by District Valuers or to landowners' concern over the effect of industrial development on the local labour market. The problem is sometimes compounded by inflexibility in local planning regulations. This latter factor is more often a problem in smaller settlements.

The quality of an area's environment has both a direct and an indirect effect on potential development. Most directly, it will influence the potential of an area to attract tourists and so provide employment and income in tourism and recreation. The nature of potential activities will be determined by the attractions which the area can offer, for instance, water sports, or skiing and the developments which are associated with these. Clearly, in this context too the location with respect to population centres and other areas offering similar attractions will be important. Indirectly, the quality of the environment will affect potential through its influence on the decisions of firms and individuals to move to the area. As suggested in Chapter 7, this factor is important in such decisions. However, it is not possible to quantify the quality of an area in terms of its ability to attract either tourists or residents. Evidence on the basis of past experience may be of some value, although the potential 'carrying capacity' of an area is hard to identify. People's responses to congestion are not always what is expected.

The availability and quality of other natural resources (minerals or energy sources) will be the sole determinant of the potential for extractive industries. However, other factors, such as scenic quality or other regional objectives will, through the planning process, influence whether such potential is realized.

Capital is often assumed to be sufficiently mobile, so that entrepreneurial activity will recognize potentially profitable developments, and organize the necessary resources; thus where there exist opportunities, capital will be found for their implementation. However, this is not always the case. There might be a lack of knowledge, especially about the potentials of remoter areas or simply a reluctance to travel to them. The lack of industrial experience locally is likely to restrict the supply of entrepreneurs, while those elsewhere tend to favour projects in areas with which they are familiar. The provision of information may help to overcome this, although some innovative action by state or local organizations may be beneficial. The organizational function does not end with the assembly of the required resources in a single location. The success of many ventures hinges on the quality of their management. Thus, when an area is embarking on some new field of economic activity, the necessary management skills will need to be imported. When an existing activity is being developed, management training may play an important role, as was illustrated by the efforts to improve farm management as part of the Fund for Rural Economic Development programme operated in the Interlake area of Manitoba (Tung *et al.*, 1976).

The first stage, then, in developing a regional approach to the development of employment, lies in the identification of the present resource endowment and its potential augmentation. The availability of resources leads to the identification of potential employment creating activities. The limits of resources, such as land of a particular quality, or the supply of labour, provide one constraint to the levels of economic activity. There are also limits based on the economic viability of the potential activities. In a mixed economy, an enterprise will not be undertaken unless it appears likely to provide an adequate return. Governments can influence the types and locations of economic activity to a large extent, by controlling the prices of inputs and outputs. The question of which activities are feasible in particular areas can only be answered on the basis of individual studies for each enterprise. From a public policy viewpoint, such studies should involve the consideration of the social costs and benefits, as described in the previous chapters.

Developing a regional strategy

Having identified the costs, benefits and potentials of individual activities, regional planning will proceed to integrate these into some form of overall scheme. MacMillan and Graham (1978) identify six steps to assist in the designing and testing of rural development plans. These are illustrated in Figure 13.3.

The steps are:

1 identification of quantitative rural development objectives;
2 construction of a model for the region with the capacity to simulate estimates of aggregate regional indicators of development with and without the projects contained in the plan;
3 completion of feasibility studies to assess proposed projects

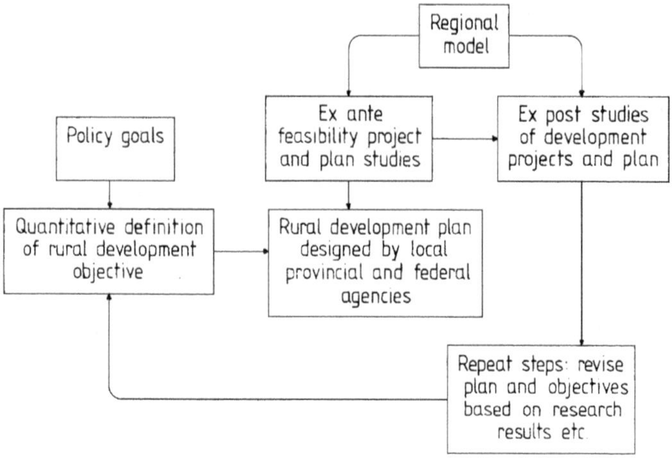

Figure 13.1 Rural development planning research activities
Source: MacMillan and Graham (1978)

relative to *ex ante* rate of return and income distribution performance criteria;

4 a plan consisting of $X million on selected projects for a fixed number of years is constructed;
5 in depth special studies of the development projects and plan are conducted to assess project results *ex post* relative to *ex ante* projections;
6 conclusions with respect to improvements in the plan and rural development objectives are made consistent with *ex post* study results.

These steps cover a number of areas which have been discussed in earlier chapters. In Chapter 3 we considered the possible objectives of public policies. As we noted then, objectives are not often specified explicitly and this presents a severe limitation to the measurement of achievement. The simulation of the impact of potential projects may be undertaken at varying levels of sophistication. In Chapter 9 we described a relatively modest approach to estimating the regional impacts of various developments. While our discussion was set in the context of *ex post* analysis, knowledge of regional interrelationships and experience of similar developments elsewhere may be incorporated for the projection of future impacts.

Inevitably, this will reduce the confidence which can be placed on the results. Currently, Hubbard and Whitby are developing this approach for the *ex ante* analysis of Development Commission expenditure in County Durham drawing somewhat on the previous *ex post* evaluation of expenditure in the Eastern Borders. More sophisticated approaches, involving such techniques as modified input-output analysis and simulation can be used (see, for example, Nelson and Tweeten, 1975; Tung *et al.*, 1976), involving considerably greater amounts of data and research effort.

Having developed an approach to estimating regional impacts and having examined the feasibility of individual activities, these may then be combined into a comprehensive plan. This may potentially be undertaken at two levels. Firstly, more fundamentally, the knowledge of regional impacts may be used so as to avoid attempting the development of more activities than may be supported by the available resources. For instance, if a regional plan involves the development of small-scale manufacturing as well as the processing of local farm produce, then it is necessary to ensure that adequate labour can be available for both these activities, as well as for any necessary growth in the agricultural sector. The second level would involve some attempt to optimize the regional plan, such as through the application of programming techniques (see, for example, Whitby and Willis (1978) for a brief discussion of these techniques). Such an approach seeks to develop a plan which will maximize some objective function, subject to the relevant resource and budget constraints. The complex nature of the objectives in rural development means that the objective function must either concentrate on a single variable, such as employment, or develop some explicit weighting between several variables. Such quantitative planning methodologies also have large data requirements. Their development could, nevertheless, assist in the understanding of regional interactions and suggest improved approaches to the achievement of regional objectives.

A model has, for instance, been constructed to investigate the conflicts between objectives in rural economic development (Williams, 1980). Efforts to maximize one particular objective are likely to lead to a fall in the level achieved in other regional objectives. A linear programming model has been used to quantify the trade-offs between alternative economic policy goals. The results show an important conflict between the interests of capital or management and those of labour. For example, more local jobs can be created, under the assumption of a given level of regional resource availability, technology and access to markets, if a region is willing to reduce the level of aggregate production of goods and services. This results from the types of industry which enable the region to achieve the various goals. Utilizing the entire available local labour force tends to involve the attraction of relatively labour intensive, low output industry. The investigation of these trade-offs can provide information to local planners in shaping appropriate objectives for development policies.

The planning process does not cease with the development of a plan, but continues with the assessments of achievement and consequent adjustments. The results of *ex post* analysis are of value both in providing feedback about the project itself which can be used for control and future development and in improving *ex ante* analyses of similar projects in other locations. The use of standardized approaches to evaluation, including the need to make explicit what approaches have been taken, can considerably improve the value of project analysis through facilitating strict comparison between alternative projects.

Planning in practice

The steps proposed by MacMillan and Graham (1978) represent an ideal. In many circumstances, such as when only a small number of sectors are involved, it will not be appropriate to develop complex regional models. Efficiency in research, as in any other activity, is achieved by concentrating resources in areas which achieve the highest pay-off at the margin.

The data problems involved in research into relatively small rural areas are well known. Generally, there is available quite a substantial amount of information relating to the agricultural sector, but data concerning other activities tends to be sparse. Edwards (1979) has recently identified a number of rural employment data gaps in the USA. While there has been a significant increase in non-farm employment in rural areas, the collection of employment data has not changed to reflect this. Other employment variables present even greater problems. Consider under-employment. While this could be an important factor in determining the size of the labour force available to incoming industry, there is often debate over its exact definition, let alone its measurement in a specific area. Population statistics also present problems. Small errors in population estimates in absolute terms may have important implications for small populations. Accurate information on migration is rarely available. Often reliance has to be placed on calculations of net migration based on the difference between current estimated populations and past populations, adjusted for natural change. Once again, in the context of small areas, errors in such estimates can produce large proportionate errors in important variables.

Two even more fundamental problems hinder the implementation of quantitative planning models. The first concerns the basic relationships between the variables which we seek to influence, such as employment or migration and those over which we have direct control, such as grants paid to manufacturing activities or the area of forestry. On the basis of our present knowledge, the observation of certain relationships in the past in no way guarantees the continuance of those relationships in the future. Other factors, beyond our control, and perhaps without our knowledge, may intervene. We have already referred to the second problem. This relates to the difficulty of specifying an acceptable objective function in the absence of any explicit definition or weighting of objectives on behalf of policy-makers.

None of these problems are specific to the development of regional plans for rural areas. They are central to most areas of public policy analysis. Their importance needs to be borne in mind, both when undertaking research and when interpreting the results, but they do not constitute a valid reason for rejecting efforts to make good data deficiencies, establish relationships between critical variables and improve the efficiency of the use of public resources. Regional research has an important role to play in improving the information available for the formulation of policies for rural regeneration.

14
THE IMPLEMENTATION OF RURAL EMPLOYMENT INITIATIVES

Throughout this book we have concentrated on one rural policy objective: raising the numbers of jobs in the countryside. Our emphasis on this issue is not shared by all proponents of rural policy. A wide range of attitudes are expressed. One extreme takes a *laissez-faire* approach, which regards the process of rural decline as inevitably associated with economic growth, and efforts to retard it as not only expensive and unjustified, but also as prolonging the agony of necessary structural change. The other takes a protective, paternalistic view of the countryside as something between a museum and a sheltered workshop where people can be shielded from the rigours of the outside world in order to maintain a traditional way of life in an idyllic setting. The majority, of course, falls between these. More significantly, a variety of objections, from both sides of the spectrum, are raised against the sorts of initiatives which we have discussed. They are largely voiced by three groups. The first two seek alternative uses for rural resources and see potential conflict between employment policies and their own demands. The third express a more general concern about the national implications.

Agriculture is the traditional, and by far the most significant, activity over most rural areas. As such, agricultural interests have an important influence over local policy making (Newby *et al.*, 1978). The introduction of new activities to rural areas to compete for the resources, especially the labour, over which agriculture has historically had a near monopoly, may, not surprisingly, be resisted. Whether this is a fair response depends upon the nature of the impact of, say, industrialization on agriculture. Are wages forced up? Does it become impossible to hire labour of a reasonable quality? Is valuable land taken out of production? We are thinking here of the impacts as they affect the individuals in the agricultural sector. The evidence reviewed in Chapter 7 suggests that, while the availability of labour to agriculture may be reduced, adjustments in farm systems are possible so that there need be no significant loss of incomes. From the point of view of farm employees, increasing costs of labour are hardly likely to be regarded as a problem. Loss of land for industrial development could present problems for a small number of farmers and clearly adequate compensation is needed in cases of compulsory purchase. Tenant farmers are potentially at greater risk and in the distant past have been surprised to find trees being planted over their grazing land without prior warning. Since that time, legislation has given them security of tenure against such developments.

More recent competitors for rural resources are those who make use of the environment, either for recreation or as a backcloth for other activities. Their objectives usually lead them to favour the *status quo* against either agricultural improvement, planting or industrialization. Their case centres around aesthetic arguments; whether an afforested landscape is more attractive than open moorland, or whether untidy, varied farms are more attractive than large fields and even crops. Perhaps the debate about access is more fundamental to the use of the countryside. The improved pastures and higher stocking rates of a prosperous agriculture face greater risks from recreationalists and therefore increase the incentive to restrict access. Such conflicts need to be faced, although the clarification of existing rights of way and negotiation of new ones (for example access agreements in the UK) can do much to provide adequate control. The intrusion of factories into rural areas is a concern often expressed about industrialization, although those who object to factory developments in principle do not even always recognise small factory premises and workshops for what they are. There is clearly a need to plan for appropriate developments, but generally lack of labour in small settlements will preclude the establishment of large industries other than for mining and quarrying.

The final objections to rural employment initiatives arise from a general concern over the costs involved; most of which will be borne by society more generally. We have already considered these. They include the costs of service provision, the potential losses in efficiency and the need for the exchequer to pay subsidies.

Each of these groups may, under certain circumstances have a case against employment policies. But it is argued that, given reasonable planning control, especially in critical areas where environmental costs outweigh the potential advantages, the first two groups of objectors will rarely have a valid case against the development of employment. The objections of the last group need to be heard and weighed against the potential benefits. These issues have been dealt with at some length.

Rural employment and rural problems

The causes and some consequences of rural decline have been described in Chapters 1 and 2. In recent years, debates over rural planning as it relates to the welfare of rural residents have been dominated by a number of issues. Those, other than employment, which have been of particular importance are: rural transport, the availability of services and access to the housing market. Our neglect of these issues is not to detract from their importance. However, they arise basically from the declining ability of rural residents to compete with urban residents in the economic and political markets for resources. This is a result both of declining population and incomes and increasing pressures on rural resources from non-residents, especially for housing and recreational space. These issues are, therefore, to a large extent the symptoms of the more fundamental rural problem. We believe that priority needs to be given to easing the main cause of these problems, by increasing rural populations and incomes and hence the ability of rural areas to compete. The availability of satisfactory employment in the longer term and the achievement of a reasonable income, are central issues in the decision to migrate. As has been shown, the creation of employment can have a significant impact on rates of depopulation, as well as on incomes. Such policies have the potential for achieving a long-term shift in the balance of power, thus allowing rural areas to become more self-supporting, and reduce the need for public assistance. However, some locations do not have the potential to achieve what might generally be regarded as adequate populations, incomes and levels of service provision. In such cases, assistance will be needed to ameliorate the symptoms, by subsidizing services and transport or by implementing strict controls over the housing market. Such a policy involves the long-term commitment of resources to the support of rural populations and clearly should not be embarked upon without a firm belief in their importance.

Evolution of local policies and decision-making

Given that there are few, if any, policies which can achieve benefits to some groups and costs to none, decisions need to be made as to how to trade-off the costs against the benefits. We have concentrated on the economic aspects and on methods by which some of the costs and benefits may be quantified. But this does not provide a mechanistic way of coming to decisions. It falls short of this for two basic reasons. Firstly, some of the costs and benefits have not been quantified and many of these factors are central to the question of whether declining rural areas do or do not deserve support. What effect does it have on the quality of life there? Secondly, we are unable to judge the relative merits of assisting different groups of people. National and local politics provide the traditional forum for the discussion and resolution of these issues, although bureaucrats, in fact, make a wide range of decisions which influence local policies. The recent emphasis on more direct public involvement in policy formulation reflects a desire to achieve a better match between local aspirations and public policy. Such discussion leads us towards a vast area of debate beyond the scope of this book. We have presented an approach to the analysis and evaluation of policies. This is one, we believe important, element of the question. The answer lies in the balancing of this against other aspects by our democratically elected politician.

Whether he will necessarily respond in the manner in which we would hope, that is to say towards the 'maximization of net social welfare', is open to question. There is a further impediment to this process, which we should not neglect, namely, the politician's inevitable objective of remaining in power. The question of how public expenditures are allocated between competing local areas may fall into the category sometimes described as 'pork-barrel' politics (Tullock, 1976). Models of the political process (especially Downs, 1957) have been projected to predict that rational political behaviour would operate to direct greater amounts of funds towards politically marginal areas than would be anticipated on the basis of needs and equity alone. To a lesser extent areas regarded as 'safe' by the party in power may expect to be treated relatively favourably while the opposition's 'safe' areas stand to gain least. In a study of the distribution of government expenditure in the USA, Johnston (1977) found that 'political' variables, describing the political security of state legislature and governorship and the numbers of members from each state on the relevant congressional committees, explained a larger amount of the variation in departmental spending between states than did the 'needs' variables.

Whether such a bias would work in favour of or against the interests of the more remote rural areas is uncertain. Evidence suggests that, at least for English constituencies, seats with relatively large proportions of agricultural workers offer very little return to either of the major parties in terms of the number of extra seats which would be won for a given increase in the number of votes won (Johnston, 1976). Alternative distributions of political preferences and electoral influence could result in different patterns of political priority. However, our concern lies less in predicting the direction or extent of any such bias than in encouraging its reduction through the promotion of open and informed decision-making.

The institutional environment

The success or failure of public involvement in the economy does not lie solely in the adoption of appropriate policies. They also need to be implemented and controlled and in this, as well as in their formulation, the institutional environment is often of great consequence.

Given a general agreement to provide support for rural regeneration, decisions need to be made at two levels. At a national level, the amount of funding to individual areas needs to be decided on the basis of their relative needs and potential. Secondly, decisions as to how the available finance is to be allocated within an area needs to be made, and the resultant projects implemented and controlled. Decisions as to how the funds are to be allocated to individual activities should be taken at the local level. The possible range of uses of funds would be defined by a legal framework and local organizations would be accountable to the national body.

As we have seen, the selection of areas should be based on regional indicators matched against previously defined criteria. The institution undertaking such work would also be required to oversee the initiatives and to monitor and evaluate the results. In order to achieve this, it would need expertise in the various fields in which employment may be developed and to have strong contacts with local organizations. Familiarity is also required with the relationship between employment and other rural issues. Such an organization bears resemblance to that advocated by a number of other writers. For instance, Green (1971) has suggested a rural development authority whose major tasks would be to initiate schemes of rural development or to guide development to the right place at the right time. Wibberley (1976) has argued for a Ministry of Rural Planning and Development which could achieve a closer integration of the statutory planning process with rural resource development. Indeed a former chairman of the Development Commission saw his organization as forming the basis for an English rural development agency which could co-ordinate rural development in a total strategy (Northfield, 1977), although at present their range of activity is limited to only providing assistance where no other statutory provision exists. However, he saw this national organization taking a fund allocating, co-ordinating and evaluating role with specific initiatives being developed at a local level.

The local functions of strategy development, implementation and control may be undertaken by a single organization, although there will be greatest need for public participation in the first. MacMillan (1977) has pointed out the need for local co-operation. Professional economists are ignorant of the day-to-day reality of regions, and regional groups are ignorant of the underlying general principles of regional development. There is need therefore for a dialogue between local interests and those developing the strategy. This is important, not only in order to set realistic objectives, but also to obtain public support for the initiative. Without this, development will certainly be much harder to achieve, and may be impossible.

Robinson (1972) has specified the characteristics which any rural comprehensive development agency should possess:

1 it should operate over an area of regional scale;
2 its concern should be to see that the economic, social and physical planning of the region is treated as a combined operation;
3 the agency should be innovative in outlook. Its research and intelligence role will enable it to become the focus for new initiatives;
4 it should have the power to intervene. Its status in the political system should be such that it has an effective influence over the disposition of major public and private investments, both with-

in the region and in closely connected peripheral areas;
5 its role should be continuing and long-term;
6 an indigenous agency is required. Planning at a distance is not likely to be successful – the possibilities of alienation, misinformation and misinterpretation are too great.

Such an agency represents the type of organization which could implement and manage local employment initiatives. Its main functions would be to assess the local resource endowment, identify potential areas for development, publicize these and the incentives which are available, help entrepreneurs through the maze of the various bureaucracies, co-ordinate activities within the area and maintain contacts with local groups. The emphasis needs to be on the development of local resources and businesses rather than on the introduction of outside enterprises, although these should be welcomed when the opportunity arises, or on the enforcement of an externally produced plan.

An organization of this nature would fulfil many of the roles of rural development boards and development corporations in their involvement with agriculture, forestry and industrial development. Several specific agencies have been set up to carry out such functions in rural Britain, and some established organizations have taken on these functions in the past decade. Most prominent in the latter case have been the local authorities, some of which have become closely involved in attempts to promote rural development at the county level. Perhaps the best-known regional agency in the UK is the Highlands and Islands Development Board. This agency was established in 1965 and can usefully be described, under the headings suggested above by Robinson. Most of the information presented is taken from the Board's fourteenth annual report (HIDB, 1980), from a paper by the Board's first chairman (Grieve, 1972) and from a book by two researchers who have been closely associated with the work of the Board (Bryden and Houston, 1976).

The *regional scale* of the Board is evident from the facts that 3 million hectares of agricultural land within its boundary accounts for nearly half the surface area of Scotland, whilst it contained only 6 per cent of Scotland's 5 million population, in 1978. Grieve noted that rates of depopulation had slowed down to somewhat below the Scottish average but that the main problem was the 'effects on widely scattered communities of 200 years' emigration which had its beginnings in the suppression of the Clans after the risings of 1715 and 1745 and in the later Clearances of subsistence peasantry from the glens in favour of sheep farming and deer and grouse shooting'. The residual population, following this process of decline was ageing and had only half the Scottish average rate of natural increase. According to Grieve it also showed 'a lack of enterprise and confidence, and a serious thinning out of communities already too small and too isolated'. However, more recently (HIDB, 1980) the process of population turnaround, noted in Chapter 2, has also been found in the Highlands. In particular the 1970s have seen a substantial net increase in population of the HIDB area. In Table 14.1 the population data are reported, showing that for the area as a whole a compound annual increase in population has been achieved whilst the Eastern Highlands in fact account for most of this growth.

Table 14.1 Population change in the Scottish Highlands, 1971–9

	Total population		*Net change 1971–9*		*Annual*
			Total		*average*
	1971	*1979*	*Numbers*	*Per cent*	*compound*
Eastern Highlands	176,729	200,571	+23,842	+13.5	+1.59
Western Highlands	121,602	124,201	+2,599	+2.1	+0.26
Total HIDB area	298,331	324,772	+26,441	+8.9	+1.07

Source: HIDB (1980)

Note: The Eastern Highlands include the local authorities of Caithness, Sutherland, Ross and Cromarty, Inverness, Badenoch and Strathspey, Nairn, Orkney and Shetland. The Western Highlands contain the remainder of the HIDB area.

The integration of *economic*, *social* and *physical* planning is one characteristic which the Board has not been able to achieve without reference to the existing powers of other agencies. For example, the HIDB has attempted, over the last few years, to obtain stronger statutory powers of land acquisition in order to alleviate 'the more intractable land use problems' in its area (HIDB, 1978). The arguments for these powers are developed in some detail by Bryden and Houston (1976) who point to the extreme concentration of ownership of land within the Highlands and to the problem landowners who manage their estates, placing a low priority on productive potential. This ordering of private objectives is seen to conflict with the Board's broad development aims and it therefore sought direct means of resolving the conflict. To obtain such statutory powers the Board had to gain the support, or at least the consent, of a large number of individuals and organizations. In the end they were not granted these powers (HIDB, 1980) which, at least the Board would claim, will constrain its propensity to integrate different forms of planning. Other activities, such as the Board's involvement in forestry, have achieved integration of effort between different agencies with different policy objectives. Indeed, the wide range of the Board's interests is evidence of its success in combining economic, social and physical planning.

The Board's propensity to *innovate* has been demonstrated in several contexts. The better-known recent examples include its efforts to introduce deer farming to the Highlands and its participation in fish farming, particularly the support for salmon production.

The Board's powers to *intervene* in the land market have proved controversial, as noted above. Nevertheless, its intervention in support of capital investment is one of its major functions, as can be seen in Table 14.2.

Table 14.2 HIDB financial assistance and employment by sector

Sector	*Grants*	*Loans and shares*	*Job equivalents*	*Weighted total assistance per job equivalent*
	£1,000	*£1,000*	*number*	*£*
Manufacturing	6,566	12,121	6,243	1,438
Tourism	18,013	7,438	3,693	5,281
Fisheries	4,125	16,990	1,422	5,290
Land	2,062	8,636	1,018	3,722
Other, including construction and services	4,599	6,993	3,739	1,604
Total	35,355	52,178	16,115	2,842

Source: HIDB (1980)

Notes: 1. All money values are in 1979 prices: sums relate to approvals, not disbursements.

2. Job equivalents consist of the Board's estimate of employment created plus one half of jobs retained. Both items are measured in terms of full-time equivalence.

3. Weighted assistance combined grants and loans and shares with weights of 1.0 and 0.2 respectively.

Tourism has claimed a major share of the grants distributed, though manufacturing and fisheries together account for more than half of loans and shares. Assistance per job equivalent shows a quite remarkable spread over the different sectors. Evidently cost per job is not used as a sole criterion in allocating funds to different sectors.

Part of this variability in cost per job may be explained by differential cost movements between sectors but such an explanation would still leave substantial differences which may be attributable to the weight given to factors other than economic efficiency in selecting industries for support. This is perfectly consistent with the Board giving some weight to the notion of equity between the sub-regions of its area. Such a concern would indicate its adoption (implicitly if not explicitly) of a social welfare function of the kind developed by McGuire and Garn (1969), which includes inter-regional equity arguments as well as the more conventional efficiency ones.

It is also notable that agriculture does not appear under a distinct heading in this table, despite the fact that it accounts for 10 per cent of the workforce in the Board's area. This underlines the fact that agricultural policies are highly centralized in Britain. Agricultural policies in the EEC reflect this same general tendency, together with a strong emphasis on the support of farm-gate selling prices. However, two important exceptions to this generalization are notable in the Highlands. First, virtually the entire HIDB area is within the EEC Less-Favoured Areas boundary so that its farmers are eligible for forms of assistance which are not so closely tied to total production as the normal end-price support system in use. Thus the forms of income support in the HIDB area give farmers less incentive to increase labour productivity and hence may contribute less to the reduction of agricultural employment than end-price support. Second, the EEC has published proposals for an integrated development project which would attract 50 per cent of its funds from the Community, amounting to £10 million, the remaining £10 million to be raised within the UK. The area designated for the scheme is the Western Isles which has a population totalling 30,000. The prior existence of an effective development agency was probably an important factor in the initiation of these proposals.

There can be little doubt about the *continuity* of the Board which has now existed for fifteen years. Having survived some early political difficulties the HIDB now seems a very durable agency. It is also manifestly *indigenous*, its headquarters being based within its area and its main links with central government being through the Scottish Development Agency.

The successes of the Board have been widely acclaimed, though it must be recognized that the effectiveness of such a body is extremely difficult to assess in any objective fashion. For example, it would be too easy to attribute the evidence of population turnaround in the Board's area to the success of its policies. In fact the most dramatic increases in population are clearly attributable to the development of North Sea oil during the 1970s. Perhaps the achievement of the very modest reversal of net depopulation in the Western Highlands is stronger evidence of the Board's success. Certainly the Board matches up well to the criteria suggested by Robinson but a more profound test of its performance will be whether it manages to retain population in the Highlands after the North Sea oil potential has been exhausted, or even after its development phase has been passed. The difficulty of reaching more precise conclusions as to the viability of such agencies ensures that their continued existence will be for politicans rather than economists to decide. Meanwhile economists may be able to assist in developing operational criteria to guide it in the allocation of its funds.

The implementation of rural employment initiatives involves a variety of changes; in people's place of work, in their lifestyles, in their relationships. In order to be successful, such initiatives need to have popular support. Those involved therefore need to both see these changes as being to their advantage and to anticipate that they will actually come about. Such perceptions will result to a large extent from how initiatives are promoted and the strategy pursued by those concerned. Much then depends upon the individuals involved.

15
CONCLUDING REVIEW

The structural change associated with economic growth in developed countries leads to the relative decline of regions whose economies are largely dependent upon agriculture. This in turn reduces incomes and opportunities and encourages migration out of such areas producing a variety of well-known and widespread problems. A number of interrelated factors will be important in influencing their relative position in the future. The most important of these will be the world prices of agricultural products, the cost of energy, the application of technological advance and changing tastes for and attitudes to rural living. Generally, in the developed nations, we see little prospect for any increase in agricultural employment and in fact a continuing decline seems most likely although the prospects for forestry, recreational and tourism seem somewhat better. The numbers of jobs located in rural areas, providing services to the local population, would also seem likely to decline. The application of new technology in the retailing and administrative sectors will both reduce the numbers employed and increase the options for organizations such as banks to centralize their staffs. These would appear to be the pervasive, underlying trends, against which efforts to sustain employment must be viewed. Despite these trends there have been significant reversals of this pattern of declining populations in a number of developed countries as we have noted earlier. The evidence suggests that the previously dominant role of the search for economic opportunity as the original impetus to migration has weakened. A variety of reasons for these changes have been suggested. They include the fact that a growing proportion of the increasing population of people of retirement age are moving to rural locations, the increased orientations towards leisure activities, the improvement of transport facilities allowing greater decentralization in manufacturing, the development of extractive industries, the spread of urban settlements into areas classified as non-metropolitan and the growth of government institutions, especially those for higher education. One further, and unquantified, factor is the impact of economic recession. While workers feel that they are unlikely to find work in urban areas, the numbers emigrating from rural areas is likely to be reduced, perhaps being retained as under-employed in the agricultural and service sectors.

Two issues determine the general importance of these trends: whether the trend continues on a long-term basis and whether similar patterns are experienced in all countries. On the whole, the factors outlined above do seem set to operate over a significant period of time, perhaps excluding the continuing improvement, or at least reducing costs, of transport facilities and the growth of government institutions, but including, according to many prognostications, economic recession and unemployment. The impact of increasing transport costs would be to tend to restrict mobile manufacturing industries to operating within closer proximity of their markets. While on the whole this will involve locations nearer urban centres, some activities may benefit from rural situations such as where the processing of primary products involves a reduction in mass or where production takes place for rural consumption, especially of products with high transport costs whose production involves only limited economies of scale. The development of alternative energy sources could be one such activity. Also technological developments may enhance the opportunities for service activity location in rural areas. However, location decisions are likely to be influenced by the quality of the environment and, until there are further improvements, access to telecommunication networks. The most remote areas would seem to represent unlikely locations for most service activities.

We may then summarize these elements of rural futures. The prospects for not-too-remote locations with attractive environments appear to be quite good. They stand to benefit from immigration of retired people and recreationalists, whose presence will in turn stimulate employment in a variety of service activities. They may also attract footloose service activities. Areas without these advantages would seem set to face continuing decline in the absence of intervention, albeit at a reduced rate if high levels of unemployment deter would-be emigrants from seeking improved conditions in urban areas.

We have been engaging in extremely general discussion about rural futures. However, the fates of individual areas will be substantially influenced by local factors. A variety of activities have been suggested as representing possible avenues for rural regeneration. We have omitted some which for some areas could be important. These will usually be associated with the utilization of such specific resources as the sea or local minerals. Each area needs to concentrate its efforts on its particular strengths. Some areas, where economic growth is occurring spontaneously will not need any development assistance. They may of course experience other problems, such as those resulting from the preponderance of older people in retirement areas. The role of analysis and planning here will be to guide and select appropriate developments. Those areas at the other end of the spectrum of economic viability will not achieve regeneration without massive and unjustifiable injections of public funds. Nobody would advocate policies to maintain population centres in the most remote areas of Australia. Between these two extremes lie those regions which are at the margin of economic viability. For these, the implementation of employment initatives can achieve, at reasonable cost, the maintenance of settlements which can offer the range of services and variety of employment which will prevent high rates of emigration. Such areas are likely to be those which have most recently experienced a decline in their economic fortunes.

In Part II, we considered the more important sources of employment in rural areas: agriculture, forestry, recreation and tourism, manufacturing and services and have tried to suggest the potential of these activities for future employment. Care is required, however, in translating past experience, which has been the subject of a variety of studies, into future expectations. Apart from a probable tendency to select successful initiatives for study, the experience is often placed in a substantially altered macro-economic environment. The most fundamental changes derived from the lower levels of economic growth and higher levels of unemployment and the slower, or even zero, rates of population growth which are current, and likely to be continued in most developed countries. Chisholm (1976) has discussed the implications of these changed conditions for regional policy. Rural areas are finding that they are increasingly in competition with urban and other rural areas for a diminishing number of mobile companies. The expansion of expenditure on regional promotion thereby becomes a wasteful process where, while each individual tries to 'get ahead', the total pool of employment remains fixed. Such resources are better devoted to developing indigenous enterprise. This shift is illustrated in the experience of the sources of new companies establishing in the Eastern Borders described in Chapter 7.

The question of whether or not these policies should be implemented turns upon the issue of whether the benefits outweigh the costs. We have at some length described an approach to the quantification of some of these elements. Our central argument is that these issues need to be assessed from a 'social' as opposed to a 'private' point of view. It is not adequate to simply measure the flows to and from the exchequer or to only take into account the profits made by private operations. There are substantial benefits to be achieved through the introduction of otherwise unemployed labour to the work force. Policy-makers must be aware, too, of the social costs: the costs of providing services to remoter populations; the potential loss of efficiency in encouraging economic activity away from its markets. Decisions need to be made in the light of such information and they can be improved through the use of standard techniques for the comparison of alternative policies. The light cast by such an approach cannot illuminate all the elements of the debate and in the final analysis decisions need to be taken by politicans on the basis of the relative importance attached to rural regeneration as against the multitude of other calls upon public funds and resources.

We have discussed the form of organization which could be most favourably placed to initiate and administer rural employment policies. The recent emphasis on public involvement in planning and the need for areas to encourage the development of their own resources and emerging companies underlines the importance of strong links between any organization and the local population. In the majority of cases, of course, institutions are not built from scratch but evolve from existing ones. A consideration of qualities which such an organization should have will be of benefit in deciding the direction of evolution.

This book has been written during a period of steeply rising unemployment in the UK, and in other developed countries. Under such circumstances its subject matter may seem to acquire a very particular relevance. However, against this two factors must be acknowledged. First, *rural* unemployment is a very old problem. Its core is in the structural changes required in rural labour markets if rural populations are to be retained. Second, to the extent that unemployment arises from deficiencies in the demand for labour (and hence for goods), it will not necessarily be solved by micro-level projects. The evaluation of which we have described in detail in Chapters 10–12 does nevertheless highlight the substantial benefits to be gained from getting people to work. The controversy over the cure for deficient demand unemployment has not yet reached the stage where a consensus is in sight. Accordingly we have not been able to say much about the relevance of macro-level management of the economy to rural areas. Despite these two reservations, it does remain appropriate to consider supporting rural areas through the labour market.

The policy alternatives to labour market management have been widely discussed and some of them enthusiastically embraced. Income support by manipulating agricultural prices has been common in the developed world since before World War II, as problems of surplus disposal and distorted asset values will testify. Attempts at maintaining populations by guaranteeing their housing through planning controls have led to rising house prices and lengthening council-house queues in scenic parts of the UK (Shucksmith, 1981). Maintenance of other public services for declining residual populations has proved too costly in many areas and, where recognition of such costs cannot be avoided, attempts to reduce their impact have tended to further accelerate depopulation. More radical solutions such as negative income tax, which has been discussed in the UK (see Whitby and Thomson, 1979) and tested experimentally in both urban and rural USA, whilst offering advantages in principle, have so far been sufficiently complex to repel politicians and administrators seeking solutions.

In such company, and under such conditions, a policy of rural revival using the labour market as its main vehicle has considerable appeal. With prevailing high unemployment there is an intuitive attraction about creating jobs. Such attractions led to the setting up of the Tennessee Valley Authority in 1933 as one (very controversial) response to the problem of unemployment. Similar arguments have produced the Highland and Islands Development Board in Scotland and other smaller-scale regional agencies. Given the long recognition and persistence of rural structural unemployment, it is perhaps curious that there have not been more such agencies established. In the UK part of the answer to that question is the traditional centralist tendencies of the UK government. Such an ethos tends to produce policies which attempt to change the environment in which private decisions are made. The resulting policies are very broad in nature and lacking in discrimination. A recent review of European regional policies (Yuill *et al.*, 1980) points out that the hey-day of such broad-brush policies is now past. The recession of the mid and late 1970s, characterized by high unemployment and strong competition from low labour cost countries, together with pressure to cut public expenditure, combine to create an environment hostile to such general policies. The essence of the smaller-scale local schemes which have been used in rural areas is that they offer scope for, or even oblige, discrimination. In Europe, the European Commission has taken a step in this direction in proposing (in 1979) three integrated development programmes, one in the Highlands of Scotland, one in France and one in Belgium. Such projects require choices as to location, type of economic activity and resources to be employed.

At various points throughout this book we have noted that governments pursue policies designed to discourage rural depopulation. We have not questioned whether such an objective is a correct reflection of society's preferences, but rather, have taken it for granted. Our contribution has been to examine different ways of approaching this objective with a view to comparing them in economic terms. Our main conclusion is that attainment of this objective will be more efficiently achieved if the labour market is used as the medium through which policies are transmitted. We recognize that administrators may prefer to operate a multiplicity of policies simultaneously, and this certainly complicates the analysis. Nevertheless, we would argue that attempts to retain viable economies in rural areas that ignore labour markets are unlikely to succeed.

REFERENCES

Adams, R. L., Lewis, R. C., Drake, B. A. and Vogely, W. A. (1973) 'Appendix A: An economic analysis', in *Outdoor Recreation: A Legacy for America*, Washington, DC, Department of the Interior, Bureau of Outdoor Recreation.

Archer, B. H. (1974) 'The Impact of Recreation on Local Economies', *Planning Outlook*, special issue (Summer), 16–27.

Archer, B. H. (1976) 'The Anatomy of a Multiplier', *Regional Studies*, 10 (1), 71–7.

Archibald, G. C. (1967) 'Regional Multiplier Effects in the UK', *Oxford Economic Papers*, 19, 22–45.

Barkley, D. L. and Paulsen, A. (1979) *Patterns in the Openings and Closings of Manufacturing Plants in Rural Areas of Iowa*, North Central Regional Center for Rural Development, Iowa State University.

Barkley, P. W. (1978) 'Some Nonfarm Effects of Changes in Agricultural Technology', *American Journal of Agricultural Economics*, 60 (2), 309–15.

Barrows, R. and Bromley, D. (1975) 'Employment Impacts of the Economic Development Administration's Public Works Programme', *American Journal of Agricultural Economics*, 57 (1), 46–54.

Basnett, D. (1978) 'North Sea Oil – A Chance to Tackle Unemployment', *Lloyds Bank Review*, 130, 1–17.

Beale, C. L. (1977) 'The Recent Shift of United States Population to Non-Metropolitan Areas, 1970–75', *International Regional Science Review*, 2 (2), 113–22.

Beale. C. L. (1978) 'People on the Land', in T. R. Ford (ed.) *Rural USA, Persistence and Change*, Ames, Iowa State University Press.

Bellerby, J. R. (1956) *Agriculture and Industry, Relative Income*, London, Macmillan.

Birch, D. L. (1979) *The Job Generation Process*, Cambridge, Mass., Massachusetts Institute of Technology.

Bishop, C. E. (1960) 'The Rural Development Program and Underemployment in Agriculture', *Journal of Farm Economics*, 42, 1196–206.

British Tourist Authority (1978) *Annual Report for the Year Ended March 1978*, London, British Tourist Authority.

Brown, A. J., Lind, H. and Bowers, J. (1967) 'The "Green Paper" on the Development Areas', *National Institute Economic Review*, 40, 26–33.

Brown, W. A. N. and MacMillan, J. A. (1977) 'Recreation Program Development Impacts: A Dynamic Regional Analysis', *American Journal of Agricultural Economics*, 59 (4), 750–4.

Brown, W. A. N. and Pearson, R. G. (1977) *The Energy Requirement of Farming in New Zealand*, Research Report No. 80, Agricultural Economics Research Unit, Lincoln College, New Zealand.

Brownrigg, M. (1974) *A Study of Economic Impact*, Edinburgh, Scottish Academic Press.

Brownrigg, M. and Greig, M. A. (1974) *The Economic Impact of Tourist Spending in Skye*, Special Report 13, Inverness, Highlands and Islands Development Board.

Bryden, J. and Houston, G. (1976) *Agrarian Change in the Scottish Highlands*, Glasgow Social and Economic Research Studies 4, London, Martin Robertson.

Buck, T. W. and Atkins, M. H. (1976) 'Capital Subsidies and Unemployed Labour, A Regional Production Function Approach', *Regional Studies*, 10, 215–22.

Campbell, K. O. (1962) 'The Rural Development of Northern Australia', *Australian Journal of Agricultural Economics*, 6 (1), 21–30.

Cawley, M. E. (1979) 'Rural Industrialisation and Social Change in Western Ireland', *Sociologica Ruralis*, 19 (1), 43–59.

Central Office of Information (1978) 'Summary Input-Output Tables for 1973', *Economic Trends*, 104, 291–6.

Centre for Agricultural Strategy (1980) *Strategy for the UK Forest Industry*, Report 6, Reading, Centre for Agricultural Strategy.

Champion, A. G. (1981) *Counter-urbanization and Rural Rejuvenation in Britain: An Evaluation of Population Trends since 1971*, University of Newcastle upon Tyne, Seminar Paper No. 38, Department of Geography.

Chisholm, M. (1976) 'Regional Policies in an Era of Slow Population Growth and Higher Unemployment', *Regional Studies*, 10, 201–13.

Cloke, P. J. (1977) 'An Index of Rurality for England and Wales', *Regional Studies*, 11, 31–46.

Cloke, P. J. (1978) 'Changing Patterns of Urbanisation in Rural Areas of England and Wales 1961–1971', *Regional Studies*, 12, 603–17.

Cochrane, W. W. (1965) *The City Man's Guide to the Farm Problem*, Minneapolis, University of Minnesota Press.

Countryside Commission (1974) *New Agricultural Landscapes*, London, HMSO.

Countryside Commission (1976) *The Lake District Upland Management Experiment*, CCP93, Cheltenham, Countryside Commission.

Cowling, K. G., Metcalf, D. and Rayner, A. J. (1970) *Resource Structure of Agriculture: An Economic Analysis*, Oxford, Pergamon Press.

Curry, J. (1972) 'Effects of Non-Farm Employment in Rural Areas', *Farm and Food Research*, 3, 4–7.

Dartington Amenity Research Trust (1974) *Farm Recreation and Tourism in England and Wales*, CCP83, Cheltenham, Countryside Commission.

Dasgupta, A. and Pearce, D. W. (1972) *Cost-Benefit Analysis: Theory and Practice*, London, Macmillan.

Davidson, B. R. (1965) *The Northern Myth*, Carlton, Melbourne University Press.

Davidson, B. R. (1976) 'The Effect of Agriculture on Country Town Population in the Grazing and Wheat Growing Regions of New South Wales', *Review of Marketing and Agricultural Economics*, 44 (4), 147–64.

Davies, G. (1979) 'Unemployment', in D. H. Gowland (ed.) *Modern Economic Analysis*, London, Butterworth.

Davis, K. (1969) *World Urbanization, 1950–1970*, vol. 1, Berkeley, Institute of International Studies, University of California.

Dawson, P. J. (1980) 'An Analysis of Wage Adjustment in British Agriculture, 1948–1975', *Journal of Agricultural Economics*, 31 (2), 201–14.

Deaton, B. J. and Landes, M. R. (1978) 'Rural Industrialization and the Changing Distribution of Family Incomes', *American Journal of Agricultural Economics*, 60 (5), 950–4.

Denman, R. (1978) *Recreation and Tourism on Farms, Crofts and Estates*, Edinburgh, Scottish Tourist Board.

Department of Natural Resources (1976) *An Outline of the Ord Irrigation Project Western Australia*, Canberra, Australian Government Publishing Service.

Development Commission (1920) *Tenth Report of the Development Commissioners for the Year Ended 31st March 1920, with a Review of the Work of the Commission during the Past Ten Years*, London, HMSO.

Development Commission (1972) *Mid Wales: An Assessment of the Impact of the Development Commission Factory Programme*, London, HMSO.

Development Commission (1973) *Change and Development in Rural Areas, 33rd Report of the Development Commissioners*, London, HMSO.

Development Commission (1976) *Thirty-Fourth Report of the Development Commissioners for the Three Years Ended 31st March 1976*, London, HMSO.

Development Commission (1980) *Encouraging Enterprise in the Countryside: Thirty-Seventh Report of The Development Commissioners 1978–9*, London, HMSO.

Dillman, D. A. (1979) 'Residential Preferences, Quality of Life, and the Population Turnaround', *American Journal of Agricultural Economics*, 61 (5), 960–6.

Doeksen, G. A. and Schreiner, D. F. (1972) 'Investments in Agricultural Processing for Rural Development in Oklahoma', *American Journal of Agricultural Economics*, 54 (3), 513–19.

Douglas, P. G. and MacMillan, J. A. (1972) *Simulation of Economic Impacts of Highway Expenditures*, Research Report No. 9, Centre for Transportation Studies, University of Manitoba.

Downs, A. (1957) *An Economic Theory of Democracy*, New York, Harper and Row.

Earl, D. E. (1975) *Forest Energy and Economic Development*, Oxford, Clarendon Press.

Eckstein, O. (1958) *Water Resource Development*, Cambridge, Mass., Harvard University Press.

Economic Associates Ltd (1967) *Present and Future Demands for Holiday Facilities in the Pembrokeshire National Park*, National Parks Commission, London, HMSO.

Edwards, C. (1979) 'Rural Employment Data Gaps', *Agricultural Economics Research*, 31 (1), 44–7.

Evans, A. W. (1973) 'Measuring the Total Impact of a New Factory in Furness: A Markovian Approach', *Regional Studies*, 7, 404–8.

FAO (1979) *Production Yearbook*, vol. 31, Rome, Food and Agricultural Organization of the United Nations.

FAO (1980) *Production Yearbook*, vol. 32, Rome, Food and Agricultural Organization of the United Nations.

Feist, M. J., Leat, P. M. K. and Wibberley, G. P. (1976) *A Study of the Hartsop Valley*, CCP92, Cheltenham, Countryside Commission.

Fernandez, M. (1977) *Evaluation of Manpower Training Programs: The Interlake Manpower Corps*, unpublished PhD thesis, University of Manitoba.

Fitton, A. M. H. (1978) 'The Reality – for Whom Are We Actually Providing?' in Countryside Recreation Research Advisory Group Proceedings, *Countryside For All?*, Cheltenham, Countryside Commission.

Ford, T. R. (ed.) (1978) *Rural USA: Persistence and Change*, Ames, Iowa State University Press.

Forester, T. (1979) 'The Great Jobs Hunt: Trying to Beggar Regional Neighbours', *New Society*, 48 (865), 252–5.

Forestry Commission (1977) *The Wood Production Outlook in Britain – A Review*, Edinburgh, Forestry Commission.

Forestry Commission (1980) *59th Annual Report and Accounts*, London, HMSO.

Forster, H. C. (1961) 'The Potential for Agricultural Development and Settlement in the Northern Territory', *Journal of the Australian Institute of Agricultural Science*, 27 (3), 115–22.

Fothergill, S. and Gudgin, G. (1979) 'Regional Employment Change: A Sub-Regional Explanation', *Progress in Planning*, 12 (3), 155–219.

Galloway, L. E. (1968) 'Geographic Flows of Hired Agricultural Labour 1957–1960,' *American Journal of Agricultural Economics*, 50 (2), 199–212.

Garbett-Edwards, D. P. (1972) 'The Establishment of New Industries', in J. Ashton and W. H. Long (eds) *The Remoter Rural Areas of Britain*, Edinburgh, Oliver and Boyd.

Garrison, C. B. (1968) 'The Impact of New Industry: An Application of the Economic Base Multiplier to Small Rural Areas', *Land Economics*, 48 (4), 329–37.

Gasson, R. (1973) 'Industry and Migration of Farm Workers', *Oxford Agrarian Studies*, 2 (2), 141–60.

Gasson, R. (ed.) (1977) *The Place of Part-time Farming in Rural and Regional Development*, Centre for European Agricultural Studies, Wye College, University of London.

Gibbs, R. S. and Whitby, M. C. (1975) *Local Authority Expenditure on*

Access Land, Research Monograph 6, Agricultural Adjustment Unit, University of Newcastle upon Tyne.

Gilder, I. M. (1979) 'Rural Planning Policies: An Economic Appraisal', *Progress in Planning*, 11 (3), 213–71.

Gilg, A. W. (1980) 'Planning for Rural Employment in a Changed Economy', *The Planner*, 66 (4), 91–3.

Goddard, J. B. and Pye, R. (1977) 'Telecommunications and Office Location', *Regional Studies*, 11, 19–30.

Green, R. J. (1971) *Country Planning*, Manchester, Manchester University Press.

Greig, M. A. (1971) 'The Regional Income and Employment Effects of a Paper Mill', *Scottish Journal of Political Economy*, 18, 31–48.

Grieve, R. (1972) 'Problems and Objectives in the Highlands and Islands', in J. Ashton and W. H. Long (eds) *The Remoter Rural Areas of Britain*, Edinburgh, Oliver and Boyd.

Hansen, Niles (1980) 'Policies for Nonmetropolitan Areas', *Growth and Change*, 11 (2), 7–13.

Harbury, C. D. (1958) *The Industrial Efficiency of Rural Labour*, Cardiff, University of Wales Press.

Hardman, H. (1973) *The Dispersal of Government Work from London*, Cmnd 5322, London, HMSO.

Harris, S. (1974) 'Changes in the Terms of Trade for Agriculture: New Plateau or New Precipice', *Australian Journal of Agricultural Economics*, 18 (2), 85–99.

Hathaway, D. E. and Perkins, B. B. (1968) 'Farm Labor Mobility, Migration and Income Distribution', *American Journal of Agricultural Economics*, 50 (2), 342–53.

Haveman, R. H. (1972) *The Economic Performance of Public Investments*, Baltimore, Johns Hopkins University Press for Resources for the Future.

Haveman, R. H. (1978) 'The Dutch Social Employment Program', in J. L. Palmer (ed.) *Creating Jobs: Public Employment Programs and Wage Subsidies*, Washington, DC, The Brookings Institution.

HIDB (1978) *Twelfth Report, 1977*, Inverness, Highlands and Islands Development Board.

HIBD (1980) *Fourteenth Report, 1979*, Inverness, Highlands and Islands Development Board.

Hind, I. W. (1977) 'Estimates of Cost Functions for Primary Schools in Rural Areas', *Australian Journal of Agricultural Economics*, 21 (1), 13–25.

Hirsch, F. (1977) *Social Limits to Growth*, London and Henley, Routledge and Kegan Paul.

Hirschman, A. O. (1958) *The Strategy of Economic Development*, New Haven, Yale University Press.

HM Treasury (1972) *Forestry in Great Britain: An Interdepartmental Cost/Benefit Study*, London, HMSO.

HM Treasury (1976) *Rural Depopulation: Report by an Interdepartmental Group*, London, HM Treasury.

HM Treasury (1979) *The Test Discount Rate and the Required Rate of*

Return on Investment, Government Economic Service Working Paper No. 22, London, HM Treasury.

Hoch, I. (1976) 'City Size Effects, Trends and Policies', *Science*, 193 (4256), 856–63.

Hoch, I. (1979) 'Settlement Size, Real Income and the Rural Turnaround', *American Journal of Agricultural Economics*, 61 (5), 953–9.

Hodge, I. D. and Whitby, M. C. (1979) *New Jobs in the Eastern Borders: An Economic Evaluation of the Development Commission Factory Programme*, Monograph 8, Agricultural Adjustment Unit, University of Newcastle upon Tyne.

Hoffman, E. S. (1967) 'Agricultural Development Projects', in D. B. Williams (ed.) *Agriculture in the Australian Economy*, Sydney, Sydney University Press.

Holland, D. W. and Baritelle, J. L. (1975) 'School Consolidation in Sparsely Populated Rural Areas: A Separable Programming Approach', *American Journal of Agricultural Economics*, 57 (4), 567–75.

Horne, J., Tweeten, L. and Holland, D. (1974) 'Alternative Criteria for Guiding the Selection of Economically Depressed Areas for Special Funding', *Annals of Regional Science*, 8 (3), 111–22.

Hutton, E. M. (1967) 'Integration of Northern and Southern Development as an Essential in Australia's Future Prosperity', *Journal of the Australian Institute of Agricultural Science*, 33 (2), 85–97.

Inglis, C. J. (1977) 'A Forest Employment Model for the Highland Region', *Scottish Forestry*, 32 (2), 101–10.

Institute of Terrestrial Ecology (1978) *Upland Land Use in England and Wales*, CCP111, Cheltenham, Countryside Commission.

Irving, B. L. and Hilgendorf, E. L. (1976) *Tied Houses in British Forestry*, Research and Development Paper 117, Edinburgh, Forestry Commission.

Janssen, L. (1974) *Comparative Profit Rates of US Manufacturing Firms by City Size*, unpublished MS thesis, Department of Agricultural Economics, Stillwater, Oklahoma State University.

Jéquier, N. (1976) *Appropriate Technology: Problems and Promises*, Paris, Development Centre of the OECD.

Jensen, R. C., Mandeville, T. D. and Karunaratne, N. D. (1979) *Regional Economic Planning – Generation of Regional Input-Output Analysis*, London, Croom Helm.

Johnston, R. J. (1976) 'Resource Allocation and Political Campaigns: Notes towards a Methodology', *Policy and Politics*, 5, 181–99.

Johnston, R. J. (1977) 'Environment, Elections and Expenditure: Analyses of Where Governments Spend', *Regional Studies*, 11, 383–94.

Jones, W. D. (1972) 'The Impact of Public Works Schemes on Farming: A Case Study Relating to a Reservoir and Power Station in North Wales', *Journal of Agricultural Economics*, 23 (1), 1–13.

Kampe, R. E. and Lindamoud, W. A. (1969) *Underemployment Estimates by County, 1960*, Agricultural Economics Report No. 116, Washington, DC, USDA.

Kaneff, S. (1979) 'Solar Energy Renews Hope for Local Economies', *Royal Australian Planning Institute Journal*, 17 (3), 182–5.

Kanel, D. (1961) 'Age Components of Decrease in Numbers of Farmers, North Central States 1890–1954', *Journal of Farm Economics*, 43 (2), 247–63.

Keane, M. J. (1978) 'Economics and the Size of Rural Schools', *Canadian Journal of Agricultural Economics*, 26 (3), 47–52.

Kelly, J. H. (1966) *Struggle for the North*, Sydney, Australasian Book Society.

Kemper, P. and Moss, P. (1978) 'Economic Efficiency of Public Employment Programs', in J. L. Palmer (ed.) *Creating Jobs: Public Employment Programs and Wage Subsidies*, Washington, DC, The Brookings Institution.

Lancaster, K. (1969) *Introduction to Modern Microeconomics*, Chicago, Rand McNally International Company.

Larson, O. (1978) 'Value, Belief and Normative Systems', in T. R. Ford (ed.) *Rural USA: Persistence and Change*, Ames, Iowa State University Press.

Layard, P. R. G. and Nickell, S. J. (1980) 'The Case for Subsidising Extra Jobs', *Economic Journal*, 90 (357), 51–73.

Lever, W. F. (1974) 'Manufacturing Linkages and the Search for Suppliers and Markets', in. F. E. I. Hamilton (ed.) *Spatial Perspectives on Industrial Organization and Decision-Making*, London, John Wiley and Sons.

Lewis, J. N. (1971) 'Land, Closer Settlement and Development Policies', in D. Douglas (ed.) *National Rural Policy*, Sydney, Sydney University Extension Board.

Lingard, J. and Rayner, A. J. (1975) 'Productivity Growth in Agriculture: A Measurement Framework', *Journal of Agricultural Economics*, 26 (1), 87–104.

Lloyd, A. G. (1965) 'The Controversy of Northern Development', *Review of Marketing and Agricultural Economics*, 33 (3), 119–25.

Lucey, D. I. F. and Kaldor, D. R. (1969) *Rural Industrialization: The Impact of Industrialization on Two Rural Communities in Western Ireland*, London, Geoffrey Chapman.

Lyons, B. (1980) 'A New Measure of Minimum Efficient Plant Size in UK Manufacturing Industry', *Economica*, 47 (185), 19–34.

McCarthy, K. F. and Morrison, P. A. (1977) 'The Changing Demographic and Economic Structure of Non-Metropolitan Areas in the United States', *International Regional Science Review*, 2 (12), 123–42.

McGuire, M. C. and Garn, H. A. (1969) 'The Integration of Equity and Efficiency Criteria in Public Project Selection', *Economic Journal*, 79 (316), 882–93.

McKean, R. N. (1958) *Efficiency in Government through Systems Analysis*, New York, Wiley.

MacMillan, J. A. (1977) 'The Need for Partnerships in Regional Development', *Canadian Journal of Agricultural Economics Annual Meeting Proceedings*, 29–37.

MacMillan, J. A. *et al.* (1974) *Parklands Region Manpower Information Study*, unpublished report, Department of Agricultural Economics, University of Manitoba.

MacMillan, J. A. and Graham, J. D. (1978) 'Rural Development Planning: A Science?', *American Journal of Agricultural Economics*, 60 (5), 945–9.

MacMillan, J. A. and Lyon, S. (1977) *The Interlake Experience: A Description and Evaluation of a Rural Development Program, 1967–1977*, Occasional Paper No. 9, Department of Agricultural Economics, University of Manitoba.

MacMillan, J. A. and Nickel, E. (1974) 'An Economic Appraisal of Urban Housing Assistance – Rental Supplements versus Public Housing', *Canadian Public Administration*, 17 (3), 443–60.

Mandeville, T. D. and Jensen, R. C. (1978) *The Impact of Major Development Projects on the Gladstone/Calliope, Fitzroy, Queensland, and Australian Economies: An Application of Input-Output Analysis*, Report to the Department of Commercial and Industrial Development and Comalco Limited, Department of Economics, University of Queensland.

Marquand, J. (1979) 'Four and a Half Myths about the Services Sector', *CES Review*, 7, 32–6.

Mathur, V. K. (1971) 'The Integration of Equity and Efficiency Criteria in Public Project Selection: A Comment', *Economic Journal*, 81 (324), 929–31.

Maxwell, T. J., Sibbald, A. R. and Eadie, J. (1979) 'Integration of Forestry and Agriculture – a Model', *Agricultural Systems*, 4 (3), 161–88.

Millerd, F. W. and Fischer, D. W. (1979) 'The Local Impact of Outdoor Recreation', in C. S. Van Doren *et al.* (eds) *Land and Leisure: Concepts and Methods in Outdoor Recreation*, 2nd ed., London and New York, Methuen.

Ministry of Agriculture, Fisheries and Food (1979) *Agricultural Labour in England and Wales: Earnings, Hours and Number of Persons, including a Report of the Wages and Employment Enquiry, 1978*, London, MAFF.

Ministry of Agriculture, Fisheries and Food (1980) 'December 1979 Agricultural Returns for England', *Press Notice* No. 111, London, MAFF.

Mishan, E. J. (1971) *Cost-Benefit Analysis*, London, George Allen and Unwin.

Molgat, P. and MacMillan, J. A. (1972) *Education in Area Economic Development*, Winnipeg, Manitoba, Centre for Settlement Studies, University of Manitoba.

Moseley, M. J. (1974) *Growth Centres in Spatial Planning*, Urban and Regional Planning Series No. 9, Oxford, Pergamon Press.

Moseley, M. J. and Townroe, P. M. (1973) 'Linkage Adjustment Following Industrial Movement', *Tijdschrift voor Economische en Sociale Geografie*, 63 (4), 137–44.

Mutch, W. E. S. and Hutchinson, A. R. (1980) *The Interaction of Forestry and Farming*, Economics and Management Series No. 2, Edinburgh, East of Scotland College of Agriculture.

Nabarro, R. (1973) 'Do Public Works Help the Uplands?', *New Society*, 26 (582), 525–7.

Nalson, J. (1968) *Mobility of Farm Families*, Manchester, Manchester University Press.

Nelson, J. and Tweeten, L. (1975) 'Systems Planning of Economic Development in Eastern Oklahoma,' *American Journal of Agricultural Economics*, 57 (3), 480–9.

Newby, H. (1977) *The Deferential Worker: A Study of Farm Workers in East Anglia*, London, Allen Lane.

Newby, H., Bell, C., Rose, D. and Saunders, P. (1978) *Property Paternalism and Power*, London, Hutchinson.

New Zealand Department of Statistics (1979) *Inter-Industry Study of the New Zealand Economy, 1971–72*, Wellington, NZ Government Printer.

Nicholson, N. (1978) 'Differences in Industrial Production Efficiency between Urban and Rural Markets', *Urban Studies*, 15, 91–5.

Nilles, J. M., Carlson, F. R., Gray, P. and Hanneman, G. (1976) *The Telecommunications-Transportation Tradeoff*, New York, John Wiley.

Northfield, Lord (1977) 'The Role of the Development Commission', *Town and Country Planning*, 45 (6), 304–7.

Oakeshott, R. (1979) 'The Call of the Shires', *The Economist*, 272 (7091), 31–7.

OECD (1978) *Regional Policies and the Services Sector*, Paris, OECD.

OPCS (1980a) *Mortality Statistics: Area, 1978, England and Wales*, Series DH5 No. 5, London, HMSO.

OPCS (1980b) *Birth Statistics, 1978, England and Wales*, Series FMI No. 5, London, HMSO.

ORRC (1962) *Prospective Demand for Outdoor Recreation*, Outdoor Recreation Resources Review Commission Study Report 26, Washington, DC, US Government Printing Office.

Packman, J. (1979) 'Rural Employment: Problems and Planning', in J. M. Shaw (ed.) *Rural Deprivation*, Norwich, Geo Abstracts Ltd.

Parsons, S. T., Rayner, A. J., Reed, G. V. and Young, R. (1978) 'Oil Price Inflation and British Agriculture', *Oxford Agrarian Studies*, 7, 105–24.

Philip, A. B. (1978) 'Creating New Jobs. A Report on Long-Term Job Creation in Britain and Sweden', *Policy Studies Institute Broadsheet*, 44 (576), 1 63.

Powell, R. A. and Mandeville, T. D. (1978) 'Analysis of Sector Interactions and Stability in a Rural Region of NSW', *Economic Record*, 54 (146), 239–55.

Price, C. (1978) 'Mechanisation or Husbandry? An Economist's Speculation', in R. B. Tranter (ed.) *The Future of Upland Britain*, Paper 2, Reading, Centre for Agricultural Strategy.

Rayner, A. J. (1968) 'Price Quality Relationships in a Durable Asset: Estimation of Constant Quality Price Index for New Farm Tractors, 1948–1965', *Journal of Agricultural Economics*, 19 (2), 231–45.

Rees, J. (1978) 'Manufacturing Change, Internal Control and Government Spending in a Growth Region of the United States', in F. E. I. Hamilton (ed.) *Industrial Movement and Change: International Experience and Public Policy*, London, Longmans.

Reilly, J. J. (1974) 'Impact of Softwood Plantations on Rural Economic Development in Australia', *Australian Forestry*, 37 (2), 142–52.

Reithmuller, P. C. and Spillman, N. D. (1978) 'Off-farm Employment in the Grazing Industry', *Quarterly Review of the Rural Economy*, Introductory Issue, 44–7.

Renborg, U. (1979) 'Energy Analysis of Agriculture: Biology or Economics – A Survey of Approaches, Problems and Traps', paper presented to 17th International Conference of Agricultural Economists, Banff, Canada.

Rhodes, J. and Moore, B. (1973) 'Evidence to the Expenditure Committee (Trade and Industry Sub-Committee). Regional Development Incentives, Session 1972–3', HC327, 162–75, London, HMSO.

Richardson, Harry W. (1969) *Regional Economics*, London, Weidenfeld and Nicolson.

Robinson, D. G. (1972) 'Comprehensive Development', in J. Ashton and W. H. Long (eds) *The Remoter Rural Areas of Britain*, Edinburgh, Oliver and Boyd.

Rowe, G. (1979) *The Hired Farm Working Force of 1977*, Economics, Statistics and Co-operative Service, Agricultural Report 437, Washington, DC, USDA.

Sadler, P., Archer, B. and Owen, C. (1973) *Regional Income Multipliers*, Bangor Occasional Papers in Economics No. 1, Bangor, University of Wales Press.

Schucksmith, D. M. (1980) 'Petrol Prices and Rural Recreation in the 1980s', *National Westminster Bank Review*, February, 52–9.

Schucksmith, D. M. (1981) *No Homes for Locals*, Farnborough, Gower Publishing.

Schuh, G. E. (1962) 'An Econometric Investigation of the Market for Hired Farm Labour in Agriculture', *Journal of Farm Economics*, 44 (2), 307–21.

Schumacher, E. F. (1973) *Small Is Beautiful, A Study of Economics as if People Mattered*, London, Blond and Briggs.

Scottish Office (1966) *The Scottish Economy 1965–1970. A Plan for Expansion*, Cmnd. 2864, Edinburgh, HMSO.

Sen, A. (1975) *Employment, Technology and Development*, Oxford, Clarendon Press.

Sinden, J. (1977) 'The Demand for Recreation and Tourism in Australia', in D. Mercer (ed.) *Leisure and Recreation in Australia*, Malvern, Sorrett Publishing.

Smith, V. and Wilde, P. (1977) 'The Multiplier Impact of Tourism in Western Tasmania', in D. Mercer (ed.) *Leisure and Recreation in Australia*, Malvern, Sorrett Publishing.

Spooner, D. J. (1972) 'Industrial Movement and the Rural Periphery: The Case of Devon and Cornwall', *Regional Studies*, 6, 197–215.

Standing Conference on Rural Community Councils (1978) *The Decline of Rural Services*, London, National Council for Social Service.

Steele, D. B. (1969) 'Regional Multipliers in Great Britain', *Oxford Economic Papers*, 21, 268–92.

Stewart, G. A., Garside, G., Gifford, R. M., Nix, H. A., Rawlins, W. H. M. and Siemon, J. R. (1979) 'Liquid Fuel Production from Agriculture and Forestry in Australia', *Search*, 10 (11), 382–7.

Stilwell, F. J. B. (1972) *Regional Economic Policy*, London, Macmillan.

Stoakes, R. (1979) *Oil Prices and Countryside Recreation Travel*, Working Paper 20, Cheltenham, Countryside Commission.

Storey, D. (1980) 'Job Generation and Small Firms Policy in Britain', Policy Series No. 11, London, Centre for Environmental Studies.

Sugden, R. and Williams, A. (1978) *The Principles of Practical Cost-Benefit Analysis*, Oxford, Oxford University Press.

Summers, G. F., Evans, S. F., Clement, F., Beck, E. M. and Minkoff, J. (1976) *Industrial Invasion of Non-Metropolitan America: A Quarter Century of Evidence*, New York, Praeger.

Thomson, K. J. and Whitby, M. C. (1976) 'The Economics of Public Access in the Countryside', *Journal of Agricultural Economics*, 27 (3), 307–20.

Timbrell, M. (1980) 'Unemployment in the 1980s', *Lloyds Bank Review*, 136, 15–29.

Tracy, M. A. (1976) 'Fifty Years of Agricultural Policy', *Journal of Agricultural Economics*, 27 (3), 331–49.

Tullock, G. (1976) *The Vote Motive*, Hobart Paperback No. 9, London, Institute of Economic Affairs.

Tung, F. L., MacMillan, J. A. and Framington, C. F. (1976) 'A Dynamic Regional Model for Evaluating Resource Development Programs', *American Journal of Agricultural Economics*, 58, 403–14.

Tweeten, L. and Brinkman, G. L. (1976) *Micropolitan Development: Theory and Practice of Greater-Rural Economic Development*, Ames, Iowa State University Press.

Tyler, G. J. (1973) 'Factors Affecting the Size of the Labour Force and the Level of Earnings in UK Agriculture 1948–1965', *Oxford Agrarian Studies*, 2, 20–45.

USDA (1979) *Farm Labor*, Economics, Statistics and Co-operative Service, Washington, DC, USDA.

Vickerman, R. W. (1975) *The Economics of Leisure and Recreation*, London, Macmillan.

Vietmeyer, N. (1980) 'Rubber Shrub for Our Deserts', *The Bulletin*, 100 (5193), 75.

Vining, D. R. and Kontuly, T. (1978) 'Population Dispersal from Major Metropolitan Regions: An International Comparison', *International Regional Science Review*, 3 (1), 49–73.

Wagstaff, H. W. (1973) 'Employment Multipliers in Rural Scotland', *Scottish Journal of Political Economy*, 20, 239–61.

Walters, R., MacFarlane, N. and Spenseley, P. (1979) *Jojoba: An Assessment of Prospects*, London, Tropical Products Institute.

Wesney, D. and Woolcock, R. F. (1978) 'The Economic Assessment of Large-Scale Irrigation Projects', in J. C. McMaster and G. R. Webb (eds) *Australian Project Evaluation*, Sydney, Australia and New Zealand Book Company.

Whitby, M. C. (1977) 'Occupational Mobility into and out of Farming: Some Demographic Estimates for England and Wales', *Oxford Agrarian Studies*, 6, 122–34.

Whitby, M. C. and Thomson, K. J. (1979) Submission to Select Committee of the House of Lords in *Policies for Rural Areas in the European Community*, 27th Report 1979–80.

Whitby, M. C. and Willis, K. G. (1978) *Rural Resource Development: An Economic Approach*, 2nd ed., London and New York, Methuen.

Whiting, L. R. (ed.) (1974) *Rural Industrialization: Problems and Potentials*, Ames, Iowa State University Press.

Wibberley, G. P. (1976) 'Rural Resource Development and Environmental Concern', *Journal of Agricultural Economics*, 27 (1), 1–16.

Williams, D. G. (1980) 'Goal Conflicts in Rural Economic Development', *Agricultural Economics Research*, 32 (3), 21–5.

Williams, J. D. and Sofranko, A. J. (1979) 'Motivation for the Immigration Component of Population Turnaround in Nonmetropolitan Areas', *Demography*, 16, 239–55.

Woodruffe, B. J. (1976) *Rural Settlement Policies and Plans*, Oxford, Oxford University Press.

Yuill, D., Allen, K. and Hull, C. (eds) (1980) *Regional Policy in the European Community*, London, Croom Helm.

NAME INDEX

SUBJECT INDEX

For Product Safety Concerns and Information please contact our EU representative GPSR@taylorandfrancis.com
Taylor & Francis Verlag GmbH, Kaufingerstraße 24, 80331 München, Germany

www.ingramcontent.com/pod-product-compliance
Lightning Source LLC
LaVergne TN
LVHW020626300926
849161LV00004B/621